DESERTER PRESENTS: TODAY SOUTH LONDON, TOMORROW SOUTH LONDON

DESERTER PRESENTS: TODAY SOUTH LONDON, TOMORROW SOUTH LONDON

ANDREW GRUMBRIDGE AND
VINCENT RAISON

unbound

This edition first published in 2018

Unbound

6th Floor Mutual House, 70 Conduit Street, London W1S 2GF

www.unbound.com

© Andrew Grumbridge & Vincent Raison, 2018

ISBN (eBook): 978-1-912618-75-0
ISBN (Paperback): 978-1-912618-74-3

Cover design by Neil Gower

Illustrations by Emily Medley

Printed and bound in Great Britain by Clays Ltd, Elcograf S.p.A.

MIX
Paper from
responsible sources
FSC® C018072

Dedicated to Anna-Louise and Rima. This is what we were doing.

Super Patrons

@MrFouldsy
Caspar Addyman
Giovanna Adriani
Stephen Allport
Anthony Alpe
Duncan Amey
Llia Apostolou
Kate Armstrong
Matt Arnold
Colin Aslett
Karen Badenoch
Chris Balmbro
Ruth Bannister
Bob Barber
Aaron Barnes
Tony Barry
The Beer Shop London
Gareth Bellamy
Jo Blackwell
James Blackwood
Peter Blair
Tony Blanden
Noel Blanden
The Blythe Hill Tavern
Jo Boffey
Al Boyd
Paul Bracey
Stephen Brandl
Stephen Brandl
Clarkshaws Brewery
Andy Brock
Andrew Brooks

Louise Brown
Lorraine Browne
David Bryan
Ian Buck
Henry Bufford
Anthony Bunge
Phil Burch
Cas Burke
Helena Burnell
Tim Burrows
Tom Cairns
Pierce Calnan
Chris Camilleri
NEil Campbell
Jessica Cargill Thompson
Adam Carrier
Jason Cattermole
Debbie Cavaldoro
Darryl Chamberlain
Paul Chapman
Rama Charma
Warren Chrismas
Deborah Clare
Neil Clasper
Marion Clayton
Ralph Clayton
Nikki Coates
Danny Connock
Neil Cooper
Andy Craig
Alex Crane
John Crawford
Mike Crilly
David Croft
Matthew Cross
Emily Darian

Sydney Davies
Anthony Denny
Rebecca Denton
Daniel Derrett
DINE
Graham Dodds
Emmet Doyle
Esther Drabkin-Reiter
Alan Dryland
Simon Dye
Miles Eames
Megan Eaves
Steve Edwards
Holly Edwards
Mark Etherington
Ian Faragher
Sarah Ferrier
Stuart Fleming
Ben Fox
Jim Frank
Alastair Frusher
Lovell Fuller
Garth Garland
William Gavin Miller
Sean Gibson
Chris Gilbart
Paul Gill
Suzy Gillett
Diane Glynn
Rich Gordon
Ginny Goudy
Nicholas Green
Laurie Green-Eames
Henri Grumbridge
Paul Hadfield
Matt Hall

Nick Hanks
Robert Harley
Duncan Hart
Guy Haslam
Paul Hastings
Brixton Hatter (cider i up!)
Leo Hemsted
Paul Higgitt
Ben Hockman
Matt Hodsdon
Nat Holtham
Les Howell
Ayo Hughes
Rebecca Hughes
Peter Ibbotson
Alastair Instone
Tom Jackson
Julian Jarrett
Matt Jelliman
Jay Jernigan
Dan Jestico
Darren Johnston
Christopher Jones
Kevin Jordan
Clare Keeble
Geoff Keen
Alex Kickham
Dan Kieran
Toby Kinder
Doreen Knight
Arec Koundarjian
Anna Lancefield
Benjamin Lawson
Jimmy Leach
Isobel LeeS
Tim Lewis

Peter Lindley
Bernadette Lintunen
Tim Livesey
Clare Loops
David Loosmore
Steve Lorimer
Daniel Ly
Cheryl Lygo (Chezovitch)
Michael Lynskey
Alan Maddock
Robert Marsh
Ian Martin
David Matkins
James Mayne
Justin Mc Carthy
Jane Mccarthy
Stephen McCarthy
Ian McClelland
Phoebe The Mistress McCluskey
Lesley McFadyen
Alec McGill
Michael McKee
Ben McNamee
Terence Mcsweeney
Elliot McVeigh
Fernando Mediavilla
Antony Medley
Keith P. Meyer
Jon Midlane
Glenn Miller
That's Mister Proktor To You
John Mitchinson
The Moge
Tony Morris
Arita Morris
Nicola Morris

Kate Mulley
James Murphy
Kate Naomi Williams
Dougie Neillands
Bryony Nester
Timothy Newsome
Caroline Nightingale
Dukes O.S.
Fingers O'Ballyer
Mark O'Neill
Kevin Offer
Mick Oldham
Mike Ormerod
Kwaku Osei-Afrifa
Renlau Outil
Julia Pal
Duncan Palmer
Andrew Parker
David Parnell
Andrew Parsons
Jason Parsons
Rima Patel
Charlotte Pearce Cornish
Helen Peavitt
Sam Pegley
Alan Penfold
Auntie Penny
Dan Peters
Anji Petersen
Janis Petke
Duncan Philpot
Will Pitman
Nick Pittaway
Ian Pleace
Justin Pollard
Andrew Potapa

James Powell
Simon Powell
Emily Power
Chris Pressley
Mike Prince
John Prince
Draught Punk
Hetty & Gwennie Radford
Jack Raison
Claire Raison
Shannon Randall
Amanda L Ranford
Mark Ratcliff
Jonathan Ratty
Raziq Rauf
Jonny Rawlings
Lisa Redding
Dave Richards
Lisa Riemers
Elisabeth Ritchie
A Robbins
Chris Roberts
Nigel Roddis
Steve Ronksley
Fiona Roper
Ross
Paul & Harriet Ruffley
Stevie Russell
Alison Sakai
Tom Sargeant
Alice Schofield
Ben Schofield
Tim Scott
Mike Shaw
Clive Shaw
Lloyd Shepherd

Harold Shiel
Corinna Silk
Mark Slater
Howard Smith
Brenda Smith
Janine Smith
Matthew Smith
Steve Spence
John Spowage
Truda Spruyt
Richard Stansfield
Lianne Starns
Pete Staves
Jan Stöver
Ian Synge
East Dulwich Tavern
Simon Taylor
Martin Taylor
Jonathan Taylor
Pudsy TheBarber
Dafydd Thomas
Karl Thomas
Tim Thomas @timofnewbury
Matt Thomson
Steve Thomson
Chris Thomson
Marcel Thomson
Jamie Titterrell
Graham Tomlinson
Tony Tony
Stephen Turvil
Jessica Tyler
Akane Vallery Uchida
Jim Urpeth
James Watson
Peter Watts

Alex Wells
Paul Whitehead
Mark Whittaker Esq
Patrick Wilson
Adam Winfield-Freed
Richard Wiseman
Louise Wkefield
Chris Wood
Paul Woodall
Ed Wray
Tim Wright
Warren Yates
Nick 陶思義

Dear Reader,

The book you are holding came about in a rather different way to most others. It was funded directly by readers through a new website: Unbound.

Unbound is the creation of three writers. We started the company because we believed there had to be a better deal for both writers and readers. On the Unbound website, authors share the ideas for the books they want to write directly with readers. If enough of you support the book by pledging for it in advance, we produce a beautifully bound special subscribers' edition and distribute a regular edition and e-book wherever books are sold, in shops and online.

This new way of publishing is actually a very old idea (Samuel Johnson funded his dictionary this way). We're just using the internet to build each writer a network of patrons. Here, at the back of this book, you'll find the names of all the people who made it happen.

Publishing in this way means readers are no longer just passive consumers of the books they buy, and authors are free to write the books they really want. They get a much fairer return too – half the profits their books generate, rather than a tiny percentage of the cover price.

If you're not yet a subscriber, we hope that you'll want to join our publishing revolution and have your name listed in one of our books in the future. To get you started, here is a £5 discount on your first pledge. Just visit unbound.com, make your pledge and type DESERTER18 in the promo code box when you check out.

Thank you for your support,

Dan, Justin and John
Founders, Unbound

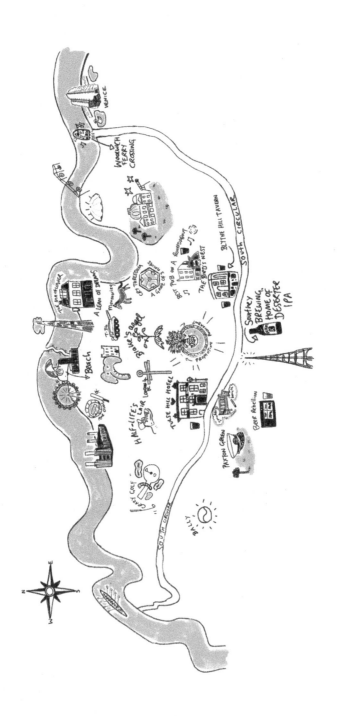

Contents

Foreword

by Ned Boulting

Outside, in the real world, South London was busily attacking the working week, hurrying along damp pavements towards late-running buses and pressing commitments. I wasn't. Being a freelance writer and broadcaster, I was smirking from underneath the duvet, as my smartphone lit up with the glorious, slovenly adventures of Half-life, Roxy and our narrators, Dirty South and Dulwich Raider. I read with growing awe and not a little envy as our heroes went about their everyday business of celebrating the ordinary via the medium of alcohol. What larks! What japes! What a waste of human potential!

That was years ago. But the habit of checking in with Deserter has stuck. Monday morning starts in the same manner every week: I check to see what our pub-crawling advocates have been up to, and I am never disappointed. Time and time again, Deserter pulls off the trick of weaving a story around the everyday habit of getting through the requisite number of hours which separate getting up from crashing out. Along the way, there are pints to be drunk, friends to make, fags to be smoked, great themes to be discussed, occasional pickled onions to swallow and places to visit.

And here's the point: during the course of their meanderings, and almost by mistake, Deserter's panoply of wastrels throw up the odd genuine revelation. Incidentally, accidentally, information is imparted with all the targeted precision of a tidal surge along the Thames, leaving a tideline of stuff on the shore of their words as the water recedes. The flotsam and jetsam of these addled minds yields up the occasional historical, cultural or psychogeographical treasure as they stumble incoherently through their fuzzy, ruminative lives. They may not mean to educate, but they do.

The real star of the show, though, is South London itself. It is, for those who don't know, the portion of the capital that sits beneath the waterline of the river, below the liquid belt, an unthinkable nether region of betting shops, weed-riddled parks and beaten-up boozers. At least, that's the common perception. My mother-in-law, for example, used to lock the doors on her car as she drove across Westminster Bridge. My friend from York describes it as an endless string of newsagents and kebab shops, the horrible prig.

So, that's one way of looking at it. I prefer to call it 'home', which is precisely the point of this celebratory book. South London, this unheralded patch of tarmacked land, shot through by the juddering vein of the South Circular, is in fact a glorious, undulating, varied, humdrum, poetic place to live and walk and breathe, stuffed with a population of people from Planet Earth who rub along just fine. It is a place to launch a life, settle in, grow roots and never leave. It has pubs, too, which helps; loads of them. And most have been visited at one time or another by our boozy tour guides.

So get under the duvet and prepare to do nothing.

Arm yourself with the requisite indolence.

Welcome to the world of Deserter.

Introduction

What are days? They are the building blocks of our lives. Do not yield them cheaply, drably, to empty rooms and offices. Put on your hat, find a couple of chums who make you laugh and see the world. Or at least what's up the road.

On these pages you will travel in the company of our favourite idiots, on trails that promise little, but deliver large. We embark in winter with a search for the world's best bar and, throughout a full year's cycle, extract as much pleasure from mucking about in unlikely places as is possible without resorting to heroin. We're saving the heroin.

Along the way, we'll reveal ways to enjoy what South London has to offer but, more than that, what we're saying is: make the most of your time; enjoy yourself, and others, wherever you are.

Life may not always be amazing, but one thing we've noticed is that it is on the short side. It's a lunatic twinkle, a brief and preposterous carnival of lust and egos, and in the absence of a master plan – or indeed any plan – 'messing around' is surely the only rational response.

Yours at play,

Dulwich Raider & Dirty South

A Little History

Once, South London's fortunes were entirely dependent on activity 'over the water'. Now, it blossoms in its own light. It's been a slum, it's been a resort. It's been a neglected, demeaned and degraded annex of a great city. It is arguably only now, in the 21st century, that it has become a playground for South Londoners, a place with its own purpose and identity. Sure, many from the north don't get it, but such is South London's confidence that now you can simply smile when they look down on you, as if they'd just cited the virtues of hard work, temperance and the rod. South London has arrived in an extraordinary place in its timeline. It may be instructive, before delving into where it is now and how to get the best out of it, to know where it's been.

From their home and birthplace at Greenwich Palace, Henry VIII and Elizabeth I expanded England's boundaries in territory, trade, knowledge and the arts. Between them they gave us a navy, an empire (sorry, everyone) and the English Renaissance, a time when you could go to the pub, catch a show and sleep it off, all in the same building. It's no wonder they called it the Golden Age.

South London is lit

By the time of Elizabeth's reign, English literature had blossomed into a vigorous and poetic champion of human expression. And its infancy, its roots, lay South.

Completed in 1386, Chaucer's *Canterbury Tales* gives us an insight into the lives and minds of ordinary people in medieval days. We learn that even the pilgrims liked a pint and a bit of sauce. It was also one of the first major works to be written in vernacular English, making it accessible to all. Its starting point was the Tabard Inn in Southwark, a place that should have been preserved for eternity but is now merely marked with a plaque. It could claim to be the birthplace of English literature as we know it, a momentous achievement that should surely be marked by a pub.

Bankside became the home of theatre in London, putting on the plays of Shakespeare and Marlowe, whose mysterious murder in a Deptford watering hole would combine South London's renown for drama and danger. Plays had been banned from the City but the stage thrived in lawless Southwark. A battle raged between the Puritan north and the louche south. The City was for the pious. Southwark was for us.

In addition, South London became central to the work of Dickens, Blake, Ruskin, Browning, Pepys, Evelyn and Thackeray. OK, I'm just going to say it: South London is the cradle of the English language. Safe.

Playground equipment

Alongside the theatres thrived the bear-baiting pits, brothels and pubs that continued Southwark's well-deserved reputation as an unruly, lively hangout where all kinds of sketchy behaviour were acceptable. Every month of the year had a holiday in the Elizabethan era, plus there were drunken seasonal fairs that would get right out of hand. Sport and games thrived. Messing about became a part of the fabric of life's struggle, a tradition which we strive to honour.

By the 18th century, places like Vauxhall, Peckham and Woolwich became holiday resorts for those who could afford it. Pleasure gardens around the world were sometimes named 'Vauxhall' after the cutting-edge pioneer of public entertainment by the Thames.

In the 19th century, South London's music halls, theatres, ballrooms and pleasure gardens made it a playground for residents and visitors from over the water alike. The first music hall in town, the Canterbury Hall in Lambeth, was legendary from the moment it was built in 1852, though the South's reputation for roughness remained.

Victorian social historian J Ewing Ritchie wrote of the area as having 'monster gin palaces, full of ragged children, hideous old women and drunken men'. Waterloo was a proper rough house too, but it did boast the Feathers Tavern, a female-only pub, at 1 Waterloo Road, known as a 'cow public house' (typical of the misogyny of the time which has now, of course, been completely eradicated). Battersea was seen as a Sodom and Gomorrah where booze, sport and gambling combined around the Red House pub, the finishing post of many Thames races.

In short, South London was brilliant.

Boom

In 1850 there were 10 commons in the old district of Lambeth. A hundred years later there were none, as building in the capital went supernova with – to paraphrase Harry Williams, author of *South London* (1949) – a brutal insensitivity to history and beauty. South London went from pastoral loveliness to dense housing, with mere pockets of its rural past. London may have been a wealthy imperial city, but evidence was scarce below the river. But a city with eight million trees can hardly be written off as purely urban. And if anything, South London is rich with parks and open spaces compared to above the river. But of course it's not rural any more: it's a big smelly glorious fuck-off city.

The Second World War had a devastating impact on South London, with the Luftwaffe donating thousands of bombs to every corner of it. The war took a terrible toll beyond the dead and the battered streets. The post-war gloom hung over South London for a generation or more, making it a darker and more insular place, no matter what anyone tells you about the good old days.

South London revival

The 1951 Festival of Britain redefined the South Bank as a place of arts and entertainment. It has truly come of age now, making it one of the most vibrant cultural centres in the world. Plus, as we shall see, it's got a few ace spots to rejoice in intoxicants.

Harry Williams decried South London's decline into urbanisation as a tragedy, partly because he was a lover of the country, not the city. Now, we contend, South London is an integral part of the capital and its part in the thrill of this great city should be acknowledged. For instance, a multi-storey car park may be an ugly thing. But a multi-storey car park with a bar, art and spectacular views over the entire metropolis, like Frank's in Peckham, is surely a moment of glory in mankind's development. Take a bow, SE15.

Our summary of South London's present is a largely positive one. It's a place full of choice, whether you want to be alone and anonymous, commune with deer in Richmond Park, taste food from around the globe, catch the finest artists or musicians, explore history, enjoy the fruits of the area's brewing boom or put dog shit in a bag up a tree; there is little unavailable to the South Londoner. Especially if he nicks off work in the arvo and gets in before the herd.

South London has waited patiently for its due credit, and now we must get on with enjoying it. Anyone fancy a pint?

Beer Triangle

It says a lot about my doctor that one of the magazines available in his waiting room is *Drinks International*. On a cold winter morning, I read an article entitled 'World's Best Bar' and almost forgot about my tennis elbow.

It named London's Artesian, based in the Langham Hotel on Regent Street, as the world's best bar for the third year in a row. At Artesian, I read, the decor is modern oriental, the atmosphere is 'relaxed' and the drinks on offer include 'experimental cocktails' with ingredients such as leather, gemstones and rice (I really wish I was making this up).

I felt a slight tension headache coming on so as a distraction exercise I pondered what elements might combine to make my own 'best bar'.

Desirable features, I reckoned, were as follows:

- Well-kept, cask-conditioned ale. Or at the very least some quality keg beer
- Small, discreet and intimate enough to encourage chat, if you're in the mood
- A good clutch of regulars
- Simple finger food
- Friendly, knowledgeable and familiar staff
- Music no louder than conversation.

I ran all the above through a mainframe pubgorithm™ (my actual mind) and the good news was that it spat out a result. That was the Beer Rebellion at 128 Gipsy Hill, SE19.

The bad news was that it had closed.

The good news again was that it had reopened, at 126 Gipsy Hill (next door). And the good news didn't stop there. Since the first Beer Rebellion had opened, under the auspices of the now-defunct Late Knights microbrewery, two further bars had been added to the family, the London Beer Dispensary in Brockley and the Beer Rebellion, Queens Road Peckham.

Obviously, I was going to visit the new Gipsy Hill Beer Rebellion. Only death could be more certain. But an idea took shape: why make it easy on myself? Why not turn it into an adventure? I could devise a walk that would take in all three of the buggers. And if I made it a triangle I'd be able to visit the first one again, making it, by my calculations, the world's first four-pointed triangle.

And what if I did it on a rainy day? In January? And then, for added difficulty, I added the edgy companionship of one Half-life into the mix.

Beer Rebellion, Queens Road Peckham

Half-life wasn't replying to texts and despite the fine coffee and lemon poppyseed cake from the Blackbird Bakery in an arch beneath Queens Road Peckham station, by 2pm I was forced to take in the first point of my triangle alone.

I hadn't been back to Beer Rebellion, Peckham, since its insanely busy opening night and now I had it largely to myself. Previously a bookie's, it's a one-room bar with a glass frontage ideal for a rainy day (though I accept, any room filled with fine ales could be considered ideal for a rainy day. Or any day).

As the rain tipped down I supped an IPA and chatted to Aidan, the bar manager. It's a feature of the Beer Rebellion family that staff are invariably open and chatty. The hiring policy is to actively seek people who haven't had bar experience so that, as Aidan put it, they haven't had the chance to develop bad habits.

I was tempted by another pint but decided to take advantage of a lull in the rain.

'Raider, you know you can get a bus to the Beer Dispensary?' said Aidan.

'Too easy, Aidan. Too easy,' I said, as I threw on my raincoat and made for the door. Outside I was greeted with an 'Oi!' loud enough to momentarily stop the traffic.

And there he was, standing in the road, hands on hips, six foot four in his shaven feet. It was Half-life, dressed in a kilt, hobnail boots, aviator sunglasses and a T-shirt that read, 'I'm the Bishop of Southwark'.

'Afternoon, Your Grace,' I said. 'You do know it's gonna piss it down all day?'

'What are you, some kind of weather cunt?' he replied. To which the answer, if I'm honest, is probably yes.

After wasting another ten minutes watching Half-life buying a small bottle of brandy in Tesco and chatting up the till girl, we finally set off up the hill towards Nunhead, just as the lull in the rain ceased.

'Where've you been, anyway?' I said.

'Hospital. Visiting Strange Martin. He came off his horse.'

'Strange Martin has a horse?'

'I like hospitals,' he said. 'I think it's all the drugs.'

Having missed his first pint, Half-life determined to have a swig of brandy for each pub we passed before reaching our next destination. So that was one at the Hollydale and one, due to an early wrong turning, at Skehans on Kitto Road. It was as we were crossing the railway, trying to get back on route, that Half-life announced the brandy wasn't agreeing with him.

'Jesus fucking Christ Almighty, my chest is on fire,' he said, belching and gobbing over the rail bridge.

'Perhaps you should have spent more than £4.50 on it,' I ventured.

'Where's the nearest apothecary?'

'Up here,' I said, having no idea, but striding on anyway. This was a ten-mile triangle, with added drinking time required, and I'd hoped to do most of it before dark.

As it happened we came across a tired-looking parade of shops where Half-life was able to procure something for his dyspepsia while I tried to work out whether we were in Nunhead, Brockley or New Cross and, more importantly, where the pub was. Still the rain teemed and drummed.

'Says take after food,' said Half-life, hunched over his Gaviscon instructions.

'I'm sure it'll be fine,' I said.

'I'll get some chips,' he said, and headed for a fish bar on the corner.

'Oh, for fuck's sake. For a renegade, you're very risk averse,' I called after him, and he flicked me the Vs.

Outside the chippy some schoolboys were taken by Half-life's wardrobe.

'*Mate*… Check the garms,' piped up one of the youths. 'What's under your dress?'

'Silence, child,' commanded Half-life, 'or I will show you.' Which shut the little fucker up.

Unable to take out my phone to check the way due to the incessant rain (that's my excuse), I took another wrong turn and we headed up towards Honor Oak Crematorium, which seemed to be in Camberwell New Cemetery, of all places. Balls.

I came clean to Half-life and told him once we had got over another railway line we would have to double back on ourselves into what I hoped would turn out to be Brockley.

'We should be there in ten,' I told him.

'Good,' he said. 'I'm not missing Kazakhstan v Czech Republic.'

London Beer Dispensary, Brockley

For reasons lost in the mists of extra time, Half-life will have no truck with the England football team. Instead he follows a frankly bewildering array of world football minnows, at least one for each federation, to which the Kazakh brothers are the latest addition.

As we dried off in the welcoming brown-wood gloom of the LBD we discussed the niche opportunity for the sports micropub, over pints of Gipsy Hill Brewery's fruity pale ale.

Like many ideas that occur on the cusp of the third pint, it seemed to us to be the best idea in the world – a micropub with a hidden TV unveiled just for the football? – and Half-life scribbled it down on a napkin to show to some 'investors'.

In fact, the LBD is less of a micropub and more of a pub pub, with its sizeable back room and beer garden. But it is different in one important respect – it doesn't have a bar. Instead when you need a refill you wander over to the chalkboard and the staff – in our case, Karolina – emerge from the throng to talk you through the ales on offer. Karolina recommended Brass Castle's Snow Eater and it was a pine-tinged cracker, which made us feel strong and forget about the monsoon.

While Half-life watched the football on my phone, I eavesdropped on a couple of ageing luvvies who had wandered in for an afternoon pint and had been amusing themselves with a selection of songs from musicals.

'Peter Hall is the most loathsome man in the world,' said one.

'At least Roger completely understood the nature of regional theatre,' replied the other.

'Fuck this shit,' said Half-life, as Kazakhstan went two down, and we prepared ourselves for the next leg.

As we strode purposefully south down a rain-wet Brockley Road I took a call from my bank, the gist of which was that the branch manager was currently concerned about three overdrafts: Japan's, Greece's and mine.

'Can I call you back tomorrow?' I said. 'I'm in the middle of a beer triangle and we're trying to make up some time.'

'I see. Very well,' replied the clerk. I could hear a hint of recognition in his voice that I was having a better time than him. I almost felt sorry for him. But I didn't have time to waste feeling sorry for bankers, I had to buy some tobacco so we could roll a massive joint.

The light was fading as we turned right onto Honor Oak Park and trudged up past the station. It seemed so very *uphill*. It's leafy enough but exhaust from the rush-hour cars clogged our lungs. So, too, did Half-life's superb weed, which we smoked on One Tree Hill while gorging on Gaviscon pills washed down with brandy. It was a welcome break but One Tree Hill, despite its catchy name, is actually home to thousands of trees, all of which seemed determined to drip us to wet death, so tarrying was not an option.

'Rainy, innit?' said Half-life. *Who's chatting weather now?* I thought, as I flipped up my hood.

Onward we marched towards the South Circular. Perhaps we shouldn't have been surprised that Sydenham Rise rose, but boy, that is some rise. Something broke inside us and when, on Sydenham Hill, the downpour became torrential, we were forced to duck into the Dulwich Wood House.

I'm glad we did, in a way. It reminded me of everything a good pub isn't. Cavernous after a recent extension, all the drinkers (and the bar) had been kicked downstairs while the lovely rooms with a view were given over to absent diners. But it was warm and dry and did a decent enough pint of Adnams' Ghost Ship. We dried off and summoned the strength to push on.

'It's all downhill from now on,' I told Half-life.

'Thank fuck for that,' he said.

'Apart from Dulwich Mountain.'

I didn't elaborate on the joke since he looked like he was going to drop me. After all, this is a man who once stamped on a mate's hamster due to a perceived slight over his dancing. (Though, to be fair, he was eight at the time.)

Beer Rebellion, Gipsy Hill

Mercifully dry once more, we cut down Rock Hill and through to Paxton Green. The lights of The Paxton pub – surely one of South London's finest pubs on a roundabout – teased and tantalised, but we girded our kilt for the final push up Gipsy Hill. And there, opposite the station, in what now felt like the dead of night, was Beer Rebellion Mark 1, its sign still up but now standing dark and empty. And next door, like a pissed-up phoenix rising from the ashes, there was light in the window and the unmistakable aura of hop-based conviviality.

Still with a whiff of fresh paint, the new place was a little more hard-edged than before with its oak bar and high tables. I missed the feature stillage standing amongst the punters but the Beer Rebellion magic persisted in innumerable details, not least the beer, and the lovely Fran was on hand to provide the best kind of continuity.

She poured us some Chelsea Blonde by local brewery London Beer Factory, and now feeling strangely peckish, we ordered a couple of their legendary burgers. Downstairs there was a little snug complete with a fireplace, where Half-life removed first his shoes and then, I'm afraid to say, his socks. But I preferred the upstairs, gazing out into the wet night and across to the station, trying to guess which of the frazzled commuters was going to come over and push on the door to paradise.

Replete, I turned to Half-life.

'Right mate, you ready for the last leg?' I said.

'Uh?'

'Back to Peckham, to do the triangle.'

'Bullshit.'

'We've got to, otherwise it's just been… a line. What about the hypotenuse?'

'You're on your own with your fucking hypotenuse,' said Half-life, finishing off his pint. 'I'm staying here.'

And so did I.

On Hospitals

It's after dark, you're on the bus home and you've just remembered there's no milk in the fridge. And even if there was, there are no clean cups, which you know because you were drinking Pernod out of the last one in the early hours of the morning. Pisspots. Is this what it's come to? You can't even have a cup of tea in your own stinking kitchen?

And then, through the steamed-up windows, a sign appears. A sign that advertises the presence of an institution where you will be sure of succour: sustenance, light, warmth, perhaps even a chat with interesting people in their pyjamas.

A sign that reads, 'Hospital'.

As Samuel Goldwyn noted, a hospital is no place to be sick. Let's face it, it's wasted on the sick. What do the ill need with the 24-hour buzz of newsagents, cashpoints, nurses, cafes, smoking areas and bistros? Yes, it's a self-contained mini-city, with all the hustle and bustle of life and, indeed, death. A million stories a day just waiting for you to be part of them, for free.

And what stories. Once in King's College Hospital, while I was assisting a porter who had got into difficulty attempting a three-point turn with a bed outside Nephrology (now Renal), a bag of blood was knocked to the floor. It burst and in his frantic efforts to limit the damage the porter slipped over in it. I've lost the photos now but in the aftermath he looked like he'd been torn apart by lions. I was subsequently called as a witness to his disciplinary hearing, which he sadly lost. But on a more positive note, I dined out on the story for weeks. And I'd only popped in for a cappuccino.

Listen, there's no point being sniffy about it, we're all going to end up in hospital at some point so we may as well give them a spin and get used to them. And in London, of course, we're never far from one, which helps. Not like in the country, where you can drive for days without seeing so much as a chemist.

The big-city hospital offers mile upon mile of warm, dimly lit corridors featuring exciting directions to wards named after songbirds, or mysterious 'wings' and coloured zones that combine to create impossibly exotic breadcrumb trails: 'You are in Nuthatch, Cerise, Keats Wing'.

In no other country in the world can you wander into a hospital, buy a Danish and a Ribena, take a lift to the TV lounge and spend 30 minutes with five strangers in slippers. You could stay there all day, and perhaps would if it wasn't for one of your new friends producing a pouch of tobacco and suggesting you all head out to the bins. Thanks, NHS.

Hospitals even have chapels if you're religiously inclined. I'm not, but I do find them an excellent place for having a good sit down and checking your accumulator. They are welcome little oases of peace in what, as we have seen, can be a quite exhausting environment.

Anyway, here is our round-up of some transpontine hospital action.

Guy's

The original 1720s forecourt at the St Thomas Street entrance to Guy's Hospital, SE1, now serves as a car park for surgeons' Porsches, sadly, but it leads on to two cloistered quadrangles, after which you find yourself in a leafy square filled with benches, ideal for exterior urban relaxation.

The forecourt itself is home to our favourite hospital bar, known simply as Guy's Bar. Home of the £4 pizza, it offers subsidised drinks and a pleasantly grimy student vibe. We liked it before it was refurbished but this low-ceilinged basement bar has still, late on, the feel of a health-and-safety disaster waiting to happen. But who cares? You're in a hospital.

As it's part of the King's College Guy's Campus, in theory you will need to know someone from King's to gain admittance. In practice, a white coat or – Half-life's favourite – a stethoscope will do the trick.

Also within Guy's is the Quintiles drug research unit which gives you the opportunity to take part in clinical trials for new drugs, offering you the apparent Deserter dream of getting paid a couple of grand for spending two weeks on your arse playing PS4. While it all sounds great in principle, after ten days of single-sex internment, headaches, catheters and dormitory sleeping you start to feel like maybe this isn't what your parents had in mind for you and that you might actually be coming last in the human race.

King's

Despite being a full-blown TV star, with its own show and all, King's College Hospital, SE5, remains friendly and unpretentious. Once famed for its legendary Penthouse Bar, sadly this much-loved local institution, where cleaners would routinely find bras and discarded Durex amongst the beer glasses and fag butts, is no more. Instead there is an integral Marks & Sparks and five (5) coffee bars to lay about in.

14

But for the best hospital coffee, you need to go across the road to the other side of Denmark Hill...

Maudsley

The Maudsley Hospital, SE5, provides healthcare not just for the mentally ill of Southwark and Lambeth, but for nutcases across the UK. But are they really mad, or have they just heard about the coffee at Café at the Ortus?

Located off a footpath called Memory Lane (who says psychiatrists don't have a sense of humour?), Café at the Ortus provides the finest coffee we've found in a hospital, as well as good grub, Wi-Fi, plug 'oles aplenty and fabulous shitters. If the weather's good, there are outside tables and even blankets available for picnics or sunbathing. It has the laid-back feel of a university campus, and student prices to match.

Lewisham

University Hospital Lewisham is worth a visit if only to cock a snook at Jeremy Hunt who tried – unlawfully – to cut the services available there in order to 'improve patient care'. It not only persists, but also offers a restaurant (with balcony) and a cafe, both of which have uplifting views out over the River Ravensbourne and Ladywell Fields.

But for the the king of hospital views we have to head back into town...

St Thomas'

Named after St Thomas Becket and relaunched by Florence Nightingale, the lady with the lump, St Thomas' Hospital, SE1, lies in Lambeth and sits directly across the River Thames from the Palace of Westminster.

And so it is that from its Shepherd Hall restaurant you can look out over the River Thames towards the Houses of Parliament while you enjoy what must surely be the best-priced riverside meal in town. It even gets five-star reviews on TripAdvisor.

What better place, once you get past the smell of iodoform, for a romantic meal *à deux*? Perhaps even a first date? You can comfort your reluctant partner with the knowledge that the patients upstairs are forgetting about their illnesses long enough to post pictures from their hospital beds on Instagram. And if you fancy heading upstairs afterwards to enjoy the view together, George Perkins Ward is a personal favourite.

So, South London's hospitals have much to offer the cold and the lonely, the thirsty and the peckish, as well as those simply in search of an off-centre afternoon out. If you do choose to accept the hospitality of the NHS, don't forget to drop a pound in the donation box. If everyone turns up for a piss-about in the hospitals they might not be able to cope. But if everyone gives a few quid, who knows, maybe we could build a few more.

Of course, another way to help the NHS cope is to look after yourself in the first place, to stay active. What we're saying is, there may just be a reason that God put distances between pubs.

Boris Bike Bender

Christmas has been and gone. The tinsel has grown flaccid. The binmen have carted off your empties, like sacks of clinky tears. A New Year, a new you. Very similar to the old you, except that you're less sure what year it is.

Should I try the gym? I wondered. But before I could respond I heard myself ask: 'Does the Full English come with toast? No? Toast, then. And a spot of black pud, if you don't mind, Doris.'

Momentarily, I considered jogging. But the thought sprinted away from me as breakfast arrived and I remembered who I was.

'Thanks, Dol.'

No, I'm not quite ready for a New Year regime of exercise, abstinence and occasional laudanum. The flesh may be weak but the spirit is completely fucked from too much booze, too much food and not enough drugs.

Luckily, there is another way, a path to virtue that allows for generous refreshment – the Boris Bike Bender. Cycling to pubs like country folk, but without running into your cousins, who may be your sisters.

There are 70-odd docking stations in South London, most within striking distance of intriguing boozers, confirmation that we are living in an age of great wisdom. Most of those bikes are in Zone 1, however, as former mayor Boris Johnson was advised that everyone beyond owns their own horse.

I plotted a route that would skirt the borders of horseland and bikeland, from Shad Thames to Kennington – the pushbike frontier. Half-life insisted on joining me, hungover and moaning about a hard night. He enjoys a cycle, though mostly so he can abuse and threaten motorists. In order to make more friends on the road, he donned the football shirt of North Korea for the occasion.

Dock 1: Curlew Street, Shad Thames for the Dean Swift

Boasting one of the finest leans in all of London, the Swift calls itself a 'Local Beer House', which sounds close enough to a pub to warrant visiting. There, I made the mistake of accepting a Scrabble challenge from Half-life, which descended into farce when he insisted on the validity of the word 'cockbiscuit'.

I gained a measure of revenge watching him try to figure out how to release the Boris Bike for the next leg of our voyage.

'You have to read the instructions,' I offered.

'I've read the fucking instructions. I've got the release code. Where's the fucking keyboard?'

'You have to read *all* the instructions. From the beginning.' Finally, he got it.

'Cockbiscuit,' he muttered.

Half-life then uncovered the first flaw in my plan as we were forced to ride past the Draft House at Tower Bridge. He moaned it was inhuman to pass a pub, but there was no docking station nearby. Well, there was, but we'd left it just one minute earlier.

Dock 2: Bermondsey St for Simon The Tanner

Simon The Tanner used to be good, then went a bit shit, then it closed. Now, it's ace again. That's progress, or similar. The couple who own it have two other pubs, all dedicated to the cask. Here, though, I made a serious tactical error. I was persuaded by the barman to taste Siren's Ryseing Tides, a beer that claimed to be 'bursting with tropical fruits and berries', something that should only occur in cocktails or somebody else's breakfast. But it was mood-alteringly superb. I ordered a heavenly pint, then realised it was 7.4%. I was supposed to be cycling, though on the plus side I now felt like I was king of the freaking universe.

A further flaw in the plan was uncovered when I realised I'd have to get another release code to get another bike. It didn't cost, but it meant more arse ache and I could see problems on the horizon if I was expected to continue this level of transport admin. Pro tip: get yourself a key if you're going to try this exercise and ale extravaganza.

Dock 3: Long Lane for the Leather Exchange

Soon we were riding again with 'Whoo hoo!'s and Half-life screaming 'Fancy a pint, sisters?' at some passing nuns. Sadly, our joy was short lived. The Leather Exchange was closed. As a Fuller's pub it was only ever going to be adequate, but now it had failed in its primary objective, which is to make me happy. Furious, Half-life then told me we had to take a detour so he could see Ollie the Schnoz and swap some ketamine for pancetta, in one of life's more puzzling barters. He couldn't understand my concern with leaving the planned route.

'It'll take two minutes! Don't be such a knob-badger,' he moaned, playing the long game for future Scrabble clashes.

We arrived on Southwark Street to find only one docking station left, and that was blocked off by a fat lad in a Crombie.

'Excuse me, mate,' said the ever-polite Half-life, 'move your lard out of the fucking way unless you want me front fork stuck up your grid.'

The obstacle explained he was minding the last available slot for his girlfriend, who was on her way.

'Not any more you're not,' said Half-life, before suggesting that, if he didn't shift, his girlfriend could dock between the man's cold, dead arse cheeks. This prompted the romantic hero to assume a boxing stance, to which Half-life responded by treading on his front foot and punching him hard on the nose, just as his girlfriend arrived. She gave lover boy a slap too and screamed at him as they went off, presumably to get married. Half-life was badly shaken, he claimed.

'I abhor violence,' he said, as indeed he had told any number of magistrates.

To settle his nerves, I got him a pint at The Sheaf (Dock: the Hop Exchange) and then another when he suffered a relapse when almost passing the Gladstone Arms (Dock: Borough High Street).

Dock 4: *Geraldine St for the Albert Arms*

Parking up in the backstreets of the Elephant, Half-life unleashed a Blue Peter (one he'd made earlier), which we proceeded to smoke in the Georgian splendour of West Square. The ancient mulberry trees in the public gardens have to be held up by bits of wood. It wasn't long before I knew how they felt.

We toddled over to the Albert, a classic Victorian backstreet boozer, with two bars, the Albert and the Victoria, ever unchanging, but... what was this? Given its humble past, I was taken aback to find it had become a gastropub, with a sumptuous-looking menu. Luckily the little front bar was still small and cosy, even if it was no longer brown, and we were able to have a nice pint to get over the shock.

Happier, wobblier, we picked up our bikes. It didn't seem like such a good idea any more, so, ever mindful of health and safety, we decided to ride on the pavement, like children. Drunk, stoned children, packing pancetta on a pub crawl.

Dock 5: Cleaver Street for the Prince of Wales

Half-life was apprehensive about visiting the PoW as the last time he'd been there, some years ago, the potty landlady had wrestled him off his stool and onto the floor, from behind, for no apparent reason. I'm not sure I believed the 'no apparent reason' bit, but it's an agreeable little pub on another lovely Georgian square, so we took our chances.

Architectural critic Ian Nairn considered Cleaver Square to be at odds with the spirit of South London, claiming it was 'always risking a bust in the mouth'. Indeed, when we arrived, there were four old boys playing pétanque in the peaceful sun-dappled square, as if they'd forgotten where they were.

The gents who agreed to play us looked like they regretted it from the moment Half-life pulled his rubber gloves from his bag and began his stretching routine. And I knew we'd won from the moment he got under their elderly skins with graphic tales of age-related incontinence and a lament on the state of the modern funeral. I dreaded to think what else was in Half-life's bag. The only thing I could be certain of, as I shelled out for another pint in the gloaming, was that it didn't contain his wallet.

Venice of the South-east

At a screening of Stanley Kubrick's *A Clockwork Orange* with fellow adventurer and Deserter regular Roxy, we couldn't help but notice how well the locations depicted the dystopian world to come. When I told her that some of it was filmed down the road, you should have seen her little feet dance.

'Let's go,' she said. 'Let's go to the future.'

And so it was that we embarked on a surreal stroll through the Venice of the South-east – Thamesmead, SE28 – to discover where the future once was. With its five lakes, a canal, nature reserves and a lengthy riverside, Thamesmead has one foot in Lombardy and the other in something else entirely; something with three prisons, a dump and a sewage works. It's not an exaggeration to suggest there is no place like it on earth.

Due to a distinct lack of hostelries, this was likely to be a nature and freaky architecture trail, rather than a pub crawl, proving that we're not one-dimensional booze hounds after all. Sometimes we have other daft ideas. And as much as she loves a pub, Roxy was up for the nature angle, being from somewhere outside London.

'Where was it you grew up, Rox?'

'Arselington-on-the-Wane, Berkshire.'

'That's it.'

We started out in Lesnes Abbey Woods, the unspoilt ancient woodlands that overlook Thamesmead, taking in the view from the 12th-century abbey ruins, the rare and wondrous remnants of medieval South London. It is speculated that the abbey was built by Richard de Luci as penance for the murder of Thomas Becket, who,

I seem to recall, once ran a boozer on the Old Kent Road. Sadly, the Augustinian monks who dwelt here didn't bother to brew any beer. Or if they did, they drank it, leaving nothing for us, other than some old stones.

From there we stepped onto an elevated walkway into the wonder of Thamesmead South, the original Thamesmead, with its '60s brutalist architecture and estates made almost entirely of concrete, like the South Bank with windows and washing lines. The grey uniformity reminded me of old sci-fi movies where everyone had flying cars and identical clothes.

'I'd so wear a jumpsuit, if I lived here,' said Roxy.

You can't get a mortgage on these concrete houses, so they are open to cash buyers only. Consequently they are among the cheapest homes to buy in London. The Raider thought about moving here once, until he discovered the lack of pubs.

'An aperitif?' said Roxy, handing me a hip flask.

'Is that milk?' I asked, incredulously, on taking a swig.

'Moloko with knives,' she announced, having added vodka to emulate the favourite tipple of Alex and his droogs in Anthony Burgess's novel about free will that Kubrick had so notoriously adapted for the screen. Ahead of us was Southmere Lake, where, in the film, Alex dumps his mate Dim in the water. Now I noticed Roxy only wore mascara around one eye, like Alex and his gang. It was either subtle cosplay, or she'd got up late.

Already excited by the otherworld-ness of Thamesmead South, Roxy squealed when she saw the horses. Yes, horses. Several little ones, scattered around the path to the lake, tethered to the ground.

'Given Thamesmead's reputation, I'd half expect the horses to get stabbed in the arse by local herberts,' she said. But the horses are owned by the nearby travelling community, which probably explains why no one messes with them. As we got closer to the huge lake, beyond the melancholy nags, we could see herons, swans, moorhens and coots. Roxy even knew which was which. In the distance lay the headquarters of Channel 4's *Misfits*, either incongruously or congruously, I'm not sure which.

Thamesmead isn't just a town, it's a social housing experiment.

Originally it was designed as a utopian ideal built to ease the over-crowding in places like Peckham and by many accounts did so happily for some time. It later developed a reputation for crime and social problems. It tried to learn the lessons from previous social housing mistakes, but made new ones, with dangerous walkways and a lack of shops and transport. There are 50,000 people living here and you practically have to get a bus to buy 20 Superkings and a jazz mag. But there is a strong sense of community, in a diverse environment where you're as likely to bump into a grime artist as you are a bird watcher.

One of the designers' innovations was water, thought to be a calming influence. It was a nice theory, but when Southmere was dredged a few years back they found no fewer than 21 vehicles sleeping with the fishes.

Things are changing by Southmere, though, starting with the demolition of old (50 years old!) housing and building of new. Peabody, the housing association which took over Thamesmead in 2014, in conjunction with the Bow Arts charity, is also getting behind the creatives already here as well as building studios at the Lakeside Centre for many more to come. It won't be just me and Roxy in the spring sunshine larking about for long. For now, though, it was ours. Between the towers and the lake we found a discarded La-Z-Boy chair, set to recline, decorated with empty cans of Stella. It was just too tempting.

'Bagsy the first hour,' I said, taking the load off. 'Where else would you find a La-Z-Boy by a lake?'

'And reclining furniture too,' quipped Rox.

From Southmere, we headed to East Thamesmead because, as much as Roxy enjoys the urban wilderness, she's a country girl at heart and it's at the Belvedere end of the 'Mead that you find the Crossness Nature Reserve.

'Fabulous,' said Roxy, fumbling for something in her bag after our lengthy hike.

'What? There's nothing here,' I moaned. 'What you got there? Is that a microscope?'

'Binoculars, you tit,' she said as she began to survey the... stuff. 'You don't find many grazing marshes around London.'

'Gosh, no,' I agreed, feigning interest. I had to admit the juxtaposition of horses and tower blocks was very Thamesmead, I got that. Reeds though? Did we need to crouch in a hide to look at what is basically long grass?

'Amazing,' she said, softly. 'Stonechat, grebe, lapwing...'

'Is this the shipping forecast?'

'These are living wetlands,' she said. 'And I've just spotted an urban ignoramus.'

'What can I say, Rox? Nature either scares me or bores me. I'm a city boy. Born of the streets.'

'Yeah, the streets of Sidcup.' A fair, if hurtful point.

It was a relief to reach the Thames. At last, something I could understand. The tide was out and you could see a vast expanse of mud flats, with waders tucking into a subterranean feast of, I don't know, not voles... Moles? Sea moles?

Here there was a vast stretch of river that we only had to share with the odd cyclist and the occasional group of old boys fishing, leaning their rods on railings, having a right old gas. Soon we were hit by the smell of the sewage works, though. Not overpowering, but definitely not date material. At the Southern Outfall, sewage is cleaned only by natural means, largely using shit-eating bacteria, then dispersed into the river where the birds go mad for whatever's left.

The Crossness Pumping Station is Grade I listed. The 'cathedral on the marsh' is striking from the outside and quite beautiful inside but its real genius is that, despite being built 150 years ago, it is still perfectly adequate today, such was the foresight of the civil engineer Joseph Bazalgette who designed it in anticipation of London's growth. Which, when one thinks of one's own contribution to the sewerage system and multiply it by a few million, is pretty remarkable, not to mention sickening.

We stopped by a bench and had some dosed milk and a go on one of Roxy's 'beasts', as she calls her joints. Very soon the river view became breathtaking. The sky was huge and awe-inspiring and we could see central London in the distance.

'We are in London,' said Roxy. 'Look, there's the tiny Shard.'

By the time we turned inland for the town centre, we were gasping. I tell you, Thamesmead is effing massive. We arrived at the town centre, the oddly modest fulcrum, with its clocktower, handful of shops and cafes, a canal and, thankfully, a pub. The Cutty Sark, formerly run by darts legend Andy 'The Viking' Fordham, is a welcoming sports boozer, with a quality darts set-up and betting tips at the bar from friendly locals. We took our pints out to the little beer garden that overlooks the canal. It turns out swans and ducks like cheese and onion crisps.

'The things you discover on a nature trail,' I opined.

'Come on then, David Attenborough. How about the Tump?' said Roxy, just as I was eyeing another pint. Tump 53 is another nature reserve in Thamesmead, but this one was closed, only open to the public on certain weekends in the autumn and winter. Something about giving birds space to hump each other in peace.

'So where are we going then?'

'Well, there is one other pub…'

It would have been quicker to walk inland to the Princess Alice, the handiest pub for HMP Belmarsh, but infinitely preferable to take the long way round and walk by the river. Despite Thamesmead's reputation for urban bleakness, the reality is that it is much more about birds, voles and bats than city life. There are no nightclubs here, and its only tourist attraction is a sewage pumping station. Its annual festival is growing and it's become the funkiest of venues for Greenwich+Docklands International Festival events, but to be honest, there didn't even seem to be many people. Some say Britain is full up. On this evidence, that isn't even close to being true of London.

But who needs crowds when you're going to the pub?

The Alice is named after a passenger paddle steamer that sank in a collision at nearby Tripcock Point in 1878. Over 650 people died, making it the greatest loss of life in any Thames shipping disaster. It's not in the best taste, is it? Would you name a pub Grenfell Tower, for instance? The Princess Alice does have a picture relating to the sinking of the ship, but it's a cursory gesture.

What isn't cursory is their devotion to roast meat, for the Alice has a carvery seven days a week, which by my calculation is almost every day. For under a fiver you can stuff yourself with beef or turkey and an array of vegetables. Best get in there quick though, as by 2pm it's all been under a heat lamp for hours and value becomes a trial. Posters proudly state that cask ales are £2.50 on Mondays and Tuesdays, which would be a bargain if they ever had any on. And yet, we sort of loved its commitment to crapness. Have you seen *Westworld*, where you holiday in another time? This is like Carveryworld. You can enjoy it as long as you know you can jump in an Uber and go to Londonworld.

And that's what we did. We'd walked enough miles on only two pints, in the spring heat, to warrant jumping in a car to Abbey Wood station and onward. At Abbey Wood though, we were tempted to have one more at the Abbey Arms. It's one of those pubs where the music seems to stop when strangers walk in, but if you take no notice, it starts again and everyone is perfectly nice. Soon they were singing along to obscure '70s tunes and making Roxy their new friend.

'It's nice that we can do something together other than pub crawls though, don't you think?' said Roxy, as we reflected on the day with a rollie in the pub's pleasant grassed beer garden.

'I suppose it is, yes. A nature crawl. Would have been nice with a few more pubs though.'

'Couldn't agree more. Pint?'

The Arts Holes

'Fancy doing some galleries later?'

A perfectly natural response to such a suggestion (though not necessarily one you say out loud) is, 'Sure, but afterwards where can we get a lovely little big pint?' Half-life, though, has more urgent requirements and he stood upon no such ceremony as his thoughts bubbled directly to the surface.

'Only if we can get a pint on the way,' he said. 'I'm fucked. Didn't get any sleep last night.'

'What were you doing?'

'Mushrooms.'

Beaconsfield, Vauxhall

We arranged to meet at Zeitgeist at the Jolly Gardeners, the German pub on Black Prince Road, but I hardly need add that Half-life failed to materialise, so I pushed on alone to my first allotted gallery, the Beaconsfield at Vauxhall, housed in the splendid former Lambeth Ragged School building.

I was pleased to find Monmouth coffee on offer in the Ragged Canteen, which I took in the sun-filled, flagstoned cafe before heading through to the darkened Arch Space, which I had all to myself. I closed my eyes and found myself wonderfully lost in a mesmeric 'sound performance' by resident artist Sean Dower.

'Arts hole,' said Half-life in my ear, freaking the living daylights out of me.

'For fuck's sake, what's the matter with you?' I said.

'What's the matter with *you*?' he replied.

'Where were you?'

'Where were *you*?'

This conversation was clearly going nowhere so we fell silent and listened some more to the throbbing bass tones echoing through the railway arch until Half-life could take it no more.

'Beer me up, Scotty,' he said.

I'klectik, Old Paradise Yard, Lambeth

My plan was to head over to the South Bank and Tate Modern via Waterloo's Hole in the Wall pub. We headed north up Newport Street, keeping to the shadows of the overground railway arches which we knew would lead us to the Holey land.

We could have walked by the river, and often we do, but sometimes the backstreets offer more stories, more grit, more tales of the unexpected. And as if to prove the point, halfway up Carlisle Lane we chanced upon a sign for something called 'I'klectik', promising 'music, art and sandwiches'.

'Let's duck in and have a look,' said Half-life. 'This wind is freezing me goolies off.'

'Which is possibly why men don't usually wear dresses,' I offered, referring to his Japanese-style gown, trench coat and hobnail boots combination.

I'klectik, despite its 'look at me!' name, turned out to be a wonderful cafe/bar/gallery/music venue, part of Old Paradise Yard, a ramshackle collection of galleries and studios in an old school house tucked away between Lambeth Palace Gardens and St Thomas' hospital.

Over coffee and wine, we chatted to the gallery director, who was overseeing the painting-in-situ of a new exhibition. Having warmed up, we repaired outside, sat in the old playground and gazed at the school building. Half-life took a draw on his spliff.

'Takes me right back to primary school, this,' he said, exhaling a cloud of toxic waste.

The Vaults Gallery, Leake Street

Back on the road, when we reached Lower Marsh we remembered Leake Street, a subterranean street given over entirely to international street artists. We stopped off to take a look and get happy on spray-paint fumes.

I've previously enjoyed evening visits to The Vaults, an underground performing arts space beneath Waterloo Station, and I was surprised now to see the doors open in the afternoon. Radka, one of the stage managers, explained it was thanks to Vaults Gallery, a new permanent exhibition space that opens all day.

Giddy with serendipity at this latest discovery, we were then saddened to learn that the giant revamped bar area remained closed until 5.30pm, so in order to toast our good fortune with something stronger than coffee from the gallery cafe, we were forced to press on to the Hole in the Wall, where we fell greedily upon an all-day brunch and pints of TEA, the ale it's OK to have with a fry-up.

The Hole in the Wall, a local institution in another railway arch – our third of the day – is a pub of many facets. The main bar, given the pub's proximity to Waterloo, can feel like a busy waiting room but the front snug bar is a cosy throwback to the inter-war pubs of Patrick Hamilton novels, where afternoons can be lost and found. Our favourite spot, though, is out back in the yard, with a couple of heaters, a partial roof of corrugated iron and a TV showing fuzzy sport. Here, shielded from the world, you feel that even in the event of a nuclear holocaust, you could continue to natter to strangers on the bench tables while keeping an eye on the handball on Sky Sports 9.

On leaving the Hole, a mysterious force drew us not to the Hayward, but to Waterloo Road. I took it as a sign.

'We could skip the Hayward,' I said, 'and go straight for another pint.'

'Fuck art, let's drink,' said Half-life.

The heart lifts as you turn into Roupell Street, partly because of its terraces of late-Georgian houses but mainly because halfway down it is the area's finest boozer, the King's Arms.

It features up to a dozen constantly changing well-kept and well-

31

chosen ales and ciders, served in classic pub surroundings. It can get very busy in the evenings but if you get there in the afternoon you stand a reasonable chance of getting the alpha tables in the side bar, with built-in seating and sight of the fire.

Half-life wafted warm air up his dress and leant on the bar.

'I was born to lean,' he said. 'Like Bruce Springsteen.'

'Or Don McLean.'

'I am the don of McLean.'

A nearby summer alternative to the King's Arms is the lovely garden-cum-cemetery of the Rose and Crown on Colombo Street, but on a cold afternoon, the King's Arms is unbeatable.

After another pint we were ready for more art. Or at least, I was, as I waited outside for Half-life to expunge brunch.

'What took so long?' I asked when he appeared.

'The grinding,' he replied, mysteriously.

Tate Modern, Bankside

After tearing ourselves away from God's very teat, we headed across Blackfriars Bridge Road to Tate Modern.

The first thing that strikes you as you enter Tate Modern is the tourists, and I mean this quite literally as you are buffeted by backpacks and poked by people from sunnier climes who have never before used an umbrella in anger.

Fortunately, the Turbine Hall is large enough to feel spacious with any amount of people. It's the kind of space worth dropping into even if you are not looking at the exhibitions, just to feed the soul. We spent a few minutes watching some people in there playing football, or a version of it.

'Am I still tripping or are they playing with three goals?' said Half-life.

After a few minutes security intervened and the game was stopped. The FA, after all, is very strict on the number of goals to be used in the beautiful game.

We took a wander around the free exhibition rooms until Juan Gris' *Bottle of Rum and a Newspaper* reminded us that there was a bar on the sixth floor which has magnificent views over the Thames to St

Paul's. However, being entirely enclosed, no smoking is permitted so at Half-life's insistence we rejected it and headed instead to the fifth-floor Members' Room where Half-life was certain we would be welcomed.

'Here, have some of this,' said Half-life in the lift and tapped out a small pile of what looked like compost into my hand from a 35mm film canister. 'Dutch.'

'What is it?' I asked.

'Ground mushrooms,' he said, as the doors opened.

'Oh, Jesus.'

'Shit just got real,' he said and we approached the entrance desk where Half-life handed over his membership card.

'I'm afraid this card is seven years out of date, sir,' said the young man at the desk.

'As if!' thundered Half-life, attempting to defy reality by sheer force of personality, which is one of the reasons I like him.

'I know that voice,' said one of two impossibly attractive women leaving the Members' Room.

'And that kimono,' said the other.

London has recently become the most populous it's been for 80 years but in the company of Half-life it's hard to believe as rarely an hour passes without him bumping into someone he knows, or in this case, two people he knew. When they'd finished a group hug he turned to me.

'Meet Rachel, my ex,' he said. 'She's an artist. And this is Rachel, another ex, she's a youth drug counsellor.' Rachel Two extended her hand.

'Hi,' she said.

'Hi,' I replied, weakly, with that sinking feeling you get when you realise you are unable to shake the hand of a beautiful youth drug counsellor because you are holding a fistful of illegal hallucinogenic mushrooms. I just about got away with a sudden proffering of my left hand and a little bow.

'Interesting,' said Rachel One when I performed the same manoeuvre on her.

'He can't use the other hand,' said Half-life. 'It's full of drugs.'

Menier Gallery, Borough

The four of us left the Tate and headed for a sharpener at the Founder's Arms, a Young's pub on the river. Not ordinarily a pub that figures large on our radar – it gets too crowded in the summer months – on this winter's afternoon it was surprisingly pleasant, with great river views and a decent selection of bottled beers. Figuring it's got to be one of my five a day, I used one of the latter to swig down my shroom compost out by the river and rejoined the table inside where Half-life was recounting a story about how his uncle had invented platform shoes.

'Reinvented, actually, because the Ancient Greeks wore them to keep their feet out of shit.'

At length, we bade the lovely Rachels goodbye and headed along Southwark Street to our final stop, the Menier Gallery at the Menier Chocolate Factory.

'So you used to go out with both of them?' I asked Half-life.

'Oh yeah.'

'At the same time?'

'Of course not at the same time! What do you take me for, some sort of pervert?'

I kept my counsel. Instead I made a joke about living in a multi-Rachel society, which he ignored, but at which, oddly, I couldn't stop laughing.

'You know, I've never noticed how beautiful this street is,' he said, gazing upon four lanes of heavy traffic.

At the Menier I went to push open the door to the gallery when Half-life demurred.

'You go ahead,' he said. 'I'll stay out here in the garden.'

'What garden?' I said.

'I mean the road.'

'Oh.'

And the road did look strangely beautiful, now. Colourful, alive, like art. If life grinds down the soul, said someone, then art at least reminds you that you have one. Also, ground shrooms greatly improve rush hour.

Leaning Tour of London

It was around six million years ago that humans first stood on two legs and made their ape ancestors look like utter berks. After about ten minutes of debilitating standing, one bright spark found a nice flat surface, just below chest height, and let a tentative elbow take the weight before exhaling with an, 'Ahhh'. Leaning was born. Humanity had embarked on something beautiful: the discovery that progress didn't always go forward. Sometimes, it went slanty.

Leaning is what sets us apart from the animal kingdom. Many animals use some kind of language. Some even use tools, something I try to avoid at all costs. What they don't do is lean most of their bodyweight on an appropriate outdoor surface, cock one leg across the other and hold a pint while complaining they're working too hard. If they did, perhaps we'd stop eating them.

In addition to the light exercise involved, if you practise the art of leaning on the *outside* of establishments you are also availing yourself of fresh air, not to mention taking on board life-giving refreshment. All in all, leaning can and should be a part of our day-to-day health regime.

But where, oh where, is the best place to have a good lean? Here, we reveal a trail offering some of the optimum places for mankind's sublime stance.

We begin at an absolute belter: the Market Porter at Borough. Not only does it provide a fine selection of booze amid the gastro-bustle of Borough Market, the leaning facilities at the outside stalls are exemplary. Plenty of space for pint and elbow, with no dangerous gradient threatening drink slide – the lean's natural enemy. I could lean there all day, if I wouldn't be reduced to clinging on by the end of it.

It's a short riverside trek east to the Dean Swift in Shad Thames, another SE1 lean of legend, but there is an emergency lean available at Tom's Kitchen, a quayside bar with a rooftop terrace, by HMS Belfast, overlooking Tower Bridge, should you feel the need to sink an in-between-pubs refresher. It's pricey, but special, so best enjoyed on someone else's tab. Otherwise follow the river from London Bridge, past Tower Bridge, till you get to Lafone Street, where your lean awaits.

Now you are at one of the outstanding leans of the city, custom built to accommodate the elbow, mankind's greatest organ. At the Dean Swift – a pub presumably named after the once-beloved race-horse of the nineteen-noughties – the sill is the perfect height to rest your glass on, so you can admire it when you're not drinking from it. Plus it's a cracking backstreet boozer, providing executive street drinking.

Pushing on, we hug the river as much as possible, but are forced to pass through curiously gated developments that hog the riverside for themselves. Presumably these citadels are occupied by people who want to say they live in Bermondsey but don't want to meet anyone else who does. On this leg there are two auxiliary leans before your destination: one on the river near Bermondsey Wall where you can email work and tell them you're still dreadfully ill, and another next to the Angel pub.

The latter spot was sadly robbed of its original public art, 'Dr Salter's Daydream', a lovely sculpture of the good doctor, which was half-inched by some gits. Thankfully, locals raised enough money to replace it, thus augmenting the experience of those enjoying diagonal comfort. Thieves will never, ever, steal the lean.

At last we arrive at The Mayflower, a jewel of a pub, with the holy grail of slanted refreshment – the Riverside Lean. The oldest pub on the Thames, The Mayflower is proper olde worlde in every regard but the prices, which are almost futuristic. But it has a deck out the back providing a superlative lean with its view of other riverside delights across the water at Wapping.

It is thought that in 1620, 65 passengers embarked here, before sailing to Plymouth and on to America. I'd like to think there was a 66th who decided to stay for one more and lean a little longer in our marvellous city.

You won't find 'a good lean' listed on a pub's website, alongside Wi-Fi, pool table or foot spa. But it can be among its finest features, promoting an ordinary pub to greatness; from a simple house of refreshment to an enhancer of the soul. As I believe the Dalai Lama once said: 'We can never obtain peace in the outer world until we make peace with our elbow.' Something like that.

On the Horses

Like all the best traditions, no one can remember for sure how or when it started. It's not like any of us are particularly drawn to horse racing as a sport. We're more drawn, I suspect, to the idea of a day spent gambling and guzzling in the company of like-minded skivers. No one can accuse us of not chasing the party. Anyway, every year we earmark a day of the Cheltenham Festival on which to abscond from mere existence, get the train going the other way, and spend an afternoon in a seaside town getting rich and soaked in Guinness.

In the early days it had been four of us. Osman – the 'Corporate Deserter' – would take a day off from the media conglomerate he was running, Spider would have a rest from not quite finishing whatever it was he was working on: his novel, perhaps, a painting, some flamboyant DIY on his Boy Georgian house. And they would join me and Dirty South for a trip out into England.

Now Osman and Spider are travelling the world: Osman on a journey to discover who will pay him the most ridiculous salary, and Spider, who will pay him the most attention. Heroically, we strive to keep the tradition alive without them. This year, though, we had other considerations.

'What about the book?' I said to Dirty South, when he floated the idea of a day on the Kent Riviera.

'What book?'

'The book we're supposed to be writing.'

'We can't let it interfere with our instincts,' he said, 'our *beliefs*.'

Nevertheless, in order to safeguard the future of literature we elected to spend the day in London instead of overnighting in the provinces. Also, we figured if we did it in London, we could include it in the book – this very tome that you are reading now – instead of doing something useful. It would double as research. Such are the mind processes of the profoundly lazy.

We picked Nunhead for the day, led there by its clutch of Irish pubs, a safe bet for Cheltenham Festival action. And in order to ensure we started with a decent pint, we were to assemble at the Old Nun's Head. But first, I took the opportunity to drop into my barber in East Dulwich, on the other side of the Rye.

'Alright, Raider?' he said. 'Do you want a beer?'

'I might as well, Pudsy,' I said. 'It's not going to make much difference, the amount I'm going to drink today.' Pudsy's real name is Sean. Really, if you're a barber, why not keep the name Sean?

'What do you want done?' he asked, as I climbed into the chair.

'Oh, take the lot off,' I said. 'Turn me into one of your magazine men.'

A chap put his head round the door.

'Do you take cards?' he asked.

'Christmas cards and birthday cards only,' said Pudsy.

'OK, never mind, thanks anyway,' said the man, and left. I asked Pudsy why he'd not mentioned the nearby cashpoint.

'I can't be bothered, Raider,' he said. 'I'm only here to get out of the house. I'm trying to read a book at the moment and people keep coming in wanting a fucking haircut.' I love my barber.

'Got any tips?' I asked him.

'Any names to do with drink,' he said. 'I once won a monkey on a horse called Another Rum. A guy was taking bets and I thought he was asking what I want to drink.' Another Rum! The very same horse our Osman had also once won big on. £40 quid on a 40-1 shot. Then he'd stood on Deal High Street giving out tenners to passers-by.

Old Nun's Head

Dirty South was already installed when I arrived at the Old Nun's Head, the *Racing Post* spread out before him.

'New barnet?' he said as I sat down. 'What do they call that, lesbian seagull?'

'You've got to keep people on their toes,' I said. 'Keep switching it up, yeah? Keep moving forward, like a Bowie or a Gaga.'

'I'm pretty sure David Bowie had more than two haircuts a year,' he said.

At the bar, a helpful and knowledgeable young woman talked me through the beer offerings before recommending a delicious pint from the last barrel of a seasonal Truman ale. Then she put the racing on. All-round top-quality service.

This year Roxy had taken the afternoon off work to join us and she arrived, breathless and excited.

'I've put five pounds on Saxo Jack!' she declared. 'When it wins I get a thousand pounds! What's happened to your hair?'

'He's being David Bowie,' said Dirty South.

'Fat White Duke?' said Roxy. 'Put that in your book, innit? Have you finished it yet? Am I in it?'

'Not any more,' I said.

'I suppose Half-pint is in it?' she said with a curl of her lip. This was Roxy's pet name for Half-life, after he once made the egregious error of getting her a half pint on a rare round. She wasn't impressed. 'Where is he, anyway?'

'On his way. Allegedly.'

The first race began, with Roxy cross because the horses hadn't started in a straight line. But she soon got into the spirit of it, providing her own running commentary: 'I can't understand a word he's saying.' 'What colour is my guy?' 'I've forgotten his name!' 'It looks like horses with tiny men on their backs, in a mad sort of way.' 'Bloody hell, how long is it going to go on for? I'm dying for a pee.' 'Did I win?'

Roxy didn't win, but Dirty South landed a 9-1 winner and our day was off to a flyer.

Man of Kent

We bade farewell to our lovely barmaid and headed over to the Man of Kent for race two, only to be disappointed. There was no big screen, as in previous years, and hardly any punters. Pudsy had told me that landlords Vinny and Sandra were selling up, so perhaps that explained it.

I told the guys about Pudsy's betting strategy and Roxy and I duly put money on Saint Calvados. But Dirty South liked the look of the favourite in the paddock and ploughed his own furrow.

Ploughing a furrow might have been a more useful endeavour for Saint Calvados, who finished fourth in a five-horse race, while the favourite, Footpad, romped home to give the Dirty One two out of two.

Pyrotechnists Arms

At first I was disappointed at our next stop, the Pyrotechnists Arms, too, as there was no sign of the free rolls I'd experienced during Cheltenhams gone by. For me, Cheltenham is all about free rolls. But what the Pyro did have was a fine collection of regulars. And by fine, I mean pissed. Completely canned at 2pm, just like you should be on a Cheltenham day.

Dirty South got stuck with Jokeman, pleased to have someone new to regale with old jokes. I avoided eye contact and went to the bar. Roxy got sandwiched between a wild-eyed octogenarian and a white patois-speaking dude in a dressing gown. Meanwhile, I was warmly welcomed by a swaying man with rheumy eyes and the softest hands I've ever shaken.

'Thank you so much for coming,' he said, quite sincerely. 'It means so much to all of us. Can I give you a hug?'

My betting strategy in the third race was quite straightforward: ask Dirty what he was on, and then bet on the same.

'Coo Star Sivola in this one,' he said.

'She sounds hot.'

'A HILF,' he agreed.

We were all on our feet as Coo Star Sivola just held on to come in at 5-1.

'Lunch is on you!' said Roxy to Dirty South, and I couldn't have agreed more.

'It will be my pleasure,' said Dirty.

Outside, on Nunhead Green, the sun was trying to come out.

'How did you get on with Pontoon Eyes?' I asked Roxy, as she fashioned a three-skinner.

'Pontoon Eyes?'

'One twists, the other sticks.'

'Don't be mean,' she said. My huggy chum from the Pyro ambled over to join us but the offer of spliff was declined.

'No, no. That stuff kills your brain cells,' he said. 'Not like getting drunk, that just hurts your liver. And you've got two of them.'

Ordinarily, Nunhead's brilliant micropub, the Beer Shop, would have been high on our list of priorities, but it didn't open until later in the day. I was gazing over longingly at it when I spotted a horse was being ridden down the road, like it was the 1920s.

'There's yours in the next race, Rox,' I said.

'Erm… Is that who I think it is?' said Dirty South.

'O. M. Fucking. G,' I said, as I made out the telltale figure of Half-life bestride the beast. And was that a cowboy hat?

'This book of yours is writing itself,' said Roxy, as Half-life rode over to greet us.

'What the absolute fuck?' said Dirty South.

'Anyone got an apple?' said Half-life. 'I'm starving.'

With his friend Strange Martin incapacitated, it transpired, Half-life had been put in charge of exercising his chestnut mare, Mmmorley. If there's a better way of arriving at a pub, I've yet to witness it. Roxy was enchanted.

'What are you doing, Rox?'

'I'm breathing up her nostrils. It's how you say hello in Horse.'

'I wish you'd say hello to me like that,' said Half-life.

'No fuckin' chance,' said Roxy.

'Are you coming up to Skehans?' said Dirty South.

'Nope, I can't stop,' said Half-life. 'I've got to drop a package off with Denmark Bill.'

'Get him to come over here,' I said. 'He'd be most *willkommen.*' Half-life looked confused.

'He's not from Denmark,' he said.

'No?'

'No, he's from Denmark Hill.'

'Oh, right.'

'And he's called Bill.'

'Got it.'

'Giddy up, girl,' said Half-life, and clopped off. Sensational. I almost applauded. But we had other horses to attend to.

Skehans

Maybe I'm being unfair as it was, after all, only three o'clock on a Tuesday, but Skehans was also not quite its boisterous, buzzing self. They were good enough to put on the racing for us, but we were the only ones watching it.

Dirty South asked at the bar for a knife and brought it over to our table.

'You going on a rampage, mate?' I said. But he removed a parcel from his bag and unwrapped it on the table.

'This,' he said, 'is lunch.' And he set about dividing an enormous pork pie into thirds.

'Courtesy of Ginger Pig?' I asked.

'No need for name calling,' he said.

Just then The Clunas arrived and we all had to shave our thirds into quarters.

'Fuckin' hell, Clunas, that was the worst timing in the world.'

'Or the best,' said The Clunas, with his mouth full.

The favourite in the 3.30 was called Buveur d'Air. After some discussion and, I'm ashamed to say, the use of a smartphone, we realised that 'buveur' meant 'drinker' in English. This was enough for me. Who cared if he was drinking air? It was still an allusion to drinking. We all lumped on and roared him past the post in first place.

'Best day ever,' said The Clunas, who'd been there all of 10 minutes.

Excited now, we craved a crowd for the last races, and the decision was made to get an Uber to everyone's favourite pub on the South Circular, the Blythe Hill Tavern. I announced that although I do have an Uber account, I was currently rated as a five-star passenger and that I didn't want my reputation sullied by drunken backseat Cheltenham chi-iking. To my surprise, this was accepted as a valid reason for not ordering one so I just waited outside while some other poor bugger sorted it.

Blythe Hill Tavern

Once, in London, it was hard to find a pub that didn't have the racing flickering in the corner. Now it's a rarity. But on racing high days, in the right pubs, it can still provide a cracking day out, full of the flavours and characters of a disappearing London.

The Blythe was busy, buzzy and convivial, as it always seems to be. Landlord Con gave us a warm welcome, bar manager Terry came over to say hello, and in a corner seat we found some more muckers: Pompey, Cyclo, Fouldsy and the Dodger, all warm and fuzzy round the edges. And finally, free rolls made a most pleasing appearance.

The Hophead and the Guinness were quite wonderful – the kind of drinks that make us all feel like winners. Though that wasn't enough for Dirty South, who went on to bag another winner in the 5.30. Perhaps the moral of the tale, I suggested to the Dirty One, is that if you're coming out to watch the racing, make sure you end up in the Blythe.

'That's probably a good rule for any time you leave the house,' he said.

Top Ten Pubs on a Roundabout

'Why the fuck would I go to pubs on a roundabout?' asked Half-life.

'Obviously, because I'd buy you a pint,' I said, obviously. But our freeloading pal is justified in questioning the attraction.

I look at it this way: there's a busy intersection, with cars rushing past in up to five different directions. Meanwhile, you're in a pub. You have just confirmed your own genius.

Below are the ten best pubs on roundabouts in South-east London. We couldn't include a closed pub in a Top Ten of anything, other than sadnesses, so The Porcupine in Mottingham didn't make the cut. But it deserves a mention after fighting off Lidl's plans to turn it into a supermarket, on a spot that has housed a pub since the 1400s. It now awaits a pub angel to return lubrication to this spherical intersection. Let's not forget, every time a pub closes, God kills a kitten.

10. The Sun in the Sands, Shooters Hill

The Sun in the Sands has the distinction of having its roundabout named after it and a whopping great one at that. It's at the junction of the main roads from London to Europe and South London to East London. Consequently it's tempting to pull off into one of its parking bays, get paralytic and sleep in the motor.

The Sun in the Sands has been cut into two, with the other half now Roy's Cafe. Handy, if you've just slept in your car and have a stonking hangover. It has no proper beer but it does have pool and Sky Sports. It's probably at its best if you're a bit stoned in the afternoon and have been walking for what almost seems like nearly a mile. So I'm told.

9. The Charlie Chaplin, Elephant & Castle

It used to be a dark, forbidding place, even for the Elephant, populated by characters left over from a Tom Waits nightmare. Now it's less dangerous but still lacking in the kind of welcome you hope for from people who have chosen a life serving the public. It's another one that only offers fizzy beer and has brightened itself up with lighter wood furnishings at no considerable expense.

Its best feature is a beautiful old fireplace near the pool table, but it takes more than that, a roundabout and a distant link to movie greatness to push it up this all-important chart.

8. The Castle, Woolwich

The Castle promises Ghanaian food all day, apart from the parts of the day when they're closed, which can surprise you. It's got a big beer garden and is a joyous place to watch Ghana's Black Stars play football. The outside tables have a view of the roundabout (get in!), the river and two beautiful art deco buildings, the former Granada and Coronet, now both churches. The Grade II-listed Coronet now hosts a megachurch named New Wine Church. Confusingly, if it's wine you're after, you're better off in The Castle.

7. The Bricklayers Arms, Beckenham

A traditional brown pub with a bit of character, cask ale, football, darts and hearty scran, The Bricklayers is perched on a roundabout offering escapes to Croydon, Penge or the High Street. But perhaps the best option is to take a table outside overlooking the hurly-burly, sup a well-kept pint and watch the world go by. To Croydon and Penge.

6. Royal Standard, Blackheath

This was the first pub to make me ask: 'What is a roundabout?' Yes, it's a circular intersection in which traffic flows, in theory, continuously, around a central island. But outside The Standard are two islands, one shaped like a giant hash brown, with closed underground toilets, dying for someone to turn them into an all-night bar.

The Standard has reinvented itself, getting rid of the football (boo!) and getting in much better beer (hurrah!) and live music (depends…). It has managed to shake off its old reputation for being a place where, late at night, misunderstandings occur, so bravo to the new regime.

5. The Greyhound, Sydenham

Having been closed for 10 years after being illegally demolished by property developers Purelake, the fact that The Greyhound even exists is a miracle of Lazarus-like proportions – though obviously much better, as it's a pub. A determined local campaign prompted Lewisham Council to force Purelake to rebuild the place, to a high spec – a rare but thrilling victory for people over bastards.

The Greyhound has a conservatory from which you can enjoy the flow of circular traffic. There are tables and benches outside so roundabout enthusiasts can enjoy a pint while admiring the confluence of humanity going about less important pursuits. And yet there's more. As an independent they are able to choose a fine line-up of cask, keg and wine. And the food menu is deeply satisfying to the comfort food seeker like myself, but also has items, most likely plants, to tempt the veggie and vegan diner.

4. The Paxton, Gipsy Hill

The Paxton has room enough to provide plenty of space for watching footy, other areas for a quiet chat about your feelings (should you have any), somewhere to eat from their trying-to-please-every-fucker menu and a garden the size of an elephant's garden. The makeover is a little unsure of itself, but a pub this big has to cater to all: people who have children, people who don't, people who can't and people who won't. It must be a godsend for parents who want to see the footy, then have some feelings, followed by some harissa lamb, before poncing a rollie in a garden large enough to hide from the offspring.

48

3. The Elephant and Castle

Though a pub is the more likely source of the name 'Elephant and Castle' than *La Infanta de Castilla*, who often gets the credit, this iteration has been a modern pub for 50 years now, if that's possible. But its 1960s-ness has always looked like bad futurism until recently.

Saved from becoming a Foxtons by local activists, squatters and the righteousness of the Lord, local pub masters, Antic, have taken it over and retained its modernist feel. Now it's thriving with decent boozes, food and a nice layout, it's hard to remember it when it was a shithole. It's got a neat outside area and several front-row seats for London's sexiest roundabout. Student-friendly, as you'd expect here, it is finally coming of age, as had, I hoped, the girls talking to Half-life.

2. East Dulwich Tavern

Not only does the EDT provide a fine pint, good food and the footy, its roundabout was the scene of wild celebrations when Dulwich Hamlet FC won promotion to the National League South, in 2018. Such was the ecstatic union of fans, players and traffic, the intersection has been named 'Promotion Roundabout' on Google Maps, as well as in the hearts of Hamlet supporters.

The EDT offers that rare luxury of supping a frothy one while sitting on (on!) a roundabout. It was almost too much for me. Half-life hated it (drinking in traffic, that is, not the EDT), but in my single-minded pursuit of the best pub on a roundabout, I was dizzied by this advanced facility.

'I've woken up on a roundabout too many times,' Half-life explained (in a way).

Nonetheless, facts is facts. This is circular-junction heaven.

1. The Birds Nest, Deptford

In the end, it was a two-horse race between the only outstanding candidates, but the Birds Nest was such an unexpected delight. From an unpromising position, it impressed in every way. Fine ales, scruffy and unfussy decor, with very good, simple, handmade food, it's a place at the heart of Deptford's cultural life.

A packed line-up of gigs, a gallery for local artists and a history that takes in not only Dire Straits and Squeeze but stretches back as far as Christopher Marlowe. Was it the deserted pub in which Mark Knopfler saw the 'Sultans of Swing', to inspire his tedious global hit? I would have asked but with happy hour and all, one tends to forget. Hats off to a worthy winner.

Streetlife: Old Kent Road

Dirty South and I had almost finished our double egg and sauté potatoes at the Elephant and Castle's Mamuśka! when Half-life appeared at our table holding his own brunch – a glass of neat Polish vodka.

'Alright, blogtards?' he said, nicking the last of my spuds. 'I haven't got all day, let's get going, they're open.' He did have all day. He always has all day.

And so, slightly hurried, we set off on our adventure: a wander down the Old Kent Road, the most famous street in South London, part of the old Watling Street, the Roman road which ran from Dover to Wroxeter, wherever that is. (If there's one thing you can criticise the Romans for, it's their choice of vital cities. I mean, Colchester? Really?)

Once a thriving Victorian boulevard, deprivation, bombing and planning catastrophes have conspired to reduce the Old Kent Road (OKR) to the status of urban highway, on which the car is king and the pedestrian a pauper. Even in the 1980s (and beyond), the OKR remained a renowned (if somewhat hairy) social destination, not something to be sped through, to get into or out of town, to just get it over with. Was there enough left to entertain us, we wondered – three blokes with nothing to do and all afternoon to do it in?

'Chaucer's pilgrims came down this way,' I said, as we made our way down New Kent Road to the Bricklayers Arms, the roundabout named after an old coaching inn (and later a train station of the same name) which marks the northernmost point of the OKR. 'And they stopped for one in the Thomas A Becket, so that's our first proper stop.'

'Good,' said Dirty South. 'It's amazing how parched you can get, walking.'

But before that I wanted to find an oddity I dimly recalled. We walked a few metres up Mandela Way, not far from the Bricklayers Arms flyover, and just as I was beginning to think I may have imagined the whole thing, from behind a screen of flowering buddleia a gun turret appeared. And then we saw it, standing proud on scrubland at the end of a terraced London street: a T-34 Soviet tank, painted in bright yellow and black stripes.

'Shit the bed,' said Dirty South. 'How did that get there?'

'I'm sure he's going to tell us,' said Half-life, not entirely enthusiastically. And so I did.

The story goes that in the '90s, having had a planning application rejected by Southwark Council, local man Russell Gray made another simpler application, this time for 'a tank'. The council assumed he meant a container of some sort and waved it through, at which point Gray purchased his tank (for £7000), parked it on his land and pointed the gun turret at the council offices. Now a well-known local landmark, it doubles as a children's climbing frame and even appears on Google Maps.

Back on the OKR, we passed a nondescript block of flats featuring a Domino's Pizza takeaway on the ground floor. An old sign affixed to what remained of the original facade read: 'World Turned Upside Down Customers Do Not Park in Access Road'. Not only was this a reminder of happier times, when folk could block side roads willy-nilly without fear of recrimination, it also told us we were standing in front of what remained of the World Turned Upside Down pub.

The World Turned Upside Down, the Dun Cow, the Green Man, the Kentish Drovers, the Gin Palace, the Frog and Nightgown… The evocative list of lost pubs on the OKR is like a poem; a surreal song, the song of Kent Street. Today's version is more like:

Lidl and Asda, Aldi, B&Q
Iceland and Tesco, they fucked it up
For you

There have been 39 pubs in all on the OKR, though not all of them contemporaneous. Now, sadly, we understood there were just two. Though more happily, we were off to one of them.

We paused at the 'White House' a vestige of the area's glorious past and former home of the Rolls family, who made a mint subleasing Crown land in the area, before feeling a bit guilty and giving something back in the form of leases for social buildings like the Wells Way Library, schools and social housing. The last male Rolls was a keen aviator and motor enthusiast who put together an engine with a certain Mr Royce.

Now the house is the 'Church of the Light of the World' or some such witchfuckery. We were to see a lot of modern-day churches on the OKR that afternoon, perhaps unsurprisingly, as they spawn to prey on the poor and the hopeless.

Heading south-ish, the next 300 metres or so functions as the area's high street, with an abundance of small, cosmopolitan shops, cafes and restaurants. It's a lively scene and one pretty much unsullied by poncification, unless you count the Eurotraveller hotel, which I don't. True, there is a cafe called Le Panier a Brioche but the outside tables were nevertheless filled with be-tattooed builders from a local site.

On the corner of Dunton Road we stopped to admire the Dun Cow building, now a doctor's surgery, but still with parts of its pub signage in place.

'And that was the Green Man,' said Half-life, looking across the road, 'where I saw my first sawn-offs.' And he didn't mean jeans.

At the junction of Shorncliffe Road we passed over the old water crossing known as St Thomas-a-Watering, from which our first destination took its name, and over which there is now a monstrous Tesco. The building presaged a lot of what we saw was wrong with recent developments along the OKR – no accessible or useful street frontage, just car parking and blind walls of brick.

But we weren't disheartened. We were thinking of our pint. A pint in one of the last remaining historic public houses on the strip, a chance to step back in time, to revel in the past, to raise a glass to long-gone carousers in the one, the only, the Thomas A Becket –

'It's closed,' said Dirty South, as we arrived.

'What? It can't be,' I cried. 'It says open noon till 5.30am.'

'This place hasn't been open for a while,' said Half-life, peering through a window. 'I can smell it.'

Our plans were in disarray. We were to lunch in another OKR institution, Frank's, a family-run restaurant that has been serving Italian food to locals for more than 40 years, but as all holidaymakers know, there is nothing more satisfying than the pint before lunch and now this simple pleasure was under threat.

Dumbfounded, we adjourned to a grassy knoll overlooking a lake in Burgess Park to regain our composure. It was all we could do to skin up.

'Nice spot for it, this,' said Dirty South.

'One of the best,' said Half-life.

Rejoining the OKR after the calming pastoral influence of Burgess Park, we were shocked by the noise and ferocity of the traffic.

'Mind you, it's been like this ever since I can remember,' said Dirty South. 'That's why the UK's first drive-through Kentucky Fried Chicken was built here. I remember being in a cab home with my ex-wife and her twin sister when it had just opened and they insisted on trying it out.'

'Hang on, you married twins?' said Half-life, perking up.

'Strictly speaking, I only married one of them,' said Dirty South. 'That's the law.'

'Bloody law,' I said.

'Unfortunately,' Dirty South went on, 'the UK hadn't quite grasped the concept of fast food and we were in the KFC queue for 45 fucking minutes, with the meter running. I had to stop the cab in New Cross in the end 'cause I ran out of money.'

'What happened after that?' asked Half-life.

'We walked home, leaving a trail of chicken bones,' said Dirty South.

'No, I mean with the twins,' said Half-life.

'Guys, I don't wish to interrupt the past,' I said, 'but what's that ahead?' Unless I was mistaken, it looked uncannily like a pub sign.

'Thank the mighty booze lords,' said Dirty South.

The pub in question turned out to be the Lord Nelson, which triggered vague memories but none of us could recall ever having been in it before. Its impressive bar and ornate Victorian interior was only undermined by the lack of any decent beer. While Dirty South and I made do with some bottled Courage Light, like it was 1970, Half-life plumped for Strongbow Dark Fruit.

'Would sir like a straw with that?' asked Dirty South.

'Cheeky cunt,' said Half-life. 'I'm not going to tell you my story now.'

'What story?' we choroused, and Half-life settled into his bar chair.

During one of his stays at Her Majesty's Pleasure, Half-life told us, he befriended a lag known as Joe Slow, a brilliant accountant turned white-collar criminal who'd landed himself inside after getting involved in a boiler-room fraud.

Joe Slow was unpopular with the other inmates, who sensed, correctly, that he felt they were beneath him. Never one to follow the herd, Half-life got to know him and soon put Joe Slow to work using his numerical skills to offer an early version of what we now know as in-play 'Cash Out', a real-time betting market that not only allowed inmates to gamble on live events (such as a game of pool or table football) but also to lock in profits or losses whenever they felt the time was right.

'If he was so smart, why was he called Joe Slow?' I asked.

'Because his name was Joe Quigley,' said Half-life.

'Of course,' I nodded.

For his part of the deal, Half-life, six foot four of imminent menace clothed in supreme confidence, saved him from a number of hidings. Over time they became close, as Half-life, a keen art lover and part-time poet, discovered they shared an appreciation of literature, design and fine art. When the moment came for Joe Slow to be moved to an open prison pending parole, he told Half-life that he would never forget his help and that when he too was released, he wouldn't regret paying him a visit in his lodgings.

'And where was that?' I asked.

'Two rooms above the Green Man,' said Half-life, leaning in for effect. 'On the Old Kent Road. Whose round is it?'

His glass replenished with more foul-tasting purple liquid, we waited for Half-life to go on with his tale. 'Back in a sec,' he said. 'Dying for a wazz.'

'You really need to work on your cliffhangers,' said Dirty South as he wandered off. We grinned at each other. 'This is brilliant,' he said.

'Tell me about it,' I said. 'I envy us.'

At length, Half-life settled back into his chair, set about refilling his empty bladder and went on with his tale.

Some time after his own release from prison, Half-life duly paid a visit to the OKR one afternoon and asked at the bar of the Green Man for Joe Quigley. He was told to talk to the bouncer.

'Who wants him?' asked the bouncer. Half-life told him and the bouncer disappeared through a side door while Half-life waited. Of the three men in the bar, he couldn't help noticing, he was the only one wearing a top.

'Quigley's on two,' said the bouncer when he returned, and as he held the door open for Half-life, a couple of sawn-off shotguns clattered to the floor from behind it. Half-life caught the man's eye.

'In case I want to kill myself,' said the bouncer, in a rare display of bouncer humour.

Half-life ascended the stairs and entered Quigley's lodging. The sitting room was decorated in the most opulent fashion, Persian rugs underfoot and thick velvet curtains keeping the traffic noise at bay.

'You should have seen the place,' said Half-life. 'All the sculptures, the paintings, the art... objects.'

'*Objets d'art?*' I offered, and Half-life flicked me his death stare.

'Do you want me to finish this fucking story or not?' he said.

'If only,' said Dirty South.

'In that case,' said Half-life, 'you will have to buy me lunch at Frank's.'

The next stretch of the OKR is predominantly housing blocks punctuated by some of the aforementioned oversized shopping outlets.

'If you squint it looks a bit like LA,' I said. 'Or some run-down US retail strip.' And we all walked along with slitted eyes until Half-life walked into a bus stop.

We stopped to admire the *History of the Old Kent Road*, a remarkable mural by Polish artist Adam Kossowski. It is on the exterior of the former North Peckham Civic Centre, now – almost inevitably in this part of the world – another oddball take on a church.

'It's not a mural,' said Half-life. 'It's a ceramic frieze.'

'Oh my god,' said Dirty South as we passed the infamous KFC, framed by two enormous and quite beautiful gasholders. 'There she is. The slowest deep-fat fryer known to man.'

On the corner of Commercial Street we paused outside the New Saigon restaurant, once better known as the Kentish Drovers pub. Looking up, we could still see the remnants of a tiled scene depicting herdsmen droving their cattle to market.

'Nice frieze,' I said.

'It's not a frieze, it's a fucking tiled mural,' said Half-life, shaking his head.

'Yeah, idiot,' said Dirty South.

Remarkably, no one had mentioned that there may now not be another pub on the OKR. I think our anticipation had turned to Frank's and my hunch was confirmed when Half-life announced 'I'm having the seafood spaghetti and a pint of Barolo' as we strolled past a giant Iceland.

'That's what you had last time, when we cleared out Dirty South's garage,' I said.

'The same,' said Half-life, and we laughed about Dirty South's text asking if we might be available to assist with some lifting, to which Half-life had responded, 'I'm not that sort of friend'.

Once again, the past was rudely interrupted by the present.

'Oh, God, no…' said Dirty South, looking up and down a parade of shops set back a little from the road.

'What?' I said.

'Where is it?' said Dirty South.

'Where's what?' I said, but I knew. I knew. 'Oh, no, *no*…'

Oh, reader. We live in the city because we love change, the constant upgrading, the movement, the cycles. Where a new gaff opens here, or someone tries a pop-up strudel bar there. To live where nothing changes, where everything simply remains, would crush our optimistic souls. But the pace is so relentless that once in a while it catches you unawares. You turn away for a moment and a dear old friend is lost forever. If only things could stay *a little bit* the same.

Yes, Frank's was gone. An OKR fixture, an Italian haven in which lunches turned into dinners and dinners into lock-ins. We stood in a forlorn huddle on the pavement and considered our options.

'We could get some tins and a sarnie from the Nisa and have a picnic on the roundabout outside Southwark dump,' I suggested, to general incredulity.

'Right,' said Half-life, taking charge, which is always a worry, 'follow me. The best burgers in town are from the van in the B&Q car park.' And we set off back up the OKR.

'I can't imagine you in B&Q,' I said.

'It's where I got my shed,' said Half-life.

'I didn't know you had a garden,' said Dirty South.

'I don't,' said Half-life. 'It's in the lounge. I sit in it to read the papers.' Since neither of us had ever set foot in Half-life's lair there was, sadly, no way of verifying this wondrous image.

But when we got to B&Q the burger van was nowhere to be seen.

'Fuck it,' said Half-life. 'Must only be at weekends.' Now rain started to fall. This afternoon was falling apart. We looked about for shelter. Looming above us were the giant golden arches of a 24-hour drive-through McDonald's. Surely not.

'Come on,' commanded Half-life. 'We're going in.'

'I try to avoid McDonald's as a rule,' I protested.

'That's because you're a snob,' said Half-life. 'It's this or Halfords.'

Confronted by that sugary nidor peculiar to fast-food outlets, Dirty South and I made do with a coke and a coffee respectively, while Half-life tucked into a Double Chicken Legend, large fries, large Coke and Big Mac on the side 'for old times' sake'. Somehow, he is as thin as a rake. (Actually, I think I know how but that's another story.)

'Do you have any demerara sugar?' I enquired of the clearer-upper at the coffee accoutrement counter.

'Twat,' said Half-life.

If you like to eat junk food while staring out at a rainy car park, then this is the place for you. Having said that, the place was filled with happy, smiling, chatty people so, really, who's the fool?

'You are,' said Half-life, never one to leave a rhetorical question untroubled.

It was with a heavy tread that we returned to the hurly-burly of the OKR when the rain eased. What if our fears came true and there were no more pubs to be had?

'We'll have to head down into New Cross,' said Dirty South.

'At some point it stops being the Old Kent Road, though,' I said. 'We're supposed to stay on the Old Kent Road.'

'Sod that. Needs must. We're not cartographers,' said Half-life.

'No, we're scientists,' said Dirty South. 'Drunk scientists.'

And then, as if rewarding our attempts at good cheer, just past the Aldi and an outcrop of stark tower blocks, we came to number 888 Old Kent Road, possibly the last building on the OKR proper. 888 is the number of Jesus, apparently, of Christ the Redeemer, and also represents triple good fortune in Chinese numerology. Who knows, maybe there is something in all that mumbo-jumbo, for 888 Old Kent Road is a pub.

More specifically, it is the Windsor Hotel (formerly the Breffni Arms). While handsome enough on the outside, the interiors have been done out like a 1980s hotel conference room, which was a bit disconcerting. But fuck it, we weren't in the mood for nitpicking. We were in the mood for booze.

We took our pints out onto the roadside terrace and Half-life once more cranked up his never-ending story.

In his rooms above the Green Man, Quigley poured two large brandies from a cut-glass decanter and the two men sat facing each other across a French-polished dining table, catching up on mutual acquaintances and bastard screws, pausing occasionally to toast their freedom. Once again, Quigley thanked Half-life for taking him under his wing, for making his stretch bearable.

'I have something for you that I know you will appreciate,' he said. 'A painting. It is yours, as a token of my gratitude. But before I give it to you, I ask that you give me something in return.'

Half-life paused in his storytelling and took a long draught of his continental lager.

'Well? What did he want?' I prompted.

'Two grand,' said Half-life.

'*Two grand?*' I said and Dirty South, who had unfortunately just taken a mouthful of beer, proceeded to spray it over the table.

'Two grand,' repeated Half-life.

'So he was basically selling you a painting,' I said, trying not to catch Dirty South's eye, who I could see was fighting a belly laugh.

'Yes,' said Half-life. 'A fucking masterpiece.'

Quigley fetched a parcel from the other room and unwrapped it on the table. For once in his life Half-life was rendered speechless. Quigley leaned the painting against the back of a dining chair and the two men stood to admire the colours, the composition, perspective and above all the light and shadow that brought the simple domestic scene to life. Then they sat down to finish the brandy.

'You didn't pay him?' I said.

'I certainly did,' he said. 'In three months, it was mine.'

'So who is it by?' said Dirty South.

'Let's just say it takes a brave man to split the bill,' said Half-life, gnomically. 'Even you two dozy cunts would recognise it.'

It turns out that art heists are a waste of time. The artefacts are impossible to sell, even on the black market, as what underlies their market value are such mundanities as provenance, authenticity and proof of ownership. But for Half-life the value was intrinsic, and well worth a couple of grand cobbled together from benefit fraud and, probably, weed sales.

We were interrupted by a grizzled old dude on a mobility scooter sporting a specially adapted umbrella arm to allow him to drink rum in the drizzle.

'Are you here for meat?' he said.

'Pardon?' I said.

'Are you boys waiting for meat?' he said. I thought about this for a moment.

'No, I'm sorry, I still don't understand you,' I said.

'The Friday meat van. Comes every week. You're not from round here are you?'

'Well, I'm from down the road,' I said. 'Denmark Hill way.'

'No, I'm from down the road,' he said. 'You're from Camberwell.'

Dirty South and Half-life went to the bar and I told the meat man about our day of closed emporiums and lost palaces – the famous old pubs, the nightclubs, Frank's...

'And Chinese Elvis has gone,' he added. 'Oh yeah, it's been getting shitter for a hundred years,' he said, which we agreed could be a promotional slogan for the OKR tourist board.

Today, though, the OKR is a designated 'opportunity corridor', with millions of pounds earmarked to make the street more pedestrian friendly and provide more community amenities, as well as thousands of new homes and jobs. The Bakerloo Line extension will even come down this way. The OKR may be at a low ebb, but if like me, you're as fond of the ebbs as the flows, now might be the time to see it.

'It'll never be the same,' said the meat man. 'Doesn't matter how much they spend on it. You can't buy the real thing.' And he motored off back to his table, to which his other half had brought more rum. Nope, you can't buy the real thing. Unless you're Half-life.

'So this painting,' I said, when Half-life and Dirty South were back. 'What did you do with it?'

'I sit and look at it every day,' said Half-life, lighting a roll-up.

'You've still got it?'

'Of course. It's in my khazi,' he said, and I retched.

'So if you could sell it, how much would it be worth?' asked Dirty South. Half-life blew his cheeks out.

'Couple of hundred, maybe?' he said.

'*Thousand*?' I ejaculated. Half-life looked hurt.

'Million,' he said, and pocketed my lighter.

Spliff Spots

They don't teach you this at school, but not everywhere is suitable for taking the herb and the hop. It's certainly *verboten* during double chemistry, to which the premature end of my academic journey stands as a testament.

Essentially, you need to be undisturbed by traffic or passers-by, but the premium spot should also afford an interesting vista, which you will find 'amaaazing' soon after ignition. So parks, cemeteries and quiet stretches of the river are ideal. Add some elevation and you're flying Executive Class, even if you are carrying value lager in a Costcutter carrier bag, in your dressing gown.

I would add that persons in authority are to be avoided, but that is surely the case at all times, unless, perhaps, in an emergency, such as when you can't find your gear.

The following are some prime locations to get dreamy with a mate.

Neglected balconies in winter

It's hard to believe that as recently as 10 years ago you could stand on the balcony of the Royal Festival Hall with a pint and a blunt taking in one of London's best sunsets without feeling the long arm of the law on your thigh. Now, partly, I fear, due to our pioneering vision, it's filled with people chatting or typing. Fine, but they are not having as much fun as we did.

In freezing mid-January, all balconies are returned to the hardy Deserters, stoically facing the freeze like woozy polar bears. The Baylis Terrace at the National Theatre was a classic neglected balcony, again with a stunning view, that due to the beautifully confusing brutalism of the Southbank nobody could ever find, except by accident. It's now been developed with less austere seating and long grasses, and renamed for its sponsor. You can still have a little of what you fancy though, if you take the NT's most easterly staircase, preferably armed with a pint from The Understudy next door, until you find a lone table in a corner, overlooking our magnificent riverside and untroubled by lovers of drama and tragedy – unless Half-life's beaten you to it.

London beach

Although you lose elevation by stepping down to the riverbank, the stretch of the Thames from the Undercroft down past the Globe Theatre provides a sensational and seldom-seen view of London. No tourists and few Londoners make it the perfect place to wobble, unseen, in a wilderness in the middle of the capital of the world, to giggle like a spoon.

Heading east, the departing tide reveals plenty of escapes along the river, where even those on the Thames Path can't see you. Though if you're smoking any of Half-life's latest batch you may as well wear a spotlight, as the stench of cannabinoids and departing brain cells alerts all in a 200m radius to your presence. Though my rule with the weed, however unreliable, is that if passers-by even know what the smell is, they probably don't care, or will want some.

Cemeteries

Is it disrespectful to crack open a cold one and spark up on a cemetery bench amid the resting dead? They don't seem to mind. For all we know that might be how they got there. On the other hand, is it respectful to pray to a non-existent being, in order that our imaginary souls may make their way to a fictitious heaven? You choose your poison and I'll smoke mine.

We could write a whole chapter about cemeteries. Indeed, we have. For they're places where peace can be appreciated by those for whom doing nothing comes easy, much like the inhabitants.

Places of elevation

Being able to take in the city from a high vantage point gives one an appreciation of its vastness, its diversity and its very high, pointy buildings. 'Wow!' I sometimes say to myself, looking out at the splendour, 'What a lot of offices.'

But, doobie in one hand and strong cider in the other, words like 'majestic' and 'sweeping magnificence' come to mind, though thankfully I keep them to myself. The two highest points in South London according to my actual guess are Crystal Palace and Shooters Hill and it is from here you can get a sense of London as a teeming mass of activity while you sit on a hill getting quietly blootered. Once in Crystal Palace Park I could have sworn I saw dinosaurs.

Oxleas Woods, off Shooters Hill, is another pleasant place in which to get confused, though that can be dangerous, should you get lost. You could spend years trying to get out of the acres of ancient woodland, if you've brought enough papers.

Parks

You need a secluded spot in a park, well away from children, and more importantly, their parents. Sitting on a fallen tree with a tinnie, looking across the green expanse of Brockwell Park, the lido reclines under the stupidly erect city. Suddenly, getting sacked doesn't seem like such a bad thing.

Greenwich Park also has vantage points where you can easily find seclusion enough to pollute the air while comparing the works of nature, Christopher Wren, Inigo Jones and the children who designed Canary Wharf for a school project for which they nearly got a C minus.

But virtually all parks are magic, in the right frame of mind. They are places of play and are very good for a game of sitting down with the vice of your choice.

Open spaces

The difference between an open space and a park is fences. And the lack of them at places like Blackheath, Hilly Fields and Clapham Common induces a giddy sensation in the city dweller. Not giddy enough to run naked in them, mind. That takes actual tequila. But enough to provoke a sense of quietude that can only be happily disturbed by the hiss of a ring pull and the foamy spit of God's love for us.

On Blackheath there are innumerable spots where you can forget yourself, all within easy reach of a pub and a pond. The views from the heath I particularly like because Canary Wharf (or whatever the fuck it's called) and the bastard Shard are cut down to size by the high plateau you're reclining on.

At the delightful Hilly Fields you can enhance your daydreams by the ancient stone circle, from the monolithic era, dragged to Brockley on the backs of sauropods from faraway Lewisham almost 15 years ago. The thirsty might like to note it is also within striking distance of the London Beer Dispensary.

By some bins

We don't know why bins attract us so much; possibly because they repel others. A favourite spot lies at the bottom of the stairs from London Bridge station to Tooley Street, which we named the Dirty Bit. With half an hour to go before kick off, I often meet Half-life here in order to get into a special condition to enjoy England struggle against Liechtenstein or similar. Nearby, just across the way from The Mudlark and affording views of the river, is its sister site, Dirty Bit-on-Sea. Somehow, over the years, we've found ourselves entering a vague sense of bliss next to hundreds of bins, the mucky little sirens.

We had five years (2004-2009) when cannabis was classified as a less harmful Class C drug, so it's naughtier now, which is nice. In this matter, as in most matters, we assume the government has no idea what is right or wrong and so we must be guided by our instincts. And our instinct is to spark up and get blissed.

A Ballad of Peckham Rye

And did those feet in ancient time
Walk upon England's mountains green:
And was the holy Lamb of God,
On England's pleasant pastures seen!
– William Blake

Peckham Rye, mentioned in the Domesday Book of 1086, developed over succeeding centuries into a playground for South-east London's workers, not just for walking about on, on Sundays and holidays, but also in the form of its legendary 'Fayres'.

King John is said to have granted the right to hold a fayre after enjoying a particularly good day's hunting there (or 'thayre'). Initially held for two or three days at a time, the locals soon realised this was much better than working and increased it first to two weeks, and then to three weeks, at which point it became such an enormous Bacchanalian romp that the authorities banned it and sent everyone back to the office.

Now Peckham Rye is limited to an annual fête in September, quite a genteel affair and hardly the place to get so bladdered you wake up the next morning on a tree stump, naked from the waist down, devoid of all bodily fluids. Which is a shame.

With this in mind I arranged with the usual suspects to get gently cajoled into ecstasy by sun, company and daytime drinking on an historico-literary parkside piss-up in honour of our revelling forefathers.

Hop Burns & Black

I met Dirty South and Roxy at Hop Burns & Black on East Dulwich Road, a shop dedicated to beer, chilli sauce and vinyl in the little parade of shops that features Zandra Rhodes' pink bus stop and kooky bollards. While ale, hot sauce and the crackle of vinyl are three of my favourite things, I do hope that they are the favourite things of enough other people so that it can keep going forever, because this place is brilliant.

We sat out front at the benches and over Siren Craft Brew's fruity Undercurrent we discussed the day's itinerary, which was: literature, pub, archaeology, pub, history, pub, pub and pub. We'd all but finished our beer when Dirty South texted Half-life to see why he was running late.

'I'm not running late,' came the reply. 'I'm eating a bacon sandwich.'

Eventually we spotted him trucking down East Dulwich Road in a Luftwaffe jacket and we scrambled to escort him down to the Rye.

Kings on the Rye

Where East Dulwich Road meets Peckham Rye there now stands a half-hearted attempt at a modern block of flats. This was once the location of the King's Arms pub. Bombed in the Blitz, it was rebuilt and latterly became a pub-cum-nightclub known as Kings on the Rye.

'Fuck me, that was rough house in there,' said Half-life. 'It had its own cab office because no one else would pick up from there.'

'Have you actually been to every pub in history?' asked Roxy.

'Does the Pope shit in the woods?' said Half-life.

The White Horse

Turning north towards Peckham proper and the northern end of the Rye we noticed immediately that this gritty little stretch was changing, with estate agents, coffee shops and health stores in evidence alongside chichi new restaurant Pedler. The White Horse pub, set back a little from Rye Lane, is one of several pubs around the Rye that get a mention in Muriel Spark's *The Ballad of Peckham Rye* and, despite a recent refurbishment, probably looks much as it did when she wrote it, in 1960.

Spark's novella is about the effect an interloper has on the mundane existence of Peckham's working class, for one of whom marriage and saving to put down a deposit on a house are the only things that matter. Ironically, this is a prospect now rapidly being denied to Peckham's working class, along with the middle class, upper class and every other class except the super-rich investor class.

'Yeah. I'm probably the most working-class person in Peckham today,' said Half-life.

'Although, strangely, you don't actually work,' said Dirty South, bravely I thought.

The Nags Head

To Muriel and me, the pub that stands at the northernmost point of the Rye is better known as the Morning Star, which it was called until the turn of the century. No one seems to know for sure, but one struggles to escape the conclusion that its name was changed to the Nags Head in order to cash in on the success of The TV Show That Must Not Be Mentioned.

This, coupled with the fact that it does no real ale, was enough for us to skip it on this occasion. I did however unearth the following review by 'Bertrand' on Beerintheevening.com, which I think bears republishing verbatim:

'we come here wiht how freinds from pekham, it was were del-boy ant rondey are form, the pum is the same as only fooles and horsers , they do'nty do pizza! here it is quiet big and it is near t'e chikceb place and cinese is ar'gross the road, thyre are bus tops here and train starton, thier are lo'ts of butcher to do shoppinge and to get stu'ff>'

I'll have a pint of whatever Bertrand's been on.

The Rye

Heading back south, now on the eastern side of the Rye, we arrived at The Rye pub, the last of Muriel Spark's *Ballad* pubs that we can still visit (a fourth, the Heaton Arms, is now demolished and the fifth, The Harbinger, was fictional). A framed picture of the book cover hung on the wall and commemorated the connection. Out back, The Rye offers table tennis and pétanque in its sizeable garden but it also has a grand interior that can get very busy (and loud) at the weekends, so we elected to sit inside and enjoy having it to ourselves – the 3pm crowd.

It wasn't long, though, before Half-life was greeted with hugs and kisses by first one striking yummy mummy and then another in quick succession.

'Come on,' he said, 'I'd better get out of here before any more show up.'

'How do you do it?' said Roxy.

'Family curse,' said Half-life, gesturing to his groin.

'Oh, God,' said Dirty South.

Opposite The Rye pub there was once a pond that was popular with local bathers and in 1923 this activity was formalised with the building of the Peckham Lido. The lido closed in 1987 and fell into disrepair, and when Southwark Council failed to find a buyer to do it up it was demolished and filled in, with the land returned to general use as part of the Rye. Recently a campaign to get it rebuilt has gathered momentum. Little evidence of the old lido remains today but we were delighted to find, hidden from view behind some trees, the tiered remains of the fountain.

'Get us,' said Half-life, sitting down on it to roll a fag. 'This is like fucking *Time Bandits*.'

'*Timewatch?*' I said.

'About half three,' he said, the idiot.

Peckham Rye is supplemented by the separate but conjoined Peckham Rye Park, into which we now mooched. Years of restoration work led by the Friends of Peckham Rye Park has paid off handsomely and the park is now once again as it was in its Victorian pomp.

The bowling green looked most inviting and we might have stopped for a game had it been open.

'Only open on Saturday and Sunday?' said Dirty South. 'That is an affront to the man of leisure.'

To the south of the bowling green lies the popular Sexby Garden. This ornamental garden was first laid out at the end of the 19th century and later renamed 'Sexby Garden' after Colonel J. J. Sexby, the London County Council's first Chief Officer of Parks. Half-life, it may come as little surprise, insisted on referring to it as the Sexy Garden for the duration of our visit.

Beyond the lake we paused on a little bridge under which ran a rivulet. We were looking at the River Peck, a stream that was mostly enclosed in 1823 but that emerges briefly into daylight in this part of the park and once filled the swimming pond at the northern end.

'Eventually all things become a sexy garden,' said Half-life, 'and a river runs through it.'

The Ivy House

There could, I suppose, be some debate about whether or not, on a tour of Peckham Rye, Nunhead's Ivy House should count as a Ryeside location. Fortunately, we couldn't give a toss either way. We love the place and walked firmly up Stuart Road, purchased some pints of Beavertown's brain-twisting Gamma Ray and settled on the outside benches like dons.

Out front at the Ivy House is a magical early-evening sun trap but we were relieved to be a little early and able to enjoy the shade on a day that was turning out to be a scorcher.

'I see you've got your sandals out of the attic, Raider,' said Roxy.

'I won't be wearing socks again until October, Roxy,' I said. 'Someone has to make a stand.'

'My hero,' said Roxy. 'So, can we just stay here all day now?'

'We've got to find Blake's tree, where he saw his angels,' I said.

'The naked angels,' said Half-life.

'I'm not sure they were naked, mate,' said Dirty South.

'They bloody were,' said Half-life, clearly enjoying a vision of his own. 'And if we find this tree I'm getting in it with 'em.'

Back on the Rye, armed with a growler of London Field's Hackney Hopster (and four plastic glasses) from the Ivy House, we took the path that runs beside Homestall Road, named after the farm that was acquired to enlarge the Rye as part of Peckham Rye Park in 1893. Here the Rye opens out to its full width with a bucolic sweep and London seems quite distant.

It was in the summer of 1765 that poet and artist William Blake, then aged eight, visited Peckham Rye and claimed to have seen visions of angels in a great oak tree. No one (least of all us) knows the location of the Angel Oak, as it came to be called, and anyway it's certainly now long gone, but in 2011 artist John Hartley replanted an oak sapling to commemorate the original.

Pictures from 2013 show the sapling in a very sorry condition and we feared it may have perished, but after inspecting a number of possible small trees in the north-western corner of the Rye, opposite the Harris Boys' Academy, we found the telltale shape of oak leaves on a tiny sapling.

True, it stood barely 12 inches high and was almost swamped by the grass in its wire plant support, but it was unmistakably an oak.

'Jesus, is that it?' said Half-life.

'That's it,' I said.

'I'd like to see you get naked in that,' said Dirty South.

'Don't encourage him,' said Roxy, and we sat down to pour beer and skin up.

Largely unfeted during his lifetime, Blake is now considered to be one of the finest artists these lands have ever produced and the critic Northrop Frye considered him to have produced a body of poetry that 'is in proportion to its merits the least read body of poetry in the English language', which I'm pretty sure is a compliment.

'Turning and turning in the widening gyre,' said Half-life, 'The falcon never hears the falconer.'

'Erm, that's Yeats, you fuppet,' I said.

'Fuppet?' said Roxy.

'I think it's a contraction of fucking and muppet,' I said.

'Nice. Who needs Blake?' said Dirty South.

'I'm on a ride and I want to get off,' said Half-life. 'But they won't slow down the roundabout. I sold the Renoir and the TV set. Don't want to be around when this gets out.'

'What the hell is *that*?' I said, and we waited while Half-life took a long draw on his spliff.

'Duran Duran,' he said, to Roxy's giggles.

'Fuppet,' she said, and Half-life pelted her with cut grass.

We watched as people came and went on the Rye: dogwalkers, joggers, strollers, mothers and children. Londoners going about their business. Roxy's eye was taken by some young men playing rugby.

'There's something wonderful about sitting here, isn't there, with the sun on your back, the smell of the grass, strong young men playing incomprehensible games...' she said.

'Yeah, it's peak England.'

'Mmm. Perfect.'

We fell silent for a moment to take it all in, lost within our individual thoughts and daydreams.

'Pint?' I said.

'Too fucking right,' said Half-life.

The Herne Tavern

With a reputation as a family-friendly gastropub, the Herne Tavern can get very busy at weekends, but at 5.30pm on a sunny Thursday it felt more like a country pub with a relaxed, airy vibe and we sat inside to get some respite from the sun and compare freckles.

The Clock House

Afterwards, we wandered down to the Clock House where I recalled many years ago grimly informing a friend that his hot nurse girlfriend was now my hot nurse girlfriend.

'Don't worry about it,' he said. 'Soon she'll be someone else's girl-friend.' And she bloody well was an' all.

The Clock House provided the official Best View of the Rye from a Pub of the day, framed by a mature wisteria and aided by the calming influence of plate-glass windbreaks or 'break-winds' as I inadvertently rechristened them.

'You don't want plate-glass break-winds,' cautioned Half-life. 'You'd lacerate your A-hole.'

The Harbinger?

The Cafe G down the road – an 'artisan kitchen and coffee house bak-ery' – is actually licensed, but as it was advertising something called 'Gymboree', aimed at pre-school children and parents, we thought better of stopping off. And anyway, we felt compelled to complete the circuit by returning to Hop Burns & Black, where the proprietor, Glenn, welcomed us travellers back for a final flourish.

At least I think it was a final flourish. On a day of visions, I do have half-remembered snatches of Half-life being a naked dancing angel at some later point. I'm just hoping it was in The Harbinger and not the East Dulwich Tavern.

Ten Best Places to be Dead

The requirements of the recently deceased are slender, at most. No, cemeteries are for the living. Places of quietude for those times when you don't want to be bothered by anyone. Away from the corruption, the filth, the blood, the shit, the mucus, the stains... I could go on.

'I do love a cemetery,' Roxy told me, on being invited to sample some of the best places to get planted in South London.

'I love the sense of peace,' I said.

'I like the booze, the sex and the drugs.'

I was out of my league, again. Of course, I've paused on a cemetery bench with a J and a Continental lager. I'm only human. But for Roxy, her hip flask and tin of ready-rolled 'beasts' have led to more horizontal refreshment with her lover *du jour* atop the remains of two poets, an admiral and an American president. And to think I was merely hopeful for a go on her beast.

As I selected which cemeteries to visit, I realised there's no point in being selfish about your own passing. If you are going to be laid to rest in South London, you may as well consider visitors. Does your final resting place provide a characterful wander through peaceful lanes? A stirring view? Interesting residents? A nice pub nearby? Or if you're Roxy, cushions?

Charlton Cemetery

Founded as a 'Gentleman's Cemetery', there are plenty of colonial governors and knights of the realm lying around, but the most interesting grave belongs to Thomas Murphy (d. 1932), who owned Charlton greyhound stadium (also dead and gone).

Prior to taking up dog racing, Murphy ran a circus act – a 13-piece monkey jazz band. One night they escaped during a burglary and the ones that remained at large caused havoc near White City. Two made a home under a Tube platform, nipping out to raid a greengrocer's and a sweet shop, while Bimbo (drums, percussion) managed to change trains and ride first class to Rugby before capture. Two greyhound statues sit at the foot of Murphy's rather grand grave, with no monkeys in sight.

Roxy seemed strangely unimpressed by the freestyling simians.

'I know I'm supposed to like jazz, but for me, it's like musical incontinence,' she said. 'I'd be more surprised if monkeys couldn't play jazz.'

Where to carry on: The White Swan, Charlton Village

Woolwich Cemetery

Not quite the saddest message amidst a solemn sea of headstones at Woolwich Cemetery declares: 'WARNING Thieves are operating in this area'.

'What the specific fuck?' asked Roxy, among the war graves and the final resting places of workers who died in explosions at the Royal Arsenal. 'What are they nicking – flowers?'

The grim honour of saddest goes to the giant cross commemorating the SS Princess Alice disaster that we mentioned earlier – 120 of the perished lie near the memorial, which was paid for by a National Sixpenny Subscription, crowdfunding by another name, to which 23,000 people contributed.

Where to carry on: The Old Mill, Plumstead Common

Beckenham Cemetery

Beckenham's cemetery is distinguished by being the only one in the collection that can be accessed by tram, at Birkbeck tram stop, to be precise. Travelling by this slick new take on an old tune, you're practically sneaking up on the dead, which is infinitely preferable to the other way round.

Another feature here is the waterfall in the garden of remembrance, adding the soothing trickle of liquid to the sense of peace. It's also a nice link to Thomas Crapper, whose innovations in flushing toilets we all honour daily.

Crapper lies in the company of W.G. Grace, one of our greatest cricketers, whose incredible career spanned 44 seasons. He eventually agreed to relinquish his place in the England team at the age of 51, admitting to his fading prowess in the field, saying 'the ground was getting a bit too far away'. Sadly, it is no longer.

Where to carry on: The Graces Bar & Grill, though on Fridays and Saturdays it's worth the 20-minute walk to Southey Brewing's taproom

Hither Green Cemetery

We liked that there were two Gothic chapels at Hither Green, one for Anglicans and another, now disused, for dissenters.

'I'm all for the dissenters,' said Roxy. 'But if they really wanted to dissent, they could have built a pub instead of another chapel.'

As green, wild and peaceful as Hither Green is, you are going to need something strong if you come across the mass grave of Sandhurst Road School bombing, commemorating the 38 children and six teachers who died in an air raid in 1943.

'Glad I came prepared,' said Roxy, taking a large glug of brandy from her flask.

'The senseless waste of young life?' I said.

'No, the nearest pub's an Antic. Doesn't open till four.'

Where to carry on: Baring Hall Hotel, Grove Park

Lambeth Cemetery

Small but charming, Lambeth hosts a number of medalled veterans of the Anglo-Sikh wars about which we are generally taught fuck all. It's hard for modern eyes to look on imperial military as heroes in the same way as we do, say, those who gave their lives defending us from the Nazis. But bravery is bravery, and I for one, have very little of it.

A more recent inductee is Mark Ashton, the co-founder of Lesbians and Gays Support the Miners, who was buried here in 1987. Ashton was immortalised in the award-winning movie *Pride*, a feel-good film in the British tradition of *The Full Monty* and *Brassed Off*.

'It didn't mention his years in the Young Communist League, did it?' Roxy said of a movie she enjoyed. 'You can't mention the c-word if you want to sell to the States. For a heavily armed country, they're awfully scared of words.'

Where to carry on: The Antelope, Mitcham Road

Camberwell Old & New Cemeteries

Camberwell Old Cemetery features some lovely overgrown stretches, home to some rare species. Acres have been lost – dug up by Southwark Council – but more are currently under threat from plans to create more burial spaces. They are being vociferously defended by the Save Southwark Woods campaign, however. You can always find more dead people, but urban woodlands like this are irreplaceable.

There's something pleasantly maudlin about strolling among 19th-century graves that being around modern tombstones can't provide. Like their inhabitants have been dead so long they're practically over it. No longer mourned, they afford the silent company my friends refuse me.

Nearby Camberwell New Cemetery is much smarter and more open, or as Roxy put it: 'Flat, with not enough hiding places.' It houses quite a few hardmen, including George Cornell, a mobster shot dead by Ronnie Kray for calling him a 'fat poofter', in a poor advert for speaking your mind.

And then there's the grave of Freddie Mills.

'*The* Freddie Mills?' asked Roxy, suddenly interested.

'Yes, *the* Freddie Mills. From *Carry On Constable* and *Fun At St Fanny's*.'

'The World Light-Heavyweight Champion of the World, Freddie Mills?'

'Possibly.'

Freddie Mills (1919-1965) lived in Denmark Hill and was the most popular boxer in post-war Britain, before going into the entertainment game. He was found dead in his car outside his Soho nightclub. The official verdict was suicide; he had shot himself in the head. Twice. As well as attracting the boxing fraternity, his funeral was attended by Bruce Forsyth, Norman Wisdom and Bob Monkhouse, so at least he was able to miss that.

Where to carry on: The London Beer Dispensary, Crofton Park

Brockley & Ladywell Cemetery

Here, you can stroll amid a wildlife haven with poets, a Cuban anarchist, a murder victim and a lady who toured the country as 'the ugliest woman in the world'.

The grave of the gifted poet and friend of Wilde and Yeats, Ernest Dowson (1867-1900), was recently restored here. Being of the Decadent movement, he was fond of prostitutes and absinthe and at least one of those was served at the Brockley Jack pub at the informal reception that followed the celebration of his work in 2010. 'They are not long, the days of wine and roses,' wrote Dowson, famously, and he was right.

The 'poor wounded wonderful fellow', as Wilde described him, died in Catford, at the age of 32, from consumption, though the drop of port he had at 6am on the morning of his death was indicative of his unhelpful alcoholism. I began to read Dowson's catchily titled 'Non sum qualis eram bonae sub regno Cynarae' to Roxy, as we walked through the cemetery's nature trail:

> *'I cried for madder music and for stronger wine,*
> *But when the feast is finished and the lamps expire,*
> *Then falls thy shadow, Cynara! the night is thine...'*

'Yeah, beautiful and all that,' she said. 'But can our shadows fall into a pub now, or what?'

Where to carry on: Ladywell Tavern

Greenwich Cemetery

'Few others can offer such a vast panorama of London, not even Highgate,' writes Darren Beach in *London's Cemeteries.*

What Greenwich lacks in celebrity and atmosphere it makes up for in aspect. It's a breathtaking view, clearly wasted on the dead. There are, however, half a dozen shelters scattered about for the living to gather their thoughts and skin up.

But what's this? They are all boarded up! You're in a cemetery, visiting your dearly departed (possibly) and you'd like to step out of the wind, rain and misery for a moment? Well, screw you. Get back to your graveside and make sure you dress for melancholy weather next time.

It's unspeakably mean. Cemeteries Manager Ken Wood (real name) said they suffered some unspecified antisocial behaviour in the shelters a few years ago and were 'monitoring the situation on a regular basis'. I do hope the errant behaviour wasn't me and the Dulwich Raider smoking a blunt in the gloaming a while back.

I could understand it if mourners were being disturbed while paying their respects, but if it was just kids with alcopops and spray cans, surely there is a better way than depriving everybody of the opportunity to take in this unique vista with a sit down, a tinnie and some Old Holborn?

Where to carry on: The Long Pond, Westmount Road, Eltham

West Norwood Cemetery

If you think a well-tended grave could be important in the afterlife, you'd best get your name down at West Norwood sharpish. It has a wealth of ostentatious tombs and vaults and 69 listed structures, many of which are grander than anywhere you are going to rest while you're alive. It's also teeming with life, ironically.

'What is that hideous racket?' I whispered, a little zubed.

'That's a sparrowhawk,' said Roxy. '*Accipiter nisus.* So the other birds are shitting themselves in case it eats them.'

'Oh, right, yeah,' I said, becalmed. 'Is that… normal?' Roxy shot me a look that suggested I wasn't.

West Norwood Cemetery contains what's left of Sir Henry Tate (sugar and art) and Hiram Maxim (light bulbs and machine guns), but our favourite spot is the Smokers' bench.

Tucked away in the north-eastern corner is a bench commemorating the lives of Bill, Ambrose and Elsie Smoker. Naturally, the bench has become a magnet for local tokers and legend has it that they leave one another special ready-rolled gifts there, though on our visit we were obliged to roll our own. Ambrose William Smoker was awarded the MBE for services to young people, and even in death, his work continues, providing a place to celebrate his family name in the most literal fashion possible.

Where to carry on: The Great North Wood

Nunhead Cemetery

Like West Norwood, Nunhead is one of London's 'Magnificent Seven' cemeteries, only this baby has it all. Probably the most beautiful cemetery in London, it has history, nature, tranquillity, views and is enjoyed by quite a lot of the undeceased. We were joined on this trip to burial-ground royalty by Half-life and the Raider.

Worryingly, it's easy to get lost in. Nunhead Cemetery sprawls over 52 acres of spooky woodland, with meandering lanes lined with overgrown graves, scattered at angles like an ogre's teeth. Despite the numerous dogs taking their humans for some much-needed exercise, it's easy to find a spot to contemplate one's significance.

There's something about the air and light here that slows you down to a sub-London pace, where you can hear your own thoughts, should you have any. You could be anywhere, with nesting birds heard above the rustle of your carrier bag as you fumble for some Neck Oil. Well, you could be anywhere that had the constant air traffic of a major metropolitan hub, anyway.

We settled on the bench that looks out to St Paul's Cathedral. Roxy shared her hip flask and lit up another beast.

'Well, I've had booze and drugs...' Half-life said, having heard of Roxy's graveyard peccadilloes. 'What's next?'

'Your days of wine and roses are gone with the wind, sunshine,' she scoffed, mixing up her Dowson.

I retracted a previous post-life desire to have myself stuffed and placed on a bar stool at my local. An eternity of being so close to a pint, but being unable to have one is, quite literally, a fate worse than death. But, I pondered in my herbal haze, providing a surface for misbehavers to enjoy a sit down, a snout and maybe even each other's flesh above my resting bones is infinitely more appealing.

Where to carry on: The Ivy House

Tramlink Trail

I bought Half-life a pint of Atlantic APA in the Brixton Brewery tap-room and put it down in front of him, next to the remains of his first. As the ale worked its magic I set about persuading him to accompany me on my latest time-wasting assignment: a day trip to visit the top three CAMRA South West London (SWL) pubs of the year.

They had been announced earlier in the month and one of them, as I pointed out to Half-life, was less than two miles from his Brixton front door.

'I dunno,' he said, 'South-west London?'

'You live in South-west London,' I reminded him. 'We're sitting in South-west London.'

'South London,' he insisted. 'We're in South London. Postcodes are a tool of repression.'

'We could take the tram,' I said, trying to jazz it up a little.

'What tram?' said Half-life.

'Isn't there a tram that goes to Wimbledon?' I said.

'I doubt it,' he said.

It's possible that, as for Half-life, Tramlink may not figure large in your life, perhaps due to its route being through some of the outer zones of South London. Despite this, the line has been around since the beginning of the century and denying the possibility of its existence is essentially futile.

Some light research revealed that it runs from Beckenham and other points south-east via Croydon to Wimbledon. And, hopefully, back again.

'Why would anyone want to go from Croydon to Wimbledon?' asked Half-life.

'Tennis?' said a friendly stranger who had joined our table.

'Balls,' said Half-life, being at once appropriate and inappropriate, one of his gifts. Finally persuaded that Tramlink was a reality, Half-life curled his lip at me.

'So, let me get this straight,' he said. 'You want to go all the way over to Fuckenham so we can get a tram all the way back to Wankledon so we can go to the pub?'

'Correct,' I said.

'That is fucking senseless,' he said, handing me his empty glass. 'I'm in.'

The Graces Bar & Grill

Tram stop: Birkbeck

In fact, we started our Tramlink tour at Birkbeck, on the Elmers End Road. Or to be more precise, the Graces Bar & Grill next door, which we espied upon arrival and into which, with an unspoken, almost telepathic thirst, we diverted.

Having been closed for years, The Graces reopened in 2014 as a sports bar – appropriately enough, as it was originally named W.G. Grace's after the famous cricketer (and early hipster), whose bones, as we know, lie in the outfield of the adjacent Beckenham Cemetery.

A partially glazed roof gives the place the feel of a conservatory, like sitting in the day room of an old people's home. An old people's home offering cask ale, big-screen sport, live music, pool and Indian food – as all old people's homes should.

As we were on an ale trail, we tried the Spitfire Gold which, despite being lighter in colour and a touch more hoppy than regular Spitfire, still basically tastes of Spitfire, which is a taste I unacquired some years ago. It wasn't bad, but we knew better was to come.

As we sauntered round to the tram stop I'm not ashamed to say I experienced a twinge of excitement. My first time on Tramlink!

I was put in mind of Belgium's glorious Kusttram and the cable cars of San Francisco. I recalled the iconic trams of Lisbon, where the number 28 takes you on a jaw-dropping ride through the Alfama, past São Jorge Castle and spectacular views of the Tejo, down into the grand squares of the Baixa, up again to the buzzing, bohemian Barrio Alto and on into Estrela, with its magnificent basilica.

Today, though, we were travelling from Penge to Croydon.

Much of the 17 miles of track runs on former railway lines, but the thrill of trams, of course, is when they appear to drift into shared spaces with cars, buses and even people, who mill about like they couldn't give a monkey's that carriages are driving all over the roads.

When we left the old rail line after Addiscombe and joined the road I even caught Half-life looking up the track out of the window.

'Exciting, isn't it?' I said.

'I was just watching that rat,' he replied.

Green Dragon

Tram stop: George Street

Our first stop – partly so we could change to Route 3 for Wimbledon and partly in order to sample the delights of the Green Dragon, a pub on Croydon's High Street that I'd heard champions real ale – was George Street.

The presence of trams, tramlines and overhead cables gave Croydon the air of a foreign town, with the town's older buildings looking their best in the sun and a backdrop of blue skies. It was a bit like being on holiday, not least as we were on our way to the pub on a Tuesday afternoon.

With up to six hand-pumped casks available and another two behind the bar dispensing via the use of Earth's gravity, it was easy to see why Green Dragon is so feted. Its handsome interiors were filled with a late lunchtime crowd, not shy of downing a couple before returning to work, sending inappropriate email and sleeping it all off in the lavs. As part of his terms of engagement, I'd agreed to buy Half-life lunch and we perused the menu.

'I'll have the beef and chorizo pie, please,' said Half-life to the barmaid.

'All our mains are half price today,' she replied.

'I'll have two beef and chorizo pies, please,' said Half-life, for whom value is paramount.

Back on the tram, at the next stop, Church Street, a group of older men joined our carriage, wearing anoraks and walking boots and taking notes on little pads. I nudged Half-life.

'Tram-spotters,' I whispered. Half-life looked over at them and then back at me, as I wrote a note on my own little pad, and he muttered something to himself.

The Tramlink section between Croydon and Wimbledon mostly follows the route of an old British Rail route that closed in 1997 so it could be converted for trams. Between Reeves Corner and Phipps Bridge it follows the Surrey Iron Railway, a 19th-century horse-drawn plateway which gives Tramlink a claim to be one of the world's oldest railway alignments.

'The Turkish writer Mehmet Murat ildan says the tram is the literary and magical version of the train,' I told Half-life.

'It's the slow version of the train,' said Half-life, possibly wearying of my jibber-jabber.

At Mitcham we spotted two old fellers in sunglasses sitting on the grass bank with a black plastic bag full of promise.

'Look at those lucky sods,' said Half-life. 'And I'm stuck on here with Michael fucking Portillo.'

Hand in Hand

Tram stop: Wimbledon

With no let-up in the spring sunshine we were faced with a dry, dusty walk up from the station to our next pub and Half-life was fearful we might not make it without taking further fluids on board.

'Here you are, let's try in here,' he said, marching into the Lu-Ma Cafe on Worple Road, despite the advertising therein of holistic therapies, juices and 'healing'.

'Two lagers please, love,' he said to the girl at the counter.

'We're a healthy-eating cafe, I'm afraid,' she replied. Half-life shrugged.

'Guinness, then,' he said.

We pushed on unquenched but it wasn't long before a right turn up Wright's Alley, a public right of way through the middle of King's College School, brought us out opposite our quarry, the Hand in Hand, number three in CAMRA SWL's pubs of the year.

A Young's pub, it is that splendid oddity – a country pub in the big city, featuring an open fire and a clutch of tables for regulars in the cottage-style original bar. Up to eight cask ales are available including, on our visit, an impressive Tower Special Pale Ale by Wimbledon Brewery, named as a nod to the original brewery building, a renowned five-storey tower brewery which burned down in 1889. We took the sun on the little front terrace, or at least I did, as Half-life lingered to make conversation with the Aussie barmaid we'd befriended, suddenly strangely happy to hear all about the trams in Melbourne.

Afterwards we paused awhile on a bench on the Common while Half-life fashioned a doobie from his magic tin. As we did so a group of teenage boys arrived at the pond and some of them began to undress. Down to their pants and with the rest filming on their phones, half a dozen of them proceeded to run into the pond shouting 'Come on, Layton!', the name of one of the houses at King's College.

'If they're our future leaders, God help us,' I said.

'I bet your school was like this, wasn't it?' said Half-life.

'Well, we did lose Simmonds over the weir during the bumps one year,' I replied. (In fact, I attended a comprehensive, but I think Half-life enjoys the fantasy.)

'Posh cunt,' he said, happily.

The Dog and Fox

We made an unscheduled stop at another Young's pub, the Dog and Fox in Wimbledon Village, when Half-life complained of a full bladder. Two other Wimbledon beers were on offer here – the Common Pale Ale and the Quartermaine IPA, which at 5.8% immediately attracted Half-life's attention. Ordinary mortals might start or finish with a 5.8-er, Half-life has them as tweenies.

'I thought you wanted the toilet?' I said, as we waited for the beer to be poured.

'I'll have a pint first, like,' he said, 'now I'm here.'

Opposite the pub stood the old fire station, which was built on the site of the aforementioned original Wimbledon Brewery. We toasted it with beer from the new. The Quartermaine was not only delicious – all musty bitterness with a hint of fruit cake (not unlike Half-life himself) – but proved a game-changer. Now we were positively aglow with that special camaraderie you get from shared travel. Not to mention drinking since lunchtime.

'If I'm not careful, I might start to enjoy myself,' said Half-life.

Back at Wimbledon station, rush hour was whirling all around us and we got tutted at by harried workers for getting confused by pink tram validators.

'Sorry, pal,' said Half-life to one of them. 'We're from London.'

The Trafalgar

Tram stop: Merton Park

By contrast, the natives in The Trafalgar, two stops back down the line in Merton, were friendly from the off. This one-roomed beauty stands alone beside some newer housing estates and is a pub where chatting at the bar is part of the experience, unlike my local Wetherspoon's, in which it is expressly forbidden.

On the beer front, the Downton Quadhop, a pale and hoppy session bitter, was so moreish that by the second pint we were planning a trip to Wiltshire to visit the brewery and spend all day lolling in the taproom.

And when a man (Richard Barrick) came in bearing a tray of the most sensational home-cooked pork pies one began to fully understand the attention to detail required to be a winner. 'The Traf' was voted pub of the year by the fine men and women of CAMRA SWL.

The Nightingale

Tube stop: Clapham South

Our final stop of the day, number two in the CAMRA SWL top three, was not on the tram route so we joined the Northern Line at South Wimbledon to head for Clapham South. Actually, we meant to get off at Balham but missed the stop because, speaking frankly, we were drunk.

'Oh, I know this one!' said Half-life as we approached The Nightingale on Nightingale Lane, yet another Young's pub, in the gloaming. 'This is near Two Thumbs Tony's.'

The place was impressively full for seven o'clock and once again there was a lot of bar-standing and chatting. It's not a small pub but the different sections give it a cosy, intimate feel and with summer around the corner it was the perfect time to be reminded of a classic winter pub experience, just before we go all straw hats and T-shirt tan. We were delighted to see that one of the guest ales was Wimbledon's Common Pale Ale. A hat-trick up! W.G. Grace would have been proud.

Given its proximity to Clapham, the pub's clientele was a surprising mixture of young and old, rich and getting by, middle and working classes – a proper community pub. The only thing that possibly told a different story was a sign offering 'Boat Race and Roast' on Sunday, referring to the upcoming University Boat Race between Oxford and Cambridge.

'Rowing?' growled Half-life.

'Toughest sport I've ever participated in,' I said.

'What, harder than bumming Jennings in the shower?' he said.

'You know nothing of my days at Nether Wallop,' I said.

'We've got a right couple 'ere!' said a regular.

We had another pint and a deranged game of darts, during which Half-life declared The Nightingale the greatest pub in the world – though he does say that a lot.

'And the weird thing is, it's only a couple of miles from my gaff,' he said. 'Why didn't you say?'

Looking for South London

The BBC recently repeated its long ting 1970s series, *The Pallisers,* a sort of Victorian-era *House of Cards,* which is based on the six 'Parliamentary Novels' of Anthony Trollope. I know this because Mrs Raider, as is her way, binge-watched the entire 26-episode series, including during mealtimes, and started wilfully discussing patriarchy, political probity and concepts of domestic dominion.

'Silence, woman! I shall hear no more of it,' I stormed finally, visibly upset, I hoped.

Secretly, I researched Trollope in order to find some dirt on him, which is to say, I looked him up on BrainyQuote (like many today, I find Wikipedia so long winded and full of paragraphs). Almost immediately I came across this: 'I can conceive of no contentment of which toil is not to be the immediate parent.'

What? And this: 'There is no human bliss equal to twelve hours of work with only six hours in which to do it.'

For real? And even: 'As to happiness in this life it is hardly compatible with that diminished respect which ever attends the relinquishing of labour.'

Oh, Jesus. That did it. Trollope clearly stood against everything I hold sacred. I grimly forbade Mrs Raider from mentioning the man's name ever again. So it came as some surprise when she brought him up *the very next day.*

We were sitting in S.i.A, the quirky cafe-bar hidden down a cobbled path off Coldharbour Lane, drinking beer for lunch and wondering where we were. We knew we were in Loughborough Junction and not Camberwell, but were we in SE5 or SW9?

I related to Mrs Raider Half-life's stance that there is only one true area south of the river: South London. Any further subdivision is, in his view, overly fussy and smacks of federal control and cuntly interference.

'I agree,' she replied, unexpectedly. 'I'm a South London girl.'

'It is odd that there is no S postcode, isn't it?' I said. 'After all, there's an N one.'

'Well you know who to blame for that, don't you?' she said.

'Is it Mark Zuckerberg?' I replied.

'Anthony Trollope,' she said, ignoring me.

'Yeah. OK, love,' I said, nodding at her beer. 'Make that your last one.'

The story of S

Can there be anything more annoying than being told something by your other half that a) you didn't know and b) is utterly fascinating? Forced to return to the Internet when Mrs Raider visited the Ladies, I read with eye-widening incredulity that Anthony Trollope had worked for the General Post Office. Furthermore, he was given the brief of streamlining the 10 London postal districts that had been introduced in 1856, and which originally included a dedicated South section. Following his report, the South district was abolished and its area summarily split between SW and SE. South London had been disappeared, and it was Trollope what done it.

Since we were already on the cusp of SE and SW we decided, having nothing better to do, to down our drinks and explore this boundary, this borderline created by the stroke of a postal clerk's pen, this course through the centre of the lands once known as South London, where east meets west.

We set off to examine, if you will, Trollope's Passage.

The Hero of Switzerland

Stepping onto Coldharbour Lane we saw road signs advertising SE24 to the south and SE5 to the north and then, retracing our steps, saw little Station Avenue opposite... in SW9. Here be magic! We turned into Loughborough Road looking to head back towards the SW9/SE5 border and northward-ish to the river.

'I think if we head up Minet Road we'll be going the right way,' I said, but Mrs Raider was crossing the road in the opposite direction, heading towards the Hero of Switzerland pub.

'Where are you going?' I called.

'Aren't we going to go into every pub on the way?' she asked and I stared at her for a moment, lost in wonder.

'I don't care what they say,' I said. 'I think you're smashing.'

Refreshed by cold beer – which had to be taken in the garden due to the regulars watching a melodramatic '80s soap opera at full volume – we walked up Minet and into Knatchbull Road, past the Minet Library that Lambeth is shamefully determined to close and turn into a gym, with a few books left in the showers as a sop to the naysayers. If ever there was something to try the resolve of an optimist it is this: libraries, filled with dreams and quietude, words and the Internet, invaded by dead-eyed bankers on cross-trainers watching VH1.

But we had less important things to worry about. On Knatchbull we spotted that while we were currently back in SE5, a road joining it from the west was actually in SW9. Dizzy with excitement, I had Mrs Raider stand in SW9 while I remained in the south-east.

'Do you feel any different?' I called.

'Yes,' she replied, hands on hips.

'How so?' I asked, preparing to jot down some notes.

'I feel slightly more bored than I did when we were at the pub,' she said.

A scientist's life, I was learning, can be a lonely one.

The Kennington

In Myatt's Fields, SE5, we forensically examined the charming Little Cat Cafe for signs of booze but were forced to leave empty handed and cut back through a corner of SW9 towards Camberwell New Road.

We passed the new and impressive Akerman Health Centre building that stands on the edge of the Myatt's Fields Estate (once known by the youth as 'The Dads' due to its resemblance to war-torn Baghdad). For a moment I thought I may have to be admitted when a cracked heel made itself known to me, but some Savlon and a plaster with racing cars on it did the trick and I was able to continue.

'Heart of a lion,' said Mrs Raider.

'Thanks, babe,' I said.

'Feet of a chicken,' she muttered.

In The Kennington on Camberwell New Road, aided by a pint of Landlord, I continued my research on Trollope and the GPO. It turned out that S wasn't the only one to suffer in the 19th-century postcode scandal. Two years earlier, NE, another of the original 'compass point' postal districts, had also been done away with and absorbed in its entirety into E!

In this case, fearing the wrath of local residents, the Post Office simply didn't tell them they were doing it. When eventually they came clean in 1869 there were petitions and protests from people and businesses who felt they would be adversely affected by being lumped in with the East End.

We were reminded of those lovable fools who a century earlier had protested at the introduction of the Gregorian calendar and the requisite overnight jump from 2 September to 14 September, 1752. 'Give us our 11 days!' they were said to have demanded and we laughed merrily at their expense. Then we remembered we were furious about the loss of our S and decided it was no laughing matter.

'Let's start a campaign to reinstate it,' said Mrs Raider, emboldened by half a Guinness.

But sadly, this cannot be. For, to make non-laughing matters worse, South London's S was picked up by Sheffield, which just happened to be passing at the right time and couldn't believe its luck when it saw it lying about, discarded on London's golden paving. (NE was pinched by Newcastle.)

Italo Deli

We pressed on up to The Oval cricket ground at Kennington, which balances on the boundary of SE11 and SW8, and we had a brief argument about whether it was a carbuncular blight on the area or a thrilling dream theatre of quintessential British sportness. Unable to agree, we left SE11 and turned into Bonnington Square, SW8, where we settled the argument through the use of wine, Coleman coffee and thick-filled Parma ham sandwiches in the late-afternoon sun. Trollope's Passage, we agreed, was stuffed full of stimulating delights. And we had yet to reach the water.

At Vauxhall, SE1 snakes out a long waterside limb and claims the last bit of SE before you hit the river, beside the huge green and white edifice that houses MI6, our secret intelligence service – though don't tell anybody. We sat on the little beach that appears at low tide and smoked a jazz fag as we looked out across the water.

'Fancy one in the Morpeth Arms for old times' sake?' I said.

'Better not,' said Mrs Raider. 'I need to be fresh for *Silent Witness* tomorrow.'

'You and those bloomin' box sets,' I said.

'Not watching it!' she said. 'I'm in it. The agency called this morning. Someone's got to pay for all this research.'

'Fair enough,' I said. We did go to The Morpeth, though.

School Run Pub Crawl

It started with a hangover. It ended with a kiss.

Spider, back in the country from a spell sorting out the Indian subcontinent, had crashed at mine, so we must have been in some state the night before. Nonetheless I had to take my little boy (six) to school that morning and, dutiful occasional uncle that he is, Spider got up and came too. Whenever he stays at ours, whether hung over or injured, Spider comes down the stairs head first, on his belly, like a slug, just to give my little guy a giggle. That's family, that is.

At the best of times, Spider looks like an exotic traveller – an adventurer, he'd like to think. In the mornings, however, he looks like a fucked-up hermit: his long hair and beard all over the place, bloodshot eyes, puffy, vague, a bit mad. When he accompanied us to the primary school, parents recoiled and teachers stood their ground at the gate. My lad gave his Uncle Spider a big hug and off to class he went.

We staggered to the Centre Cafe in Lee Green, in the doomed Lee-gate shopping precinct (UK's Worst Shopping Centre, 2010) where a soothing full English restored us. It was there that Spider became intrigued by the building opposite us: the Edmund Halley, Lee's Wetherspoon's.

'As a scientist, I feel compelled to pay my respects to Edmund Halley,' he announced.

'I thought you were a philosopher.'

'I am part scientist, part philosopher.'

'You're neither,' I told him. 'You're a gaudy dilettante.'

Some would take that as an insult. It's to Spider's credit that he took it as a compliment and gave the world the big, theatrical laugh of a

wanton dandy, before mincing about shouting, 'I'm a gaudy dilettante!' to the bemusement of the builders peering over *The Sun*.

Spider wanted to know why the pub was called the Edmund Halley. He's buried nearby, I told him, along with two other Astronomers
Royal. Lee is practically a ghetto of dead stargazers.

'We must go in there immediately and we must do so now,' he
boomed.

I knew it was unwise, but surely a pint at 10am would convince us
it was time for a nap to restore our senses to something approaching
equilibrium. My only appointment of the day, picking up Our Kid
after school, would be in safe, sober hands. Unfortunately, the pale
ale was fresh, delectable and cheap. It was so refreshing that we were
powerless against the lure of another pint. Thankfully, we soon began
to notice the smell of piss emanating from the intricate 'Spoon's carpet
and felt compelled to depart after two.

Now we had a mission. Spider wanted to see the graves of the three
astronomers: Halley, Nathaniel Bliss and John Pond, all residing at St
Margaret's Churchyard, nearby. It was our misfortune to discover that
the path to the graveyard would take us past the Old Tiger's Head.
Worse, it was now open. 11am is a semi-respectable time for a pint,
though perhaps not if it's going to be your third.

However, we persevered. It's an historic old pub that was a soldiers'
stop-off on the way to the Battle of Waterloo. It had been a boxing
and horse racing venue and – who knows for sure? – could even have
once refreshed Karl Marx during his brief spell in Lee, picking up
some lumpenproletariat insights.

We only stopped for one though because science doesn't sleep.
Sadly, neither does geography, so on the way down Lee High Road,
we were unable to pass the Duke of Edinburgh – with its lovely beer-
garden lean over the trickle of the River Quaggy – without popping
in to test the waters. A substandard ale there though led us out fairly
swiftly into the loving embrace of the Dacre Arms, a country pub in
the backstreets of South London, all hanging hops and incomprehensible brass items, and our last stop before church.

From The Dacre, there's a little alley through to St Margaret's and,
despite Spider mounting several graves, no comet-botherers were in

evidence. It was only when we discovered the Old Churchyard across the road where the remains of the original, medieval, church lie that hope was restored. Unfortunately, the gate was padlocked, though this is no barrier to an inveterate climber like Spider. It was more of a challenge for someone like me. I am less resistant to the call of gravity, but I got over in the end, accompanied by involuntary grunts of protest. It's a shame they find it necessary to lock away what's left of a church dating back to circa 1080 and its numerous notable dead. You might be forgiven for thinking it's a sign of the times, but, back around the turn of the 19th century, when Lady Dacre was offering her nightly prayer at her late husband's tomb here, she was robbed of her gold watch and chain by a highwayman.

At length, Spider was able to find satisfaction and spark up a fag by the bones of a great mind. Despite publishing a pioneering catalogue of the stars of the southern skies and making breakthroughs on planetary orbits and navigation, it was Halley's identification of a recurring visiting comet that ensured his immortality, along with his successful prediction of when it would return, after his death. Halley's Comet will next appear in 2061.

'Knackers, I'm going to miss it,' said Spider.

'Man, your diary gets packed, doesn't it?'

'I'll be dead, you prune. So will you,' he said. 'We're just too late. Another generation and we'll crack mortality, you watch. We can live forever.'

'Not the way we're going, we can't.'

'Yeah, well, we might as well enjoy ourselves. We're all going to die.'

'Cheery little fucker, aren't you?'

'Mind you, in the future, you might as well enjoy yourself because you're *not* going to die.'

'Lucky buggers. And they'll have robots to clean the bog and tell them their hair looks nice.'

'Yup. Well, if we're going to miss his comet, I'm glad we went to his stinky pub.'

At this point, I still had time for a nap and strong coffee in order to sober up enough to pick up the nipper from school without disgracing myself. Heath Lane took us towards Blackheath but fate conspired against us once more. Someone had placed the Hare & Billet in our way, standing invitingly by a pond, like a pub by water, somehow. And through the window I could see the golden tresses of my favourite barmaid, Emma, behind the bar. Fortuna, you merciless mistress!

The Titian beer nurse laughed at the state of us. She was used to seeing me appear a little second hand, but not by lunchtime. As it so often does, the H&B provided the best ale of the day. We explained our tortuous journey from school drop off to school pick up, via science. She took notes.

A nap was now off the agenda, but a double espresso at Hand Made Food would help right this listing vessel a little, before facing the stern harbour of dry land. But Spider had other ideas and insisted we pop in The Crown, a pub I tend to walk past despite its lovely aspect, it being a Shepherd Neame house. And on the way to the Hare.

'One for the road, come on.'

There we met a lovely, elderly Communist couple – modern-day rebels – who gave Spider a copy of the *Morning Star*, right there in 21st-century Blackheath. Of course we were metres from where Wat Tyler, Jack Cade and the Cornish rebels camped before their various battles. But those rebels were ruthlessly slaughtered by forces loyal to the Crown (the royal family, that is, not the pub. Though by the look of that barman…).

'You know what the next class struggle is going to be, don't you?' began Spider, who, after a few pints, had become Chatty Spider, who, in my experience, was a prelude to Sloppy Spider, then Sleepy Spider.

'Immortality. Once we've cracked it, there'll be them that can afford it and them that can't. The toffs and the deadetariat.'

'Right. I've just remembered a subsequent appointment,' said the male of the couple, getting up.

'You know what the morning star is?' asked Spider, no longer listening to incoming words. 'It's Venus. Which is also the evening star, confusingly. Funny, because the Latin name for morning star is Lucifer, though Jesus called himself the morning star and, hey, where are you going…?'

Spider's new friends waved as they hurried out of the door.

'What a lovely couple,' sighed Spider.

I parted with him at the station, just in time to make it to school. After six pubs, it was time to be a responsible parent. I kept my head down and made sure not to make eye contact with any adults and certainly not to engage in conversation. I kept comms to a minimum even when I got a hug and kiss from my boy.

'Is Druncle Spider still here, Daddy?' my lad asked.

'No,' I said. 'He had to go home.'

'Where does he live?'

'On another planet.'

'I knew it.'

My boy will hopefully be around to see Halley's Comet in 2061. I hope he'll get to see the southern stars that Halley mapped for his catalogue as well. This tale may not provide me the kind of immortality afforded to Edmund, but it too is a catalogue of southern stars, albeit only six of them (and one of them is a Wetherspoon's).

We could have spent the day watching daytime TV, or doing some of those things that always need doing around the house. Or, God forbid, working. But we chose to spend it living. Exploring pubs, science, life, death and socialism. But mostly pubs.

Knights of Dulwich

I'm not sure what we expected when we started Deserter – we were quite drunk at the time – but one thing we certainly didn't expect was press invitations. Really, the only invitations we were expecting were those that involve 'stepping outside' to settle it like men, and even that was mainly down to the loud and never-ending opinions of one Half-life.

But arrive they did. As born outsiders, we reserve the right to take the piss out of anything and everything so we didn't feel able to accept freebies to various plays, pop-ups and 'food fayres'. As fast as they arrived, we turned them all down and went to the boozer instead. And what's more, it felt good, like bunking off work.

Then, a little while ago we received an invitation to attend an exhibition preview at Dulwich Picture Gallery. Two things struck me about it: firstly, the opportunity for a dreamy wander round the world's first purpose-built public art gallery, on a Tuesday afternoon, gratis. And secondly, the word 'refreshments'.

Mmm. Lovely refreshments.

It might be morally iffy to pitch up to press events, load up on the vol-au-vents and then churn out glowing reviews. Equally, accepting such invitations and then slagging everything off could be construed as biting the hand that feeds you. But what if I were to simply drink the hand that fed me? That would almost definitely be OK.

Half-life was keen to join me and so I'd contacted the gallery to enquire about a 'plus one'.

'I'm afraid we don't do plus ones for press events,' came the reply from Louisa. Of course not. I felt a fool for asking.

'Twat,' said Half-life, upping the ante, when I told him the bad news. 'Why are they inviting you anyway?'

'Because of the blog.'

'Oh,' he said, with a curl of the lip. Half-life remains firmly of the opinion that the Internet will soon fizzle out. 'What's it called again?'

'Google.'

'That's it.'

Winifred Knights

The preview in question was for an exhibition of the work of Winifred Knights, a South Londoner, born in Streatham in 1899, who attended James Allen's Girls' School in Dulwich and then the Slade School, before becoming the first woman to win the coveted Rome Scholarship with her anti-war masterpiece, *The Deluge*. Despite being feted as a genius in her lifetime, she is little known today and the exhibition was, incredibly, her first retrospective.

I alighted from the P4 bus as the skies above Dulwich Village began to darken with storm clouds. Let it rain, I thought to myself, as I padded up the path to the main entrance, I'm in with the Art Crowd.

The Art Crowd turned out to be a smart, mostly elderly bunch who as far as I could tell were all from proper publications and not at all charlatan freeloaders. Put it this way, I was the only one wearing shorts, sandals and a four-day stubble.

As Sacha Llewellyn, the curator, began her guided tour of the exhibition – lots of drawings and cartoons as well as the major works – it quickly became apparent that Knights' art, much of it with a nod towards early Renaissance style, was rare and exquisite. By the time we'd all shuffled into the second hushed room behind Ms Llewellyn, I was enraptured, and I was only on strong tea.

Themes of sisterly love, female independence and emancipation were combined with atheism and a burgeoning love of nature and the simple pastoral life. The latter was expedited by Knights' traumatic first-hand experience of a Zeppelin bombing Streatham in 1916 and the explosion of a munitions factory in Silvertown the following year, which caused her to have a nervous breakdown and spend a subsequent period of convalescence in the country.

The work of this delicate, sensitive woman, inadvertently caught up in war, was very moving. I was reminded of those butterflies that got embroiled in the frankly rude Industrial Revolution, and were forced to adapt or die. Being white, they were easily picked off sooty backgrounds by the birds and only a genetic mutation to a blacker hue saved the species. Or was it a moth? I wasn't certain.

My reverie was interrupted by the sound of someone behind me clearing their throat. Perhaps they had been similarly moved. I looked round only to see Half-life, wearing a boater, cravat and what looked like nasturtiums in the buttonhole of his linen jacket. What the hell?

'What the f–?' I began.

'Hello,' he said, shaking me by the mitt. 'Leslie, from Google. Pleased to meet you. Wonderful.'

'But–'

'Quite, quite wonderful,' he said, crushing my lovely hand to prevent further interrogation.

An overhead crack of thunder sent a ripple of excitement through the crowd as we made our way into the final room where we learned that after she had spent many happy years in Italy, the Second World War once again plunged Knights into despair and although she began working again, slowly, after 1945, she then died suddenly of a brain tumour in her forties.

Half-life flicked me a look that said, 'What did I tell you?', in reference to his avowed position that life is there to be maxed out, along with my credit card, before there is none of it left. He doesn't just live every day as if it's his last, he often seems actively determined to make it so.

Now rain was hammering down on the roof, as if in lament for Winifred and unfulfilled promise.

'Does anybody have any questions?' asked Sacha, as she brought her excellent talk to a close.

'Yes, love,' said Half-life, 'where are the drinks?'

'There's tea and coffee by the cafe, I think,' she said, sounding a touch deflated at the mundanity of the query. Perhaps she expected more from Google. Half-life caught my eye again, looking worried now and mouthing '*Coffee?*' at me.

He was right to be concerned. I'd hoped for a table piled high with champagne flutes and ice buckets, but it was all cups, cafetières and mini-muffins.

'This is bullshit,' said Half-life, throwing a blueberry muffin into his gob and putting two in his pocket. 'Where's the booze? You said bubbles.'

'Sadly not,' said a woman next to us. 'They haven't had alcohol at press reviews here since the Age of Enchantment.'

'That sounds like a long time ago,' I said.

'2008,' she replied. 'The man from the *Mail* was sick in the umbrella stand.'

'Good lad,' said Half-life.

Disappointed, Half-life and I took our coffee into the long, glazed corridor and gazed mournfully at the rain.

'We're trapped,' I said. 'What shall we do?'

'It's time for you to put on your big-boy pants and buy some bubbles from the bar,' said Half-life, nodding towards the cafe-restaurant.

We were on our second glass of prosecco when the sun came out and we were able to take our bottle onto the terrace that looks out over three acres of manicured lawns. A cabbage white butterfly fluttered over our table and landed on Half-life's buttonhole, lured to him, as many of us are, by his colourful appearance and the promise of a good time.

'Get off, you flappy bastard,' said Dr Doolittle, 'that's for me salad.'

I told Half-life my Winifred Knights/butterfly analogy and he indulged me.

'I might use that, now I've thought of it,' he said. 'Christ, this wine is giving me wind, and not in a good way,' he went on, finishing his third glass in a gulp and holding his belly. 'I couldn't half go a pint.'

'Come on, then,' I said, getting up. It was only a matter of time, after all. 'Where? The Fox? The Phoenix? Hermit's Cave?'

'All of them. Let's not fuck about. Let's do it for butterflies. Do you know they only live for 24 hours?'

'I thought that was a myth.'

'No,' said Half-life, 'it's definitely a butterfly.'

Walking to London

When my friend Wally dropped out of polytechnic in the '80s he was chuffed to land in a squat off Blackfriars Bridge Road, central London, minutes from the river and perfect for strolling home after a night at Mud or the Wag Club. Some years later a housing association took pity on his household and Wally & co were relocated to the Walworth Road. It was little further out, and there was some rent involved, but it was still central enough to feel like he was in the thick of the metropolis.

When he and his partner came to buy a house for their young family (this was in the days when buying a house in London wasn't solely the preserve of oligarchs and 50-somethings), the estate agent showed him round a sturdy semi in East Dulwich, SE22. Wally quite liked it and the house ticked a lot of boxes. Then the agent made his mistake.

'And the great thing about East Dulwich,' he told Wally, 'is that London is just 20 minutes away on the train.'

'London?' said Wally, the blood draining from his face. 'I thought this *was* London.' The agent gave him a quizzical look. Wally moved to Majorca.

Nowadays East Dulwich is unmistakably in London's sooty embrace, but back then everyone thought of it, if they thought of it at all, as the 'burbs. Even estate agents trying to lure 'Londoners' by any means necessary. This was too much for Wally. It was London or *nada*.

I get similarly vexed by a signpost near where I live. It stands at the point where three hill roads meet, each offering a name for the same hill, as far as I can tell, depending on which way you approach it: Herne Hill, Denmark Hill and Red Post Hill. The post has signs stating 'Camberwell 1' (mile), 'Brixton 1', 'Dulwich Village 1' and so on. And then there is one that reads 'London 4'.

What? I thought this *was* London.

I decided to walk for four miles in the direction of the signpost to see where and what they were talking about. Or at least that was the plan before Half-life ruined the surprise.

When I arrived at the signpost someone was taking a photo of it. He smiled and moved out of the way so I could take a photo, too.

'London 4?' he said, with a shrug. 'What are they on about?' I liked him.

Setting off northward at a brisk pace, I was pleased to be picking up Half-life at the Fox on the Hill on Denmark Hill. It's surprising how thirsty you can get after almost nearly a whole kilometre.

'I wonder where we'll end up,' I said to the big man, over a fine pint of ELB's Pale Ale in the afternoon gloom.

'That's easy,' he said. 'Charing Cross.'

'Oh,' I said. 'How do you know that?'

'Education?' he offered, a little unkindly.

A quick look at Google while Half-life was in the khazi showed him to be correct. Distances to and from London are measured from Charing Cross, a junction just south of Trafalgar Square, where Whitehall meets Strand and The Mall. The point is marked, now, by a plaque and a statue of King Charles I on horseback.

Oh. Well. The mystery of our destination may have been solved, but at least we now had a target. Anyway, it was too late to pull out. If we pulled out now, we'd have to find something else to do, which could take hours.

'It still doesn't explain why they felt it necessary to call it 'London',' I said, as we marched down into Camberwell. 'If they mean Charing Cross, why not just put 'Charing Cross'. It's not clear, is it?'

'It could confuse a stupid person,' said Half-life.

'Yes,' I said.

According to Google Maps, it is in fact 4.1 miles from the Red Post signpost (as it is known) to Charing Cross, via The Oval, Lambeth Bridge and the Houses of Parliament. But Half-life was having none of it.

'I'm not going near Westmonster,' he said, as we came out of Greggs with some traveller's fare.

'Why not?'

'Why not? It's fucking teeming with rozzers and K-9s, that's why not. I'm going this way,' he said, gesturing towards Camberwell Road and Walworth Road. 'And it's faster.'

'That way is 4.3 miles,' I heard myself say.

'Balls. I'll race you. Last one there gets them all in.'

So I set off up Camberwell New Road alone. When I looked back after a few seconds I half expected Half-life to be hailing a cab or flagging down a bus. But no, I saw him ducking into the Old Dispensary pub, the daft sot.

Camberwell New Road is not a pleasant road for the walker and it was a relief to veer off onto Kennington Oval and round the back of the cricket ground, past the lost and lamented Cricketers pub. Round the corner, on Vauxhall Street, I came across Gasworks, a community art space which advertised an exhibition therein called *Contra-Internet*.

What a shame Half-life had chosen the way of Guinness. Not only is he fond of his art, he too is against the Internet, believing, like a *Newsweek* article from the mid-'90s, that it's just a flash in the pan born of collective hysteria. Ordinarily I would have looked in, but I just cursed the big idiot for turning my walk into a competition and pressed on.

As I crossed Lambeth Bridge and approached the Palace of Westminster I saw what Half-life meant about the security. Police were everywhere, many of them with automatic weapons. Surely they wouldn't shoot a man for carrying a pinch of weed and half an E left over from Lovebox, I wondered to myself. I crossed to the other side of the road, just to be sure.

On Whitehall I passed Banqueting House where, in 1649, the man whose statue I was approaching was put to death for treason. A clock opposite, above Horse Guards Parade, carries a black mark at the hour of two, the time when the executioner struck off Charles I's head with a single strike of an axe, and the people pushed forward to dip their handkerchiefs in royal blood.

Charlie's equestrian statue stands on a traffic island, reached by means of a crossing policed by 'gay traffic lights' (an uplifting legacy from London Pride, 2016, in which the green men have been replaced by symbols of gay pride). I had studied his reign at school, so he cut a familiar figure atop his nag. Charles I: king, martyr, truculent tyrant. Talking of which, Half-life was nowhere to be seen. I texted him and stood for a while, admiring the statue.

Commissioned by Charles's Lord High Treasurer, Richard Weston, it is cast in bronze and is the work of French sculptor Hubert Le Sueur. Soon after the Parliamentary victory in the Civil War the statue was sold to a Holborn-based metalsmith, the splendidly named

John Rivet. He was under orders from Parliament to break it up and melt down the bronze but, perhaps sensing a chance to turn a slow buck, instead buried the statue on his premises.

He produced some scraps of brass as evidence that he had followed his instructions, and made a killing selling brass-handled cutlery (to both Royalists and Parliamentarians) which he claimed was made from the remains of the statue, like a 17th-century Del Boy.

But Rivet's big payday came after the Restoration in 1660. The recovered statue was purchased from him by the new king, Charles II, and in 1675 it was placed in its current location, replacing the famous Eleanor cross that had stood on the site for three-and-a-half centuries (and which led to 'Cross' being added to the name of the hamlet, Charing).

'What did I tell you, Rodders? After the Restoration we'll be millionaires!'

I decided to drink a toast to him in the nearest pub I could find, the Silver Cross on Whitehall. It's been a pub since around the same time as Charles. Indeed, he also granted it a royal licence to operate as a brothel (which, incidentally, has never been revoked). It was the sort of place, I imagined, that Mr Rivet might have gone to spend some of his windfall.

'Where the fuck have you been?' said Half-life from an armchair, as I walked in.

'At the statue,' I said, 'waiting for you.'

'Bollocks. I've been here yonks. No shame in a silver medal, pal, but it's your round. It's like the tortoise and the hare, this.'

'Is it?'

'Yeah, the hare's all in a hurry, smart-arse fucker, bit of a cunt. The tortoise takes it easy, stops for a pint, smokes a J, still comes in first.'

'I'm not sure that's how the story goes.'

'Whatever.'

I bought us a couple of pints of forgettable ale and a plate of sausages.

'What a dull pint,' I said. 'You coming to this beer festival next week?'

'Maybe. Where is it again?'

'Kidbrooke,' I said.

'Kidbrooke? Yeah, that could be handy. Here, what do you know about storing cheese?' he said.

Before I could ask him what the bejesus he was on about, my phone rang. It was Roxy, wondering what we were up to.

'Tell her to ditch the boyfriend and come and play,' said Half-life.

'Half-life says ditch the boyfriend and come and play,' I told her.

'Where are you?' she said.

'We're in London!' I said.

'Ri-ight. Whereabouts?'

'*London!*' I said. 'Don't tell me you don't know where that is!'

Thirsty in Kidbrooke

I should have known something was up when Half-life agreed to visit Kidbrooke without swearing. My suspicions were further raised by the sight of him helping an attractive woman with a trolley bag off the train, as if he were a gentleman. Then she hopped back on and I realised it was *his* bag.

'Ta, love,' he said, passing her his number. 'And don't fucking ring before midday, alright.'

Turning to me on the platform, he said: 'Are you gonna help, or what? You know about my back.' I didn't, but still.

'Jesus, this is heavy. What's in it? Have you offed someone's dog or something?'

'Don't even joke about that. Anyone can have an accident. Listen, you'll have to stash me cheese.'

'I beg your pardon?'

Half-life had 'acquired' a wheel of Parmigiano Reggiano from an unmanned pallet in Borough Market. He realised he could not sell it anywhere in SE1 without the victim, a good friend of his, finding out. So he wanted to pass it on to his cheese fence, Johnny Blisters, who, last he heard, lived in Kidbrooke, but who he hadn't managed to contact.

'I thought I'd stash it at yours to make it easier for you to pass it on,' he said, thoughtfully. He'd only been here a minute and the day was already out of my hands.

I was going to Kidbrooke with the Raider for the beer festival at Charlton Park RFC, partly because old mate and ex-pat Ivan Osman was in town. Surely nothing could better reveal what a fucking awful idea it is to leave England than a display of our fermented might? I was a little nervous about introducing him to Half-life, who is notoriously belligerent towards new people, recently threatening to stab a friend of mine in the eye if he got his name wrong. But, fuck it, there are always risks stepping out with Half-life.

Having dragged this three-year-old lump of milk to mine, Half-life then delivered painfully detailed storage instructions before pulling out what looked suspiciously like a handgun.

'OK, OK! I'll keep it between four and eight degrees!' Half-life told me he never goes to Kidbrooke unless he's packing, as everyone there is armed.

'What the pissing fuck are you on about?' I said.

'I know they are, pal. I made a grand selling shooters in Kidbrooke.'

'When?'

'Couple of years ago. In the '90s.'

I explained that Kidbrooke had become a place for unarmed professional couples and small children with names like Gladiola. That they lived in homes with balconies overlooking the new Cator Park or the nature reserve at Sutcliffe Park in what is now known as Kidbrooke Village. He would not be needing firepower unless the Sales and Marketing team were tooled up with more than utopian brochures. He agreed to leave his Desert Eagle 9mm behind, so now I was harbouring his stolen cheese and a gun. And I only came out for a pint.

On arriving at where the Ferrier Estate used to be, Half-life was completely lost. There was not a single old building still standing.

'I'm never gonna find Johnny Blisters now,' he mourned, as I considered the implications for my dairy safe house.

Gone was the grey, dystopian, concrete fear factory. In its place was an investment opportunity. Many things have been done well on the development. There are plenty of benches and vantage points looking over the Quaggy River, where you could be left undisturbed as there's hardly anyone around, given that so much is still to be built.

'That river's new,' said Half-life.

Actually that wasn't as daft as it sounded. The Quaggy has been reclaimed from the pipe it's been in for the last 50 years. The covering up of our rivers is one of the things that London got badly wrong.

Sitting in sunshine, before water, Half-life did what came naturally and pulled out a Blue Peter and sparked it up. Suddenly, it wasn't all so bad, relaxing in a Teletubby-landscaped wonderland.

'I fucking love Kidbrooke Village, me,' Half-life declared, mesmerised by improbable water features. 'Which way to the village pub?'

Now for the bad news. There is no pub. Shame, because Half-life would have loved the Wat Tyler, the Ferrier's flat-roofed estate pub. It was lively. Once, someone threw a smoke bomb inside. When the smoke cleared the fruit machine was missing. Alas, both Kidbrooke's pubs had long since closed down, leaving only sports and social clubs to save the place from being dry, or to put it another way, worthless.

'Village' is, of course, a marketing term, not a description of something one up from a hamlet. Of the completed builds most are six to eight-storey blocks. After initial plans for the development had been agreed, Berkeley Homes applied for permission to build more homes, claiming that otherwise it would not be viable. So they were building 4000 homes, 15 minutes from London Bridge, with a £45 million grant for demolition and were unable to make a profit...?

'Or a pub,' added Half-life, sagely.

So rather than fire whoever came up with an unviable plan in a goldmine, Berkeley Homes persuaded Greenwich Council, whose own planning guidelines recommend a maximum of 15-storey buildings, to dismiss vociferous local objection and approve a 21-storey tower at the centre of the 'village', along with several 17-storey buildings.

The plan does include new bars, restaurants and shops around The Hub at the station. The dread with any newly built heart of a community is that it will lack soul and be populated by dreary chains and braying City types. My fear for the distant future of the country is that Britain will develop into a giant Canary Wharf, a hideous, characterless void where bland is beautiful. My hope is that there'll always be a scruffy South London.

Kidbrooke Village will have 35% 'affordable housing', whereas the Ferrier's 1900 homes were pretty much 100% social housing. It was one of London's toughest estates. Now it has concierges and £1 million penthouses with champagne fridges; now it has waterfalls. The old residents were 'decanted' – the vile euphemism councils use for removing people from their homes and depositing them elsewhere – to other social housing schemes at a rate of one household every day for five years. The last time I visited the Ferrier, there was just a small part of it left standing, forlorn, sad and tatty. I knew then I was going to miss its unique grimness, though I also knew I would not miss the sense of foreboding I used to get when visiting.

But before Kidbrooke Village gets finished off, it's not a bad spot for some peace and puff. Everyone's a winner, unless you've been recently decanted, as Johnny Blisters had, it turned out, to Hastings.

But we did at least have a beer festival to attend. We found the rugby club entrance tucked discreetly between two semi-detached houses, like it was having a sneaky fag and hiding from its mum. The club buildings opened out onto playing fields with a nice vista of Oxleas Woods, struggling up Shooters Hill, and there was a lovely wood-panelled bar with TV sport. The function room was lined with casks, many local, but also some welcome guests from around the country. We found the Raider trying to get into festival organiser Anna's private sampling room (not a euphemism) and Half-life looked around, observing the beards and bellies.

'Fuck me, it's like the *Lord of the Rings* catering tent in here,' he said.

Osman, who had made the world's first journey from New Zealand to Kidbrooke, arrived and was beside himself.

'Fifty beers!' he cried, with the same joy he had once exclaimed, 'It's a boy!'

'Yep. If we want to try them all we might have to have halves,' I joked, lamely.

'I was thinking two of each. I fucking hate the spare hand thing,' replied Osman.

'Respect,' said Half-life, probably for the first time in his life. They were going to get on fine.

Taproom Trail

The Bermondsey Beer Mile (BBM) is a stretch of brewery taprooms between Maltby Street, SE1, and South Bermondsey, the visiting of which has become something of a badge of honour amongst beer aficionados. I have a confession: I've never done it.

I know. Shoot me.

Last year I visited a couple of the breweries en route to a Hamlet away game. With the excellent beer and the convivial atmosphere, I was reminded fondly of Czech *pivovar* halls. The other similarity was the amount of tourists. I don't mind queuing for beer, but queueing for the toilets was an unexpected chore. As larger and larger groups turned up it occurred to me that perhaps I was too late to the party, that the BBM was now too popular.

At Deserter we're contrary buggers, prone to giving the herd the finger, so to celebrate some of the newer breweries that have opened and, well, just because we love beer, we took it upon ourselves to devise an alternative beery walk, to dig a little deeper into South London, where you will be drinking with locals and unlikely to be jostled by stag dos and rugby clubs. For now.

And so we present our alternative South London Taproom Trail, running from Gipsy Hill to Brixton via Herne Hill.

Gipsy Hill / West Norwood

Once, there were few reasons to head to Gipsy Hill. Now there are at least three, and they all involve beer. Yes, there is the Beer Rebellion but, splendidly, there are also two breweries, which formed the start point for our Saturday wander.

I spotted Half-life from the bus, asleep on Paxton Green, dressed in an admiral's uniform.

'All-nighter at Strange Martin's,' he said, by way of explanation once I'd roused him.

'Fancy dress do?' I asked.

'No,' he said, confused, and straightened his cap.

'You alright? You look a bit rough around the edges.'

'Fine,' he said. 'That last E was probably a mistake, mind.'

'Right. When was that?'

'About an hour ago,' he said. 'I need a drink. I'm parched.'

Half-life mournfully eyed The Paxton pub as we passed it but he cheered up immensely on Hamilton Road when he spotted an enormous sign reading 'London Beer Factory', and even more when we sauntered into a small industrial complex where makeshift tables and seating were being prepared on two sides of the forecourt.

'Beer,' he breathed.

Hamilton Road Industrial Estate is home to two fine breweries, Gipsy Hill Brewery and the aforementioned London Beer Factory. Half-life slaked his considerable thirst with a cold pint of Beatnik at the GHB and then we crossed the yard for a more relaxed sup of the LBF's Chelsea Blonde. Really, it brought home that all you need in life is an industrial estate and some ale.

As we sat, it began to fill up with local beer fans and Half-life, now a little perkier, fell in love with a pretty girl with a limp.

'I'd spend the rest of my life with her,' he declared.

'Only because she wouldn't be able to run away,' I said.

I bought a couple of tins from the LBF bottle shop and we headed on up Hamilton Road. At the top – for information purposes only – lies the Bricklayers Arms. It's not a stop for a real-ale tour, but it's a friendly locals' pub which still shows sport, so worth noting. We might have dropped in had anything of note been on but instead we pressed on and opened one of our cans.

'Why are new beers in these tiny tins?' moaned Half-life, waving it around. 'What the fuck is that all about? Have we got less thirsty? Am I a dwarf? Look at me. Am I a dwarf?'

'You are not a dwarf,' I confirmed, looking him up and down. 'You are the captain of the Costa Concordia.'

West Dulwich

On Martell Road we passed the mightily impressive Parkhall, the old Pye Electronics building, now transformed into a 'creative industries hub', home of IWOOT and the excellent Volcano Coffee Works, who also run an on-site cafe. Again, on another day, we could have paid it a visit, but today was about beer. Beer and quality conversation.

'Thing about dwarves is,' said Half-life, continuing a discussion I hadn't realised we were having, 'they're obsessed with fucking.'

'What are you on about?'

'Yeah, when they get together they only have one thing on their minds, apparently. Strange Martin had to photograph a load of 'em. Said it was a nightmare. Every time they wanted to start the session they had to stop them fucking in the kitchen or the toilets. Even in cupboards.'

'Don't be ridiculous.'

'For real. Everyone knows it. That Peter what's-'is-name, did *Lord of the Rings*, he said it was mental, they were out of control on set. Terry Gilliam reckoned they lost a week's shooting trying to stop all the shagging on *Time Bandits*.'

'They were all men, weren't they?'

'They don't care. They just want to fuck. They bloody love it.'

There is no one else in the world, I thought, with whom I would have this conversation. But I was wrong.

At this point, we were passing the splendid old Victorian coaching inn, The Rosendale, where Mrs Raider goes for 'bridge nights' (which I'm pretty sure is a poker school). This would be a useful stopping off point for those who don't have the foresight to stock up on supplies in advance. James, the manager, is a beer lover and he makes sure there are always interesting ales on.

We headed down the enchanting Rosendale Road, the width and grandeur of which are purportedly due to its original conception as a grand processional route to the Crystal Palace in Upper Norwood. We paused for a swig outside number 164, once the home of great British eccentric, Vivian Stanshall (and where his band, the Bonzo Dog Doo-Dah Band, were formed in 1962).

If Rosendale Road is grand, then the colossal All Saints Church that stands on it is spectacular, and unsurprisingly Grade I listed. I suggested a look round it but Half-life thought otherwise.

'Is it a brewery?' he asked, not unreasonably.

Herne Hill

This stretch would until recently have been a little on the dry side but that all changed with the opening of the Bullfinch Brewery site in a couple of arches at the northern end of Rosendale Road. Bullfinch once shared a site with Anspach & Hobday (on the Bermondsey Beer Mile) but have now taken up residence in Herne Hill, for which we gave thanks with a toast of session pale at one of their outside tables.

Rosendale Road opens out onto the glorious Brockwell Park and we took the opportunity to familiarise ourselves with trees before pushing on to Herne Hill's other brewery, Canopy, which operates in an arch on the Bath Factory Estate, behind the shops on Norwood Road.

Here the set-up is a little more make-do, a little more organic, a little more – we thought – us. We drank pints of Sunray Pale Ale in the little courtyard and watched as a group at the next table compared their lawn bowls sets, possibly before heading up to the bowling green in Brockwell Park.

'Great game,' said Half-life.

'You play bowls?' I said, trying not to sound too surprised.

'Yeah. Basement of Brixton Rec. Every Tuesday, like clockwork. When I remember.'

Aleheads should also note The Florence in Herne Hill, which has a brewpub heritage. Currently it houses Craft Academy, which offers apprenticeships for new brewers, and it usually has some of their creations on tap.

Brixton

Heading now up Railton Road towards Brixton, Half-life paused for a moment outside the little shop on Shakespeare Road which was once his local.

'It was so civilised,' he wittered, all misty-eyed. 'You'd pop in on a Saturday morning for a paper, a pint of milk and a £10 bag of weed. Just like it should be.'

'What happened to it?' I asked.

'Society,' he said, obliquely.

From here it's not far to Coldharbour Lane and a cut-through brought us onto Brixton Station Road, home of Brixton Brewery. Founded in 2013, it's the oldest taproom on our trail, which just goes to show we are truly in the midst of a revolution.

There is little or no outside seating available in this tap, but it's a compact and cosy experience and in their American Pale Ale and Electric IPA they have two of the best beers it was our privilege to experience.

Loughborough Junction

From here it was a short hop to our final stop for the day, Clarkshaw's Brewery in Loughborough Junction. Owners Ian and Lucy, perfect hosts, encouraged me to try a new batch of their classic New World IPA while Half-life found a seat at one of the outside tables that spill out of the arch and onto the pavement.

He was holding court at a table of nurses when I returned with our pints.

'I think it's because they don't get to see each other that often,' he was saying. 'So when they do they just want to make the most of it. It's beautiful, really.'

'Yes, it's cute,' said one of the girls.

'What are you talking about?' I asked her.

'Dwarves fucking,' she said. 'Apparently they shag in wheelie bins,' she added, with a lovely smile.

'Right,' I heard myself saying. 'I understand Peter Jackson said it was quite an ordeal on *Lord of the Rings*.'

Ah, sweet conversation, the mark of civilisation. Though to be fair, I had been to six taprooms.

The only slight disappointment with our trail is that, like the BBM, the only time all of the taprooms are open at the same time is, currently, on a Saturday (though most open during the latter part of the week, too). Obviously, these places have to find time to actually make some beer, we accept that, but through our combined patronage maybe we can encourage the taproom doors to open for more of the week. We'll beg, if necessary.

When Clarkshaw's closed, as it does, at dusk, Half-life told me off for not doing the walk the other way round so we could end up at Beer Rebellion until closing time, but I was shot. If you've more stamina than me that might be an idea, but I was happy to slip away and get outside a baked potato.

I still awoke on the sofa at 2am, but at least I wasn't in a field.

Dial M for Marlowe

South-east London's most mysterious murder may not have been murder at all, or so goes one of many theories on the life and death of the poet and playwright, Christopher Marlowe (1564-1593). The wildest of them has Marlowe fake his death in a Deptford guest house before escaping to France to produce the plays attributed to William Shakespeare, along with Wang Chung's 1986 hit, 'Everybody Have Fun Tonight'.

The coroner's report states he was fatally stabbed by Ingram Frizer, in self-defence, following a row over the bill. But the two witnesses were spies, and therefore professional liars. Frizer also had form in the fibs department and may also have had reason to want him out of the way. Marlowe was staying with Frizer's client, Thomas Walsingham, and Marlowe's reputation as a bawdy, drunken atheist could have damaged his business interests. So might his alleged rogering of Walsingham, up the Chislehurst, of all places. Marlowe had also been a spy. And there are plenty of reasons for bumping off spies, all just as plausible as a fight over who ordered the fruits of the forest cheesecake.

Marlowe was already effectively out on bail as investigations continued into allegations of heresy and blasphemy. Atheism was a dangerous belief in the 16th century, close to treason. People couldn't quite get their head round it and thought it 'anti-God'. As if atheists really *did* believe in an omnipotent, supernatural creator, but just thought He was a knob.

Deptford

In tracing the footsteps of Kit Marlowe, we started at the end.

'You can tell the football season's over,' opined Roxy. 'This is the second literary walk in a month.'

Indeed, after a recent sozzled afternoon helping 'research' another literary tour, round Peckham Rye, I expected attendance to suffer. Today it was only me and Rox and she only came because she'd run out of gear.

'When did you lot become book wankers, anyway?'

'After the Champions League Final,' I told her. 'What are we supposed to do? Talk about feelings?'

We met at St Nicholas' Church in Deptford, where Marlowe (if it was him) is buried in an unmarked grave. He'd spent all day at Eleanor Bull's house, a sort of private pub – not open to the public, exactly, but someone's home where you could eat, nap and drink all day with friends. Sounds lush. I say bring them back, though without the stabbing, thanks.

The account of the brawl that led to Marlowe's death didn't sound terribly convincing, but Frizer was given a swift pardon by the Queen and went back to work for Walsingham, whose best mate he had just killed. It must have made for an interesting employee appraisal that year.

Marlowe was being investigated by the Privy Council at the time and, though he had escaped previous brushes with the law, including accusations of murder and counterfeiting coins, he must have been terrified that the future promised gaol and torture, like so many of us are of a Monday morning.

After visiting the plaque that commemorates him, we headed towards Deptford Strand, the riverside site of Mrs Bull's house. Roxy insisted on a detour to the Dog & Bell, despite my vehemence that there was no proof it was a pub in Marlowe's day.

'It's what he would have wanted,' said Roxy, supping a fine pint in a pub that epitomises the phrase 'hidden gem'. It's a special place to those who know it and it was all we could do to drag ourselves away. Roxy may have been right, too. Anthony Burgess wrote of Marlowe in the (fictional) *A Dead Man In Deptford*: 'He ate little, but drank much and vomited proportionally.'

Marlowe was also a keen smoker, being a pal of fellow alleged atheist Sir Walter Raleigh, who had just brought the stuff over from the New World, with little idea what he had started. Consequently, we had to stop in Upper Pepys Park and honour them both with a biftoire.

'Booze, boys and baccy,' sighed Roxy. 'My kind of writer.'

Simultaneously calmed and excited, it was time to stare at water. From the Strand we could see the Old Royal Naval College, where, in its previous incarnation as Greenwich Palace, Marlowe had reported daily while the Privy Council figured out a way to punish him for being a clever clogs.

Our last stop in SE8 was the Birds Nest, not only, as we have seen, South London's finest pub on a roundabout, but also once the site of Deptford Theatre. Its claim to have some connection to Marlowe is feasible, back when the pub sat next to the theatre and was known as the Oxford Arms. Happily, it remains dedicated to booze and the arts, though mostly of the noisy, punky variety. It's opposition to orthodoxy seemed refreshingly appropriate on a Marlowe stroll.

For the sake of completeness, we went on to the Naval College, where Marlowe quite possibly began his final walk, along the river to his doom in Deptford. If the Old Brewery had been there then, we would like to think he would have stopped, had a drink and smoked on the lawn while composing a couplet.

Predictably, I began quoting Marlowe:

'Come live with me and be my Love,
And we will all the pleasures prove...'

'Get me a pint and skin up and I'll think about it,' interrupted Roxy, without the slightest intention of thinking about it.

Scadbury

At the time of his death, or living end, Marlowe was staying at Scadbury, the Walsingham estate. I was astonished to find it was only eight miles from Deptford, in leafy Chislehurst, Kent. While little remains of Walsingham's moated manor house, the grounds have become Scadbury Park, a lovely 300-acre nature reserve of ancient woods and grasslands. It's a dreamy place to pause, with the scents you only get in old woods and the constant racket of birdsong. I hastened Roxy towards the exit as she started on about chiffchaffs and chaffinches. You can take the girl out of the country, but you can't stop her warbling. Thankfully, we found the Sydney Arms, a pub that looks like it was once pretty but has had too much work, like a pouty actor. I could only date the pub back to the 18th century, so we only stayed for one (meaning two).

At Chislehurst Common though, there are several more boozers, including the 18th-century Tiger's Head on the site of a 15th-century pub that was owned by the Walsinghams. It's hard to imagine Kit didn't have a drink there before watching the cockfighting on the common. Today, you can celebrate his poetic spirit with their gourmet chicken burger.

Dulwich

One of Marlowe's great friends in the theatre was Edward Alleyn, the renowned actor who played the lead role in many of his plays. Alleyn was also a successful businessman, part-owning several theatres and bear pits and, possibly, brothels. With his fortune he founded the College of God's Gift, at Dulwich, inspired by Marlowe's experiences at school in Canterbury, where he, a shoemaker's son, won a scholarship to Cambridge. The college began life as a school for the education of poor scholars, a tradition that was honoured well into the 20th century, by which time it had become Dulwich College. It produced such comedy giants as P.G. Wodehouse and Nigel Farage.

The college has a day house named after Marlowe, making it a genuine Marlowe tour destination, but given it doesn't have a bar, we thought Kit would not approve. Furthermore, Roxy said, 'Balls to that' when I suggested it.

Bankside

'The sight of London to my exiled eyes,
Is as Elizium to a new come soule.'
– Christopher Marlowe, *Edward II*

We didn't make it to Westminster Abbey's Poet's Corner, either, where there is a memorial to Marlowe, giving the dates of his life as 1564–?1593. Shame, as St Stephen's Tavern is always worth a visit, even if it is in the north. We kept it south, on Bankside.

Built by Alleyn's father-in-law, Philip Henslowe, the Rose Theatre put on several of Marlowe's plays, including *Doctor Faustus*, a play which summons the Devil to the stage, spooking and thrilling audiences that had never seen anything like it, like an Elizabethan Channel 4. Southwark was the heart of louche London then, with theatres, animal baiting and whorehouses all over the shop. The pious thought theatre immoral and it was banished from the City of London, suggesting that the latter has always been full of bores, as suspected. The church in Southwark, by contrast, ran the brothels.

The Rose was excavated late last century and its remains are open to the public. There's no bar, so we left immediately and had one outside The Swan, next to Shakespeare's Globe, with its stunning view of St Paul's and the Thames.

The oldest tavern on Bankside though is The Anchor, now a tourist Mecca for those wanting to experience an authentic British pub with unreal prices. It's still a lush place to have a riverside pint, especially in winter when you can do so without half the world for company. In Marlowe's day it was called the Castle-on-the-Hoop and was also a licensed stew (brothel). There, we drank to his bones, wherever they may lie.

It felt strangely noble following the echoes of such a powerful, fearless, groundbreaking writer, who liked booze and fags and offered his middle finger to the mighty and Almighty. Doubtless his death was suspicious, but the Marlowe-as-Shakespeare theory still seems outlandish. And anyway, we had come to praise him, not bury him.

Sports Day

I had just sat down for an important talk by the Dulwich Society about why there are no pubs on the west side of Lordship Lane, when my phone buzzed. It was Cousin Max. Since he now lives in Manhattan, I decided I should take the call and slipped outside to answer it.

'Raider! I'm in town for the holidays! Let us rejoin in sporting combat!' he cried. If Cousin Max should ever decide to change his name to a symbol, like Prince, it would surely be an exclamation mark.

'I'm studying at the moment,' I said. 'Where are you?'

'Outside your house!' he said.

'Meet me in the Dulwich Plough in an hour,' I said, figuring we could at least spend the afternoon making use of the pubs on the east side of the Lane.

As it happened, in pursuit of physical fitness, mental well-being and drinks, I had already arranged a summer sports crawl with Half-life and Dirty South for the coming week, but I was wary of asking Max along, for a couple of reasons. Firstly, there was Half-life's renowned volatility with strangers. Only the week before he'd threatened to give an acquaintance of mine a 'Scottish disembowelling'. And that was at a funeral.

And then there was the fact that Cousin Max would beat us all. At everything. My simple game plan had been to get Half-life and Dirty South drunk or stoned, or both, and then crush their sporting dreams without them even realising. To introduce into the mix a man whose refrigerator is used primarily for the chilling of tennis balls was asking for trouble.

But in The Plough, Cousin Max's relentless enthusiasm melted me and over a pint (me) and an 'elderflower spritz' (him), I let him in on the plan. And anyway, I figured, I could always pair with him.

'Oh, amazing! Which sports?' he asked, and got out his PDA to jot down some notes, like it was the '90s.

'Boules,' I said.

'Pétanque, yes,' he said scribbling with his stylus.

'Erm, table tennis...'

'Whiff-whaff, good.'

'Bowls...'

'Crown green or flat?' he said, looking up.

'Flat, I suppose.'

'I see,' he said, slightly disappointed. 'Yes?'

'And crazy golf.'

'Ah, putt-putt! Splendiferous!' he said, rubbing his hands together, his time in New York having done nothing to soften his plummy tone. 'Quite the quirky quadrathlon!'

I smiled at him.

'So, you're here for the holidays, you say?' I said.

'Yes! On hols now till September.'

'Until September? Good effort,' I said.

'Abso-bloody-lutely. Fires the soul! Frees the spirit! Forges the imagination!'

I got myself another pint. This could be a long summer. Or 'Summer!'

Boules

As previously noted, the Rye pub, at the north end of Peckham Rye, gets very busy at the weekends, but its airy interiors, Rye views and vast back garden (featuring a boules court) make it an ideal weekday play space, as discovered by mummies, people working 'from home' and daytime vagrants like us just looking for a good time and a game to go with it. Dirty South, Half-life and I were gorging ourselves on Southwark Brewery's Mosaic when Cousin Max appeared through the door in a striped sports blazer and a Panama hat.

'Chaps!' he ejaculated. 'I say, nice hat!' he said to Half-life, who, as fate would have it, was also sporting a Panama. He glanced at our pints. 'Ah, I see, *ante bellum* refreshment. The last sup, as it were. Jolly good, jolly good. Not for me, no, no. I'll stick to soda. Must stay focused. *Alors, où est le boulodrome?!*' And with that he strode purposefully towards the back garden.

'Who's the cunt?' said Half-life.

'That's Cousin Max,' I said.

'Christ,' said Half-life.

Picking up the house boules from behind the bar, we found Cousin Max pacing the court in the spring blossom.

'Isn't this quite the best time of year?' he said. Cousin Max pronounces 'year' as 'yurr'.

'Best time of what?' said Half-life.

'I mean, all these people who say they prefer winter, or the aromas of autumn, or whatnot, who are they kidding? Spring is the best season, it's obvious. Spring is the best season, blue is the best colour, beef is the best meat, Bordeaux is the best wine, strawberry is the best Starburst. Am I right? *Max*,' he said, extending a hand to Half-life. 'Probably best that we partner, given our taste in hats. Do you wish to cast the *cochonnet?*'

Balls. This was a disaster. Half-life, despite years of abuse, mostly self-administered, is a quality gamer himself. We didn't stand a chance. I glanced at Dirty South just as he contrived to drop a boule on his foot.

'Ow,' he said. 'Note to self: no good for keepy-uppy.'

The rhythm of boules suits the thirsty, with a mouthful of ale available every two ends, as you return to base. This proved insufficient for Half-life, however, who insisted upon keeping a pint at both ends. It seemed to do the trick, too, as he and Cousin Max raced into a predictable 2-0 lead in our best-of-five session.

'Petit à petit, l'oiseau fait son nid,' said Cousin Max as he landed yet another boule next to the jack and advanced to inspect his handiwork.

'Too right, pal,' said Half-life.

'What did he say?' said Dirty South.

'I've no idea,' said Half-life, 'but I'm winning.'

3-0 soon followed and the acrid stench of elderflower filled the air.

Bowls

'So, what do you get up to in New York, Max?' asked Dirty South as we wandered down East Dulwich Grove towards our next stop, Brockwell Park.

'Oh, this and that. That and this. Busy, busy, busy. You know how it is,' said Cousin Max.

'Not really,' said Dirty South.

And I was unable to fill in the blanks for him. I knew there was a company, of which Cousin Max was the chairman and CEO; a company that offered an eclectic melange of legal, real estate and creative services. 'We're fixers,' he'd once told me. But in truth, I know next to nothing about him. He's not even my cousin.

Having marched up to the top of the hill in Brockwell Park, we were disappointed to find the bowls hut firmly locked and shuttered. And despite putting out a call on Twitter and trying to get the hashtag #emergencybowls trending, closed it was to remain. It later transpired that we were simply too early – the bowls club hut does open on Thursdays, but later in the day, what with people having to work and everything.

'That's a shame,' I said. 'I was looking forward to that.'

'*Dulce bellum inexpertis*,' wittered Cousin Max.

'Pardon?' said Dirty South.

'War is sweet, to those that have yet to experience it,' said Cousin Max, the cheeky bugger.

'Oh, I thought it was something about pudding,' said Dirty South.

Walking into Herne Hill on our way to our next destination – the whiff-whaff table in Ruskin Park – our attention was taken by The Commercial public house, where we elected to stop in order to assuage our disappointment with some essential fluids.

Is drinking a sport? The short, sad answer is 'Probably not'. Though it does make us feel like winners. Even Cousin Max was persuaded into having a half of Thwaites' Wainwright as we sat outside and surveyed the piazza, though he barely took a sip of it.

'I bet you 10p I can make your beer disappear without touching it,' said Half-life to him at length, seizing the opportunity for further gaming.

'Oh, jolly good. This I must see!' said Cousin Max, whereupon Half-life picked up Max's beer and drank the lot in one go.

'I owe you 10p,' he said, wiping his mouth as Cousin Max's confusion gave way to genuine joy.

'Oh, my!' he said, between guffaws. 'Wait till I show them that at the club!'

Table tennis

At Ruskin Park I passed round the job lot of cheap bats I had purchased that very morning from Peckham's Sports Direct, in an attempt to keep Newcastle in business.

'That won't be necessary,' said Cousin Max, producing a small briefcase from his bag, releasing the clasps and removing some sort of holy paddle.

'What the fuck is that?' I said, my heart sinking.

'Behold... the Stilo 7,' he breathed. 'Carbon shaft, five wood layers, impeccable spongework.'

'Oh, Christ,' I said, and Half-life chuckled happily to himself.

'This calls for a celebration,' he said and proceeded to skin up on the table as the rest of us took in the blue skies, the aroma of fresh-cut grass and the magnificent trees, now approaching full leaf.

'Isn't nature wonderful,' said Half-life, sparking up a beast and coughing out a cloud of smoke.

'What is it?' asked Cousin Max when Half-life passed it on to him.

'It's like a cigar,' said Half-life. 'A magic cigar.'

Cousin Max took a tentative toke.

'Oh, that's rather pleasant,' he said, and took a couple more.

'Not for me,' I said, when he passed it over. 'Must stay focused.'

'Oh, my giddy aunt,' said Cousin Max, as the cannabinoids began to raddle his perfect mind.

If ever there was a lesson in the dangers of doping in sport, this was it. First Cousin Max failed on a number of occasions to strike the ball *on his own serve*, then got a fit of giggles experimenting with the pen-hold and finally got the fear when a dog came over to chase the ball, at which point he climbed onto the table and refused to come down as the world was spinning too fast.

'Hold on, chaps! Hold on for dear life!'

We were all less than excellent, to be honest, but having talked Cousin Max down to *terra firma,* Dirty South and I were duly able to take the whiff-whaff leg and level the series. Job done, we sauntered into Brixton.

Crazy golf

The Duke of Edinburgh on Ferndale Road is a beautiful, Grade II-listed boozer with a wide selection of fine beer, pool, sport on the telly and another enormous garden. There aren't many ways to improve such places, but sticking a crazy golf course out back might just be one of them.

This one was a pop-up course from the guys at Plonk Golf, housed in a large marquee in the garden. We collected our putters and took a ball each, all except Cousin Max, who produced one from his pocket. For crying out loud. Who has their own golf ball?

'Well, it really is the most amazing thing,' he said. 'Incredibly rare.

There's only a handful in existence. After each shot it emits a high-pitched pulse which means it can never be lost.'

'Blimey,' I said, 'where did you get it?'

'I found it,' he said, looking very pleased with himself, before convulsing with wet-eyed giggles, in which he was joined by Half-life. 'I found it!'

It was a short course and despite some valiant attempts at interesting pipework, wasn't the greatest I've ever played (though to be fair, I've played an awful lot of 'em). And at £7.50 it wasn't cheap either. But it was in a pub garden, and amongst the Tiki stylings were plenty of places to rest your pint while you paused to address the ball or stand in your opponent's eyeline. There must surely be better crazy golf options in the Glorious South. I made a mental note to research them. Which is me all over – always working.

I don't know if it was Cousin Max's magic ball, or our inability to putt straight after four pints, but Dirty South and I fell short of that which was required and the putt-putt point went to Team Max-life.

Afterwards we took a table in one of the new outside booths and Cousin Max and Half-life suggested that the day belonged to them, two to one, and engaged in some rather vulgar high-fiving. I felt compelled to point out that the four-game series was obviously null and void since one of the sports had not even been played. To my surprise, they agreed and a replay was mooted for the following week.

'I'm in,' said Half-life, slapping Cousin Max on the back. 'Best fucking day out I've had all yurr.'

Rise of the Bottle Shops

Yes, there is more to life than pubs. There are also micropubs, the boozer's tiny sibling, proliferating in the outer reaches of London. And now, as we have seen, brewery taprooms are popping up across the Chosen Boroughs like spring daffodils. From Wimbledon to Woolwich and Peckham to Penge, ale can be enjoyed in the place of its making. And as if that wasn't enough, now bottle shops – those dedicated craft beer emporiums – are blooming too, making shopping interesting for the first time.

Some simply do takeaway, and many do growler refills from the tap and 'meet the brewer' events with tasty freebies. But not only can you take lovely booze home to drink alone with daytime TV, there are shops that you can sit in and drink with other humans. You can explore a world of hoppy creativity and return home having forgotten the bread and milk, again. Here are some of South London's outstanding reasons to put on your shoes.

waterintobeer, Brockley

waterintobeer has established itself as a welcoming little beer temple to complement SE4's already strong pub scene. The Dulwich Raider and I once visited to listen to radio commentary of a Dulwich Hamlet FA Trophy replay and were joined by several pink-and-blues. Despite the disappointing result, it was a special night. A special night, spent in a shop.

It felt a bit like being in a library, with shelves packed with classics and uncharted pleasures. But it was a library where all the books were exquisite beers. Admittedly, you can't exchange them freely, and nor will long hours of attendance make people consider you highbrow, wise or sexy. But somehow there's an unspoken encouragement to better yourself, increase your knowledge and try the nine percenter that's made from rhubarb funghi. Every time you visit the fridge, you feel you should try something different, with the pioneering spirit that made this country, if not great, then happy.

Hop Burns & Black, Peckham

The start and end point for our Peckham Rye tour, some would class Hop Burns & Black as the daddy of South London bottle shops. Kiwi couple Jen and Glenn opened their beer, hot sauce and vinyl shop in 2015 and it quickly became a fixture, pioneering drinking in shops, something we've always aspired to. They will also fill your flagon full of ale to take home, offering a choice of fine session beer or something special and strong for those nights in with someone you love, like yourself.

Outside the shop, their benches sit in a suntrap. It's one of those places you get talking to strangers at. After all, your fellow customers have already established they're discerning characters with a handle on the more important things in life.

Park Fever, Hither Green

A different take on the bottle shop phenomenon sees a canny combination of craft beer and fine chocolate, though the owner, Adrian, was surprised to see people consuming them together.

On opening night there was another smattering of Dulwich fans and a jolly vibe of discovery. Locals could not believe their luck, because Hither Green has precious few outlets serving joy in a glass. Park Fever is opposite the only pub, the Station Hotel, but offers a much stronger field of finely crafted brews in cooler, cosier surroundings. It's quickly become a focal point for those with thoughtful thirsts.

Craft Tooting

A noble venture in Tooting's Broadway Market, Craft Tooting is a shop just big enough for one little table and dozens of gorgeous beers – just about the right ratio. When I arrived I was met with an enthusiastic welcome that only Americans can deliver with sincerity. Canh, a lovely guy from Colorado, headed off my ponderous deliberations by announcing, 'Oh my god, I just put on this awesome session IPA. You gotta try it.'

It's difficult to resist somebody else's beer excitement, so after giving me a taste, he poured me a refreshing, zesty pint of Alphabet's Charlie Don't Surf. And being in the middle of a superb market, I was able to use it to wash down some honey pork belly and rice from Hi-Ki, the Robata Grill and Sushi Bar next door.

In common with all the bottle shops above, Canh has a relationship with his customers, waving a Siren stout at one who popped in to say hello, knowing he would be compelled to buy it, even at £7 a pop.

'I'm terrible at remembering people's names,' Canh confessed. 'But I know what they like. Anyway, it's been so nice to meet you... Broderick.'

Art & Craft – Streatham & West Norwood

Like Hop Burns & Black and Park Fever, Art & Craft has combined craft beer with another, unrelated, product, in this case urban and contemporary art. I can only really remember the beer though.

I visited the branch of Art & Craft set in a small, sweet old building by Streatham Hill station. Again there was one table, a fridge full of magic and someone passionate and knowledgeable behind the counter: in this case, Amy, assisted by the grumpy shop cat, Spud. The bar/shop is run by Inkspot Brewery, whose work I've yet to come across in my SE ends.

I tried a recommendation from each bottle shop I went to. As Amy liked DIPAs and sours, I went for a DIPA – a Brew By Numbers 55|04, to be precise. Quite astounding, though at 8.5% not to be taken lightly. Fruity but bitter (the beer, not Amy) it's made with Citra and Ekuanot, the hop formerly known as Equinox until it was forced to change its name after a trademark dispute, presumably with either the sun or the equator, or most likely a combination of the two.

We Brought Beer – Tooting/Balham/Clapham

The smallest of the We Brought Beer branches is tiny and in Tooting Market, yet still claims to have 200 beers. There wasn't anything to tempt me on tap, so I went for a bottle recommendation – a Brighton Bier Freshman Vermont IPA. It's a style of beer I was completely unaware of. Now we're best friends. Pine. Sweat. Grass. Biscuit. You do the math.

Their Clapham Junction branch has a dedicated tasting room upstairs and a beer garden, but at Tooting customers are more likely to take their brew to the communal area of the market, where they can mix with the gin and cocktail drinkers – a happy and promising meeting of clans.

With London rents making micropubs difficult to sustain in the middle of the capital, bottle shops are filling the gap for us city folk who like tiny rooms with big flavours. Each one is run by someone with a love for and knowledge of this emerging art form that has raised drink from being a mere provision to something life affirming.

These shops also provide ample evidence that we're seeing the Return of the Can – an old, bad idea, turned into a new, good one that's making bottles look a little old fashioned. Today's cans also often look gorgeous, giving a lot of talented designers gainful employment. Plus, they're lightweight, stackable and don't make that telltale clinking sound when you're forced to deal with grown-ups.

So, bottle shops are now everywhere, from Bermondsey to Brixton to Bromley, with at least three on the South Circular Road alone, surely making our once-derided orbital a potential holiday destination. Each provides a different offering to nearby pubs. The standard pint might be mother's milk, but how are we to grow if we don't try Mango IPAs, mummy?

Bottle shops represent bold, brave moves now that supermarkets are getting in on craft and undercutting everyone. While I'd never argue for more expensive beer, the bottle shops offer a much greater variety and level of expertise than, say, Tesco. If you don't believe me, try cracking one open in aisle 44 and discussing the Equinox/Ekuanot conundrum with the approaching security staff.

I don't believe bottle (and can) shops are a threat to pubs. Property developers, rapacious pubcos and poor management are a threat to pubs. The pub will never die, but now it has a friend, occupying a space between pubs and micropubs, but without all the rules.

To conclude: Dear Beer – you're so hot right now.

Streetlife: Bermondsey Street

With its upmarket restaurants, galleries, delis and boutiques, Bermondsey Street is as if a strip of Chelsea has been laid upon the SE1 badlands, where sallow-faced purse-snatchers still lurk, ready to pounce from their two-wheeled steeds.

But the gentrification must be more than street deep, because Bermondsey Street is filled with people with new coats and clean shoes, eating, drinking and discussing which is better, art or property prices. Presumably they are residents of the blocks of new flats that have sprung up in the area. In addition, the street hosts visitors to Bermondsey Antiques Market (Fridays 6am-2pm) and nearby Maltby Street Market (Saturdays), the insider's alternative to Borough Market.

It used to be something of a stamping ground for me, back before The Garrison went gastro and when The Woolpack was still the London Scotia Bar, installing and servicing hangovers for Scots in search of a better life, in a pub. I may as well state right off that I liked Bermondsey Street in the old days, when it was a sparse, windy backwater with a pub at either end and another couple in the middle. I'd heard much about its ascent into the gentrisphere, how it had become a foodie destination, and now it was time for it to stand up and be counted.

Antico, Zucca, Ticino, Jose, Pizarro... Am I counting in 'Modern European'? Don't be daft, I'm listing the restaurants on B-Street, as I would like to believe the locals call it (they don't). Jesus, I thought to myself, I can't eat in all these places. With a glass of drink, I wouldn't get out from any of them for under a score. I had a brainwave.

'Hello,' I said to the young man in Tanner & Co. 'I'm from a blog about doing fuck all. Can I have free food, please?'

'You would need to book ahead for something like that,' he said.

'I am congenitally unable to do things like book ahead,' I replied.

'Then I'm afraid we won't be able to help you,' he said with a smile.

'May I speak to the manager?'

'I am the manager,' he said. And there followed a short silence while I considered my response.

'Can I have free food, again?' I said.

Back out on the street, it started to rain. Well, that was the food reviews stymied. In a way I was relieved. Now I could do something else. I wondered what. I decided to go to a pub and have a drink about it.

With all the lovely bench seats in The Woolpack taken by roaring diners, I took my pint up the spiral staircase and tried to settle into the 'faux baroque' upstairs room with its elaborate black and gilt wallpaper, golden chandeliers and unavoidable ceiling mural. Think 'Jedwardian'.

A woman at the next table with a North American accent asked me if I knew the way to 'Burrow Station'.

'Burrow Station?' I said. 'What are you on about? You mean Borough. Borough. Bor-ough.'

I wondered later if I might have been in a bad mood. I mean, it was raining, I was still coughing up the last of the Widowmaker, and, really, that ceiling. Anyway, I got over myself and had a nice chat with the American lady and her simple (or mute) husband about the area. I told them locals call it B-Street.

I lunched at Al's Cafe, the last greasy spoon on B-Street, where a fine egg, bacon and chips sets you back a mere £3.60. So, even if there is no hope for the poor, at least there are fry-ups and hot tea.

Fortified, it was time for The Arts.

Inexplicably, Half-life had free-entry vouchers to the Fashion and Textile Museum. I met him there and we spent a pleasant half hour watching girls watching knitwear. Then we headed to White Cube, the swanky gallery run by Jay Jopling and to which, marvellously, entry is free.

It featured an exhibition by someone who 'explores glass beads' by creating lifeless monochromatic 'canvases'. The process is, apparently, demanding and arduous and after the third room it became clear that the artist's time would be better spent doing almost anything else. Worse, the North Gallery was showing works created from 'pantyhose, masking tape and found objects'.

'Oh my fucking god,' said Half-life, a little bit too loudly. 'Have you ever seen anything so shit? I've got to get some of this.' And he started snapping away with his phone.

'Mind the guards,' I said.

'What are they going to do, throw me out?' he said. 'They'd be doing me a favour.'

As it turned out, you are allowed to take photographs in White Cube, as you should be in any gallery. You are not, however, permitted to smoke. Not even while watching a short film in the auditorium. Not even if you're Half-life.

'Art fascists!' yelled Half-life, as we were escorted from the premises. 'Where to now?'

'You fuckoffee?' I said.

'Do what?' said Half-life.

'You for coffee?' I shot back, quicker than Dynamo, slicker than Derren Brown, the mind-mixer.

'Whatever,' he said.

There are a decent amount of coffee shops on B-Street. Hej, on Bermondsey Square, is excellent, with friendly staff and a lovely colour green. The Watch House at the entrance to Mary Magdalen Churchyard is charming. But, inevitably, the one everyone is talking about is Fuckoffee (*née* Bermondsey Coffee), with its candid slogan, 'Come happy, leave edgy'.

A little while ago they stuck up the sweary sign, made of Lego. When I first heard about it I thought it was a bit naff, a bit obvious, even. Then people started complaining about it and now I think it's brilliant. I'm contrary like that.

'I had to shield my children's eyes as we left the White Cube gallery,' bleated some dreadful red-trousered twunt on the Internet.

Oh, please. Get out of my town, and take your godawful children with you.

'I'm thirsty,' said Half-life, despite actually drinking a large coffee while moaning. 'You owe me drink for the free ins to the girl museum.'

But I was way ahead.

'Absolutely. I know a great place on Bermondsey Square,' I assured him.

We walked down via the churchyard, a lovely bit of local green space, where we tarried by a bin, lit up and lamented the loss of the horizon now that Bermondsey Square, once the site of Bermondsey Abbey, had got itself all built on and ruined.

'Imagine being a monk,' I said. 'Actually taking a vow not to enjoy yourself.'

'Nutbags, the lot of 'em,' said Half-life.

'Listen,' I said, when we reached the square, 'I've just got to make a quick call. That's the place I meant,' and I nodded at the Bermondsey Square Hotel. 'Amazing cocktails. Order whatever you want, I'll be there in a tick.'

Off he went and I pretended to make a call. Oh, this was going to be good. You see, the Bermondsey Square Hotel does not sell alcohol. Not a single drop on the entire premises. Any second I expected an ashen-faced Half-life to reappear at the door, or perhaps to be forcibly removed by security, shouting about boozes.

I gave it five minutes. I gave it ten. Where was he? After 15 minutes I went in to find him. He was sitting at a table eating steak.

'Don't sit down,' he said. 'Cunts have run out of grog so I got the rib-eye. Can you pay the geezer and we'll fuck off.'

In the warming bosom of The Marigold pub, back up the road, I told Half-life about the hotel's non-alcohol policy.

'Explains why it's empty,' he said.

I reminded him of the old joke: what do you call a meal without wine? Answer: breakfast. But he didn't laugh. Largely, I suspect, because for him this isn't always the case.

The Marigold – in which the ceiling is reassuringly brown – is, along with the Shipwright's Arms at the northern end, the most 'pub' you'll get on the street. But this end, you're away from the numbers. There is only one ale, but it offers basic, reasonably priced grub, shows the football and if the kitchen's shut you can order in whatever you want, which we duly did.

As Half-life helped himself to my pizza, I reflected on a day spent on this good-looking, wonky Victorian street, with its jumble of ex-warehouses, factories, townhouses and shops dating back to its days at the forefront of the leather and wool industries, and beyond. Now, despite the gentrification, it services a healthy mix of suits, artists, luvvies, entrepreneurs, tourists, well-heeled incomers and bemused locals. If you've got the money, it's got it all. It could only be improved by offering more in the mid-price range and by getting rid of the traffic that forces visitors and locals alike onto the narrow pavements.

After a long day we were heading off to Burrow Station when Half-life's sixth sense twitched and he spotted a light coming from a public convenience near where Bermondsey Street meets Tower Bridge Road. But it was no longer a public convenience, or rather, it was, but now in the form of an underground bar called the Bermondsey Arts Club & Cocktail Bar. We descended the tiled stairwell, pushed open the door and ordered a warming nightcap amongst the lively throng.

'Must be the first time I've ever had gin in a toilet,' I said.

'Fucking lightweight,' said Half-life.

Vinyl Frontier

'The two things that really drew me to vinyl,' runs the caption to a *New Yorker* cartoon of a man showing his friend his hi-fi set-up, 'were the expense and the inconvenience.'

Despite the sad truth in this, a few years back half a dozen like-minded muso-nerds and I began to get together for an evening of vinyl delight and, I hardly need add, getting trolleyed. Gawd only knows we've had our various problems with valves, turntable belts and pre-amps since that time, but when it all works, slipping a record out of its sleeve and lowering a needle onto it is a glorious way to listen to recorded music.

Each month at Vinyl Club, the host picks a record to play, which is listened to 'blind' and in silence, at least until the end of side one, when 'bio breaks' are allowed (or, as we say in the UK, going for a wazz and another beer). If the music is unfamiliar, guesses are allowed before the record is turned over and the album cover is passed round along with, hopefully, a lovely fat joint.

The variety of music played has been extraordinary: from the Velvets to Chic, Boards of Canada to The Streets. True, one member left after a Focus album, never to return, and even I blanched on spotting The Wombles' difficult second album *Remember You're a Womble* on the top of the host's pile (it turned out to be a beard cover to throw us off the scent). But one thing I've learned is that I can happily listen to one album's-worth of anything. Even Mongolian throat singing. Apart from anything else, it's 45 mins of dream time, combining the twin pleasures of soft furnishings and a tinnie.

With my turn coming round again soon, I decided to do a mini-crawl of some local vinyl shops to see what I could turn up. Half-life's eyes lit up when I told him and he decided to tag along to offload some surplus records and see if, like some kind of wonky Jesus, he could 'turn music into beer'.

Rat Records, Camberwell

We met in the Old Dispensary in Camberwell, where I was surprised to be introduced by Half-life to Cousin Max.

'What ho!' said Max.

'Raider, meet Max, my "vinancial advisor",' he said, looking pleased with himself.

'Er, yeah, you met him through me, remember?' I said.

'He's helping me with my vinyl salary pension,' he continued, ignoring me, and they chuckled happily together.

'Thanks for having me along for Record Store Day!' said Cousin Max and proceeded to tell us about his extensive record collection back home in NYC. 'I have one room you literally cannot get into because of the wax,' he said, 'and I only have two rooms!'

Our first port of call was Rat Records, the popular second-hand record shop across the road from The Dispensary. Appropriately enough, since we were in Camberwell, the very first record I saw in the racks was the third release by ex-locals and proto-shoegazers the House of Love. The cover even features the Camberwell Beauty butterfly – by the look of it, a treated shot of the large mosaic on the side of Lynn Boxing Club on Wells Way.

Confusingly (and, somehow, excellently), the first three House of Love releases were all called *The House of Love* and they featured the distinctive psychedelic guitar work of Terry Bickers.

'I shared a flat in Camberwell with Terry for a while,' I said.

'Bonkers Bickers?' said Half-life.

'One time we got fed up with him not doing his washing up and left it on his pillow when he was out.'

'Jesus. No wonder he had a fucking meltdown.'

'Or was that someone else?' I said. 'Anyway, he was a lovely bloke.'

'Is that it?' said Half-life. 'Is that your rock 'n' roll story? "Terry was a lovely bloke"?'

I apologised and pressed on through the racks. Ideally, I was looking to find something from this century, a period somewhat under-represented in the Vinyl Club historical spreadsheet. But this is not always easy, and rarely cheap.

Obviously, a lot more vinyl was made pre-CDs. A million seller in the '70s would mean a million records. Now a million seller might include a run of just a few thousand 'vinyls', as the young 'uns call them (and which actually strikes me as more sensible than 'records'), and they immediately become rare and expensive.

Rat Records is a 'pile 'em high, sell 'em cheap' type of place, relying on volume and fast turnover. Indeed a sign on the wall proclaims 'Every Saturday is Record Store Day here', when at 10.30am they put out everything they've been picking up all week from around the country. It's certainly cheaper than Soho, which is great, but it caters mainly for the older music fan and the dance crowd.

While Max was busying himself with Heavy Rock/Metal and Half-life was hunched over Punk and Indie, I came across an album by another South London lad, David Bowie.

I was transported back to a cold Brixton day in January. The day the news came out that Bowie had died. I'd gone down to Brixton in the morning, met Half-life and Dirty South and stayed all day.

'There's a wake party planned for 6pm!' someone had said on Twitter, excitedly. Fuck that, we thought, we're here already and the party's started: a once-in-a-lifetime impromptu outpouring of love and respect, a celebration – by people of all ages – for this extraordinary man who touched and inspired so many, on such a personal level.

His death stills ties me in a knot when I think about it, still catches me by surprise: 2016, the year David Bowie died. It scarcely seems credible, even now.

I stared some more at the album cover and the Thin White Duke stared back at me.

'Come on,' said Half-life, 'let's get you out of here, you soppy get.'

On the 68 bus to West Norwood, Half-life flipped open his record bag and showed us his wares. Along with some Whitney, a Sinead O'Connor and a No Doubt was a copy of The Beatles' *Rubber Soul*.

'God, they loved a pun, didn't they?' I said.

'Original mono,' said Cousin Max. 'There's 40 of your British Pounds right there. At least.'

'Blimey. So where'd you get that lot?' I asked Half-life.

'The Actress left them at mine,' he said, referring to one of his exes. 'Along with her handcuffs and her dignity.'

The Book & Record Bar, West Norwood

Yes, it's got books and yes, it's got records, but the special thing about the Book & Record Bar is that it also has booze. So while Cousin Max's eyes lit up at the vinyl, Half-life and I made a beeline for the bar.

After hearing several 'Wonderful!'s and a trademark 'Oh, my giddy aunt!' from Cousin Max we joined him at the racks. This was more like it, for my purposes at least: Röyksopp, Aphex Twin, Nick Cave, Hot Chip, PJ Harvey...

'Ah-ha!' I said.

'No thanks,' said Half-life.

'The stock! So much stock!' breathed Cousin Max, picking up an original EMI pressing of Kate Bush's *Hounds of Love*, one of the records to which I have treated the boys of Vinyl Club.

'My uncle used to live on her road in Brockley,' said Half-life. 'Said she was crackers. Up all night, wailing at the joanna. He reckons *Running up that Hill* was written about him having to traipse over to her gaff every night to get her to use the fucking soft pedal, the mad witch.'

'I take it you're not a fan,' I said.

'Fucking love her.'

Meanwhile, Cousin Max had got talking to the owner, Michael:

'You see, I've got Led Zep Four, utterly mint, original Atlantic colours, in the original outer sleeve... *but no inner sleeve*. Honestly, I've been looking for a spare inner sleeve for years. I must have asked in every shop in London and NYC.'

'Do you know, I think I've got one downstairs,' said Michael, and Cousin Max looked over at us, his bottom lip trembling.

Turnstyle Records, Streatham

From West Norwood we walked up and over Streatham Hill and down Streatham Common to Turnstyle Records (now sadly closed) on the High Road.

We wondered if the name Turnstyle was a portmanteau of 'turntable' and 'stylus', but it turns out it was much simpler than that: owner Chris was a Crystal Palace fan and sitting at the front of his shop, in pride of place, was a turnstile from the original Crystal Palace Park stadium.

'The Eagles – Their Greatest Bits,' I offered, to no acclaim.

Chris's shop, not far from Streatham's famous Hideaway Jazz Cafe, majored on jazz but also had a meaty rock section and Cousin Max pointed out an AC/DC album.

'Another local connection,' he said. *'Highway to Hell.'*

'Why, is it about the A23?' said Half-life.

'Picture a dark and freezing February night, 1980,' began Cousin Max, solemnly. 'A Renault 5 makes its way from a gig in town to a flat in East Dulwich. Number 67, Overhill Road, to be precise. On board, asleep in the passenger seat, is the charismatic singer with AC/DC, Bon Scott.

'Arriving at his flat, the driver is unable to wake him and so he reclines Bon's seat, gives him a blanket and leaves him to sleep off the night's excesses. The next day, wondering where he'd got to, he steps outside to find Bon, now wedged down against the gearstick, dead from a lethal cocktail of booze, hypothermia and a throatful of vomit.'

'Oh, my giddy aunt,' I said.

'Highway to Hell was the last album he made with AC/DC,' went on Cousin Max. 'The very day he died he had been due to start work on the band's next album, *Back in Black*, the record that would define the band. That album opens with the tolling of a bell and the title and cover – plain black – were chosen by the band in memory of their lost friend and colleague. The album went 22 times platinum in the US alone and is the second-biggest-selling album of all time.'

'Now that's what I call a story,' said Half-life, and looked at me: '"Terry was a lovely bloke."'

Half-life and Cousin Max approached Chris to talk through the records they had to sell and I waited outside, like the coward I am, to avoid the uncomfortable money talk.

'How much did you get?' I asked, when they joined me.

'Well...' said Half-life and opened his satchel to show me an album by The Adverts, the first Monochrome Set LP and the new one by local boys Fat White Family.

'I used to play with them in Stockwell,' he said.

'Maracas?' I said.

'No, it's true.'

'I thought you were turning music into beer?' I said, and Half-life shrugged.

'Got the bug now, innit. Can you lend us a score?'

And with that we headed round to the Earl Ferrers where Half-life persuaded the barman to let him use the decks to put on The Adverts and celebrated by buying me a pint with my own money.

Ales of the Riverbank

The plan was to visit every riverside pub between Charlton and Wandsworth, on mobility scooters. However, once Half-life started customising his steed with an ashtray and optics, the hire-shop sales guy got twitchy about the Ts & Cs. When Half-life attached some Irish whiskey and dropped his bag of weed we were asked to take our custom elsewhere.

So, a cycle crawl along the Thames, then. The 16 halves we'd planned in 16 pubs would have to be reduced to a simple pint in the eight boozers between Charlton and Bermondsey, for health reasons. A lovely riverside ride nonetheless, with no cars to worry about. Just drowning.

Anchor & Hope, Charlton

Who doesn't like drinking in an industrial estate? And this, an industrial estate by the side of the river, with views of decaying jetties, cable cars and corrugated iron fencing. Surely we had found our Shangri-la. As we leant in the sunshine with our first pint, accompanied by the gentle sound of light industry and the sight of Mother Thames, tantalisingly hitching her skirts to reveal her muddy bottom, nothing could kill my vibe.

'Just round there a couple of mile, it was,' said Half-life, pointing past the Thames Barrier towards Thamesmead. 'Seven hundred of 'em, nearly. Gone.'

'Yes,' I sighed.

'The Princess Alice,' he said, answering a question that never came. 'She sank after smashing into a big fuck-off coal ship. Six or seven hundred dead. The worst shipping disaster on the Thames ever, apart from when I lost my Telstar football.'

'Awful,' I said, and recalled sitting amongst the interred remains of many of them in Woolwich Cemetery with Roxy.

'Yeah, I loved that ball,' he said, with feeling. 'Most of them drowned. Trapped in the fucking bars.'

'Doing what they loved,' I said, trying to keep spirits up.

'The rest died swimming in their own shit from the raw sewage that had just been pumped into the river.'

'Jeepers. How's that pint going down?'

'There were a few survivors. Like Long Liz.'

'Well, I'm glad there was a happy ending.'

'A few years later, Jack the Ripper slit her throat. Get 'em in and I'll tell you more.'

I had a better idea. Playing 'Silent Pint' at the next stop.

Cutty Sark, The Yacht, the Trafalgar Tavern and the Sail Loft, Greenwich

We forged ahead by Bugsby's Reach. No one knows for sure who Bugsby was and why his name has been retained in the area. Bugsby's Hole was once a riverside place of execution, we know that. The main theories suggest he was either a devil, a pirate or a gardener. Could he have been all three, looting his neighbours' allotments to stuff his treasure chest full of marrow and cabbage, out of his mind on rum?

We rode on past Greenwich Yacht Club, The O2 and the floating art of A Slice of Reality – a vertical cross-section of a ship – through the fast-changing vestiges of the river's industrial past. It's usually disappointing to have to come inland on the Thames Path, but I love the crazy machines, chutes, vehicles and piles of aggregate that make this section of the Thames Path the most romantic industrial wasteland in the capital.

We emerged into riverside willow trees and a wealth of fine spliff spots, one of which we took advantage of before arriving at the lovely Georgian Cutty Sark pub. Our criterion for this day was to only stop at pubs from which you can see the river, which cruelly ruled out the Pelton Arms, the jewel of East Greenwich hospitality. You've got to have rules. For some reason.

For double bliss, some outside space by the water is desirable. The Cutty Sark has it all. Several ales, a stone floor, a huge ancient fireplace downstairs and the Crow's Nest room on the third floor with superb views of the river – and there are plenty of tables by the water, across the cobbled street. It used to be too far for Greenwich tourists, but the secret's out now thanks to tossers writing about it.

Our appetite had sailed upstream for the time being, which was a shame given that the next pub, The Yacht, offered Wagyu burgers. Food only returned to our agenda after a pint there and next door at the mighty Trafalgar Tavern and a ride to the last of the Greenwich riverside pubs, the Sail Loft, by which time the ship had returned.

Half-life had been partial to The Loft's haggis Scotch eggs before but the barman told us that as half the staff were Spanish, they'd ditched the Scottish Scotch egg in favour of a chorizo version.

'You fucking what?' bellowed Half-life. 'Alright, I'll have two.'

The Thames Path then threw us rudely into the gusset of Deptford, though temptingly past the backstreet classic, the Dog and Bell. But as it is some distance from the water, we were duty bound to press on, holding back our considerable emotions. I didn't mention that I'd dropped in there with Roxy just the other week. He'd only get jealous and insist on a pint.

The Salt Quay and The Mayflower, Rotherhithe

If you don't have your wits about you, this stretch of the Path could see you lost in some inscrutable housing estate, which is exactly what happened to us. At this point it was worth reminding ourselves that we were on a bike ride as much as a pub crawl, principally because there was lots of riding and no pubs. Someone had forgotten to build any on the river between Deptford and Rotherhithe – a planning catastrophuck. Somehow we emerged at Greenland Dock, confused and thirsty.

I'd had four barren miles of bland housing, slow pedalling and Halflife banging on about his irrational fear of eels before we reached the recently scrubbed up and very welcome Salt Quay pub. It's got lots of outside space and a generous balcony overlooking the great river. We enjoyed a surprisingly good Molecule of Life, a sweet brown ale.

'I'm getting notes of vanilla,' I said.

'You're getting a fucking slap if you're not careful,' returned Halflife. Indeed, I should have recalled once having to restrain him from twatting a stranger, who had described his wheat beer as 'totally marmalade'.

Next it was a short ride to the daddy of riverine watering holes – The Mayflower. Previously featured in the Leaning Tour, it is worth mentioning again. And again. It has that special light peculiar to very old pubs; the rays sucked into the ancient dark wood, sunshine apologising into the gloom through the latticed windows. Good beer here is a given, plus its assured place in American folklore.

'We have sailed from the pub to practise our religion in freedom,' the Pilgrims may have announced on arrival in Massachusetts.

'Did you say, "pub"?' replied the natives, I expect. And the rest is, literally, history. Many Americans are still mesmerised by religion, but the US has also become a cradle of the new brewing, proving that the trip wasn't such a waste of time after all.

The Mayflower's candlelit upstairs restaurant has wondrous views of the river, looking across to the tempting, ancient boozers of Wapping, but it's the covered jetty that allows you to be in a pub and on the river at the same time, like some kind of wizard. That strikes me as ironic because it's the alignment of the earth, the moon and the sun that causes the Thames tides; an explanation that sounds too hocus-pocus to possibly be true.

The Angel, Bermondsey

It was then a short hop to The Angel for our final pub. Despite being a Samuel Smith's pub, The Angel is another must-visit for riparian refreshment. Here, on its gorgeous balcony over the water, the full tide would splash our feet and be told 'Fuck off, Neptune' by Half-life, echoing the sentiment of our old friend, King Cnut, the dyslexic king. He and Half-life share a similar mastery of the elements. Cnut himself was once thwarted from capturing London just upriver at London Bridge when the crossing was torn down, an episode later immortalised by a tedious nursery rhyme.

It had been a special trip, punctuated by some fine watering holes. I love how the river meanders, forcing you to take the long, slow way round (though, did I mention there was, like, four whole miles without a boozer?).

The Thames has been a source of pleasure for centuries. The law of the land, including licensing laws, used not to apply here, which is why it used to be packed with boozy boats, sailing to Gravesend and Sheerness and back for the joy of drinking on the water. The Princess Alice disaster brought an end to that and heralded new safety regulations, an upgraded Marine Police Force and a rethink about excrement in the river.

It has always been a place of contrasts, of life and death; a river for poets and prison ships; a highway and a barrier; a place for celebration and suicide. Life became absent in the tidal river at one point, only to return in the late 20th century, proving its capacity for change and renewal. Now it is home to 125 species of fish, 123 of which, according to Half-life, are eels.

Crazy Golf Tour

Tired, weak and hung over and in dire need of an emergency fry-up, I was disappointed that my car was nowhere to be seen.

'Where's the motor?' I enquired of Mrs Raider.

'In Kent. Where you left it,' came the reply with just a hint, I thought, of satisfaction. Ah, yes. Kent. It was all coming back to me. Some of it.

A couple of nights previously I'd been in town with Roxy:

'It's my day off tomorrow,' she had said, waving a tenner in the direction of a barman.

'Great, wanna do something?' I replied.

'Sure, as long as it doesn't involve Lambeth Reuse and Recycle Centre again,' she said, referring to a recent dreamy afternoon we had spent in each other's company. And steady drizzle.

'How about golf?' I said, and she screwed up her lovely, shiny face.

'I haven't got the trousers,' she said.

'Ah, but crazy golf,' I said. 'Flukes, windmills, waterfalls, ptero-dactyls…'

'Pterodactyls?'

'Maybe.'

'Pick me up at noon,' she said.

Wandsworth Park

On the face of it, proper golf has a lot going for it. Invigorating country air, views, horizons, hip flasks, the 19th hole and three full hours of twatting a ball about with a stick… It sounds dandy. And yet I've

156

played only a handful of times, largely due to concerns about donning the correct footwear, having to borrow clubs, being shouted at by officials about unfathomably alien protocols and all the associated tutting and head-shaking.

But crazy golf is another matter. Like me, it's designed to be silly. Which is why it demands to be taken very seriously indeed. The best courses are the brain dumps of surrealist games masters who have followed their time-wasting dreams for the general benefit of humankind.

Landscaped 'pitch and putt' courses began to appear in the UK during the 19th century, using hillocks, water features and plants to add both to the difficulty and, more importantly, the nuttiness. Even Mark Twain, who famously referred to golf as 'a good walk spoiled', is said to have enjoyed the foreshortened game, which he played with Woodrow Wilson in Bermuda.

In 1912 a game called 'Gofstacle' was manufactured and offered for sale in the *Illustrated London News*, complete with hoops, rings, a bridge and a tunnel with which to design your own course in the garden. But it was the Americans who, in an entirely unsuitable metaphor, really picked up the ball and ran with it.

Tens of thousands of 'putt-putt' courses opened and, astonishingly, there were at one point more than 150 courses on the roofs of New York skyscrapers. Millions of people were playing the game and by the end of the 1920s an estimated four million people were playing each night, causing alarm at Hollywood studios as movie theatre attendances fell away. Studio bosses ordered their stars not to be photographed playing the game.

I told Roxy all this in the car over to Wandsworth Park's Putt in the Park.

'Can we have some music on?' she said.

Research had revealed that our closest crazy golf courses were the two Putt in the Parks at Wandsworth and Battersea parks and another more established course in Beckenham. South London transport has come on leaps and bounds in recent years but the Beckenham to Wandsworth golf express is still a way off, so I'd plumped for the car over public transport in order to establish this three-course tour.

For those who thrash blindly up and down the A3 on a daily basis it may come as a surprise that the leafy, riverside Wandsworth Park is just a few hundred metres from the multi-lane wastelands of the Wandsworth gyratory. I recommend anyone stuck in traffic on the way back home to Guildford or Portsmouth to stop off there and wait for the rush to pass. We parked in the new Riverside Quarter and strolled through the gates to Putt in the Park.

'Everywhere's a Quarter now, isn't it?' said Roxy.

'I know. It can't be right. Strictly speaking there should only be four of them.'

As soon as you approach Putt in the Park you know you're in safe hands. It's cleverly landscaped using the latest materials and – a couple of more straightforward holes aside – the designers have had some real fun. Of particular note were the artfully placed stones that open up unexpected rebound shots. For £8 I would have liked to have seen a few more par threes on the card, but you do at least get a tiny pencil to keep.

In my view, one of the key principles of crazy golf is that every hole should offer the possibility of a hole in one, no matter how ludicrous or unlikely that route might be. This serves the dual purpose of allowing those behind the chance to catch up and those in front – thinking themselves now masters of the game – to indulge in trick shots. I had been doing exactly the latter as we approached the ninth and I realised with a start that there were only 12 holes and I was now two shots behind. Putt-putt just got proper.

'How's Jan?' I enquired (this is Roxy's boyfriend, or 'current boyfriend' as I like to call him).

'Fine, yeah,' she said, lining up a tricky shot over the water.

'And the titanium prostatic stent?'

'Coming out next week.'

'That's good,' I said. 'Really. Imagine having one of those jammed up your urethra.'

'I am trying to take a shot here,' said Roxy.

'Fine. Just asking,' I said, and watched as her ball first plopped into the water and then as she got one of her canvas shoes wet trying to retrieve it. My work was done.

'Couldn't happen to a lovelier bloke,' I said.

With the game won and the series 1-0 in my favour Roxy suggested a pint in the nearby Cat's Back, one of London's two Harvey's Brewery pubs (the other is the Royal Oak in Borough).

'I've got the car, though,' I said.

'Bloody hell, you can have a Harvey's,' said Roxy. 'It's only 4%. That's driving beer. Pilots are allowed that in the cockpit.'

And so we sat out front on a wooden bench drinking a gorgeous pint of Best and looking at annoying architecture. Sadly, the Cat's Back is the best thing about the Riverside Quarter.

Battersea Park

If anything, Battersea Park's course is even better than its sister in Wandsworth, and not just because of the decent pizza on offer in the cafe. Roxy ordered a beer, too, and I regretted bringing the car.

'Dump it,' said Roxy. 'Then we can get trashed and party. Who has a fucking car, anyway?'

She was still a little aggrieved at a match-winning hole-out of mine which had involved my ball spending most of the shot in a shallow stream, only to pop out onto the green for a wholly undeserved victory.

'Oh, fucking hell,' she'd said.

'You make your own luck, Rox,' I'd said, with a shrug. 'Just be open. Trust your instincts. See disruption as a force for positive change.' And she had flown at me with her tiny fists.

Hither Green

Back in the car we set Google Maps for the south-east and as we headed for Beckenham I told Roxy another bit of crazy golf history, while she 'rested her eyes'.

In 2010, a professional bridge player and crazy golf fanatic, Nick Sandqvist, opened The Green, the UK's first indoor crazy golf course on the site of the old Hither Green Hospital. He toiled for 18 months designing and building the course, which he based on Nordic championship courses he'd known back home in his native Sweden, and reportedly spent £700,000 on the project. Sadly, as far as I can tell, the course closed around a year later. But not before it had hosted the 2010 London Open. Which was won by one Nick Sandqvist. Legend.

More crazy golf courses is in my Top Three Things That Could Improve South London (at number two, behind 'Seaside') and it is a great regret that I never made it over to play in Hither Green and shake Mr Sandqvist by the hand.

But the past is a foreign country: they play golf differently there. The future, on the other hand, was a municipal course in a public park, although, as it turned out, also in a foreign country.

Kelsey Park, Beckenham

Beckenham is in a London borough (Bromley) but the postcode for Kelsey Park is a somewhat disconcerting BR3 3LS.

'Is it in London?' asked Roxy. 'Or is it in England?'

'I think it's Kentland,' I said, which it was until 1965, when London annexed it.

I had never been to Kelsey Park before and what a bucolic splendour it is, teeming with wildlife and with two lovely lakes at its heart. The sun came out as we strolled towards the crazy golf course by the cafe and all was set fair until we arrived to find the gates locked and the golf hut firmly shuttered.

'Yep, it's Kent,' I said. 'If it was London, it'd be open.'

Through the fence we were able to see several of the holes on the course. I'd read that, while reasonably simplistic in conception, many of them in fact offered a stiff and unforgiving challenge. I tutted.

'I was looking forward to that. What shall we do?' I said, turning to Roxy. Roxy, though, seemed unconcerned. In fact, if anything, she seemed to be rolling a joint.

'I've got an idea,' she said.

And that's why my car was in Kent.

Execution Site Crawl

It was already 27 degrees at 11am. On a Tuesday, of all days. I put on my Poundshop Panama and made a dash for the Morley Gallery on Westminster Bridge Road.

'Don't forget to hydrate!' called Mrs Raider from her eyrie.

'I shan't!' I replied, and smiled a little smile to myself as I pulled the door to behind me. Oh, I was going to hydrate alright.

At the Morley, I took in an exhibition called *Between Dog & Wolf: A South London Twilight*, a collaboration between artist David Western and writer Jon Newman. It used archive material, words and contemporary urban landscapes to chronicle, in three distinct parts, lost or forgotten Battersea, Herne Hill and the execution sites of the Brighton Road from Kennington to Croydon.

The latter was an idea, surely, that would lend itself to a pub crawl. This simple but powerful notion was given added resonance as I learned that condemned criminals were, by tradition, allowed to stop for an ale or a gin on their final journey to the gallows. A civilised pause, pewter on the lips, before their necks were broken and, in some cases, their limbs torn asunder.

'Maybe I could walk to Croydon,' I said aloud to myself, startling a well-dressed woman who was in the gallery with me.

'You are *not* walking to fucking Croydon in this heat!' I replied to myself, sternly, and the woman in the gallery left.

But with my interest piqued, I wandered down to the old Kennington Common anyway, devising a more manageable South London execution crawl on the way, from my own half-forgotten memories of the area's history.

Kennington Common

Now known as Kennington Park, the original common was where the infamous Surrey gallows was located (the area was part of Surrey before the formation of the London County Council in 1889). The Surrey gallows was the South London equivalent of Tyburn, the principal place for execution of London criminals, and stood where St Mark's Church now stands, near Oval Tube station.

The first person to be executed here was Sarah Elston (burned at the stake in 1678 for killing her husband) and the last was a chap from Camberwell known as Badger, who was hanged for forgery in 1799.

Between times, in a remarkable admixture of barbarism and civilisation, more than 140 people were executed here, alternating with the cricket matches that the common also hosted. Indeed, they were often more of a draw for the crowds than the cricket – people would come down for a killing, bring a picnic and make a day of it.

I imagined the crew getting together for a mead or two on just such an occasion: Dirtie Southe, perhaps, Roxanne, Spyder, even Halfpike, possibly with some knitting.

'What are you knitting?' I might ask him.

'Cock muff,' he would announce. 'It's like a hand muff, but it's for your—'

'Verily, I get it,' I would reply, while he frisked me for clay pipes.

My faux historical reverie was interrupted by the A23, across which I had to get to visit St Mark's, where a raised mound would have stood, featuring the dreaded gallows. Once across, I mooched around for a bit before remembering the ritual of the condemned's final pint. What a perfect way not only to honour the dead, but to keep my promise to stay hydrated.

In the Hanover Arms I placed my hat on the bar and asked if they had a pint of something nice for the heat.

'I'm attempting to rehydrate using beer alone,' I bantered.

'Beer is between 90% and 95% water,' said the barman, 'but the diuretic effect of the alcohol makes it net negative in terms of hydration.'

'Just pour the frickin' pint, Professor,' I said. Everywhere you go, experts.

Horsemonger Lane Gaol, Newington

When the public executions on Kennington Common ceased, the killing moved, as I did now, up to Newington Causeway at the Elephant and Castle, to the Horsemonger Lane Gaol. They may not strictly speaking have been performed in public, but since they took place on the specially built flat roof of the gatehouse they were clearly and intentionally visible to anyone who cared to watch, and plenty did.

The first person to be executed here, in 1803, was Colonel Despard who was convicted, along with several other men, of a half-baked conspiracy to do away with the king and take over government, though as the group was arrested in a Lambeth pub, it was possibly just beer talk. Who hasn't wanted to take over the government after a few pints?

Despite an intervention and character reference from no less a person than Admiral Lord Nelson, Despard and his men were found guilty and informed by the judge that they were to be 'hanged by the neck, but not until you are dead; for while you are still living your bodies are to be taken down, your bowels torn out and burned before your faces, your heads then cut off, and your bodies divided each into four quarters, and your heads and quarters to be then at the King's disposal'. Which is really going to ruin lunch.

The site of Horsemonger Lane Gaol is today Newington Gardens, a little park off Harper Road and, appropriately enough, tucked behind the Inner London Crown Court. It's still known locally as 'Gaol Park'. I sat here for a while, reading the above on my phone before finding myself once again driven to honour the dead through the medium of booze.

I looked in at The Ship on Borough Road, raised a glass of London Pride to Despard and his not-so-merry men, and read some more about another local prison.

Marshalsea, Borough

Just up the road, on Borough High Street, stood the notorious Marshalsea prison (and, nearby, its hit sequel, Marshalsea 2: The Dickens Years).

The original Marshalsea was a fine-looking building that gave cover to an elaborate extortion racket, not to mention immense suffering. Before the 19th century, prisons were not considered places of punishment, they simply housed people until they had paid off their creditors or had had their fate decided by judges. They were run privately for profit and inmates who could afford it were made to pay for food and lodgings, while the poor languished in the fetid conditions of the 'Common side'.

While it wasn't an official place of execution like Horsemonger Lane and Kennington Common, the poorer inmates nevertheless faced starvation and torture as their debts increased. It was a killing machine in all but name. In 1729 a parliamentary committee reported that 300 inmates had starved to death within a three-month period, and that eight to ten were dying every 24 hours in the warmer weather.

I looked at my phone. It was 33 degrees. At that moment, Half-life called to say he was in Borough and did I fancy a pint.

'Sure. Royal Oak? I'm looking for the remains of the second Marshalsea, then heading over to Wapping,' I said.

'Marshalsea?' he said.

'The debtors' prison,' I said, and I swear I heard him shudder. Maybe it was the grand he owed me.

'Is there beer involved?' he said.

'Verily,' I said.

The second Marshalsea – built just up the road at what is now 211 Borough High Street, to replace the crumbling first – opened for business in 1811 and if anything became even more notorious than its predecessor. Charles Dickens' father was incarcerated there for a minor debt, which greatly affected the young Dickens. He made Marshalsea world famous as the place in which Amy Dorrit's father is imprisoned for debts so complex no one is able to work out how to secure his release. (Opposite the site of this second Marshalsea is Little Dorrit Park.)

I gazed for a while at the last remaining wall of Marshalsea, which runs along the unmarked Angel Place beside St George's Churchyard Garden, and went to meet Half-life in The Oak. He was outside on the pavement fanning himself with a beer mat.

'You look hot,' I said.

'You don't look so bad yourself,' he said.

After a restorative pint of Harvey's Sussex Best, we wandered down Snowsfields towards Tower Bridge. The afternoon heat was stifling.

'I wish it was a bloody snow field,' grumbled Half-life, flapping his shorts. 'My bits are on fire.'

I thought of telling him about his cock muff, but figured it would only encourage him.

Execution Dock, Wapping

Some of the inmates of the Marshalsea were held under the legal jurisdiction of the British Admiralty, who had their own special killing site at Execution Dock, Wapping, where we now headed, over Tower Bridge and through St Katharine Docks.

Execution Dock was used for more than 400 years to execute those convicted of serious crimes at sea, such as piracy, mutiny and pushing in at the queue for the duty free. The 'dock' was a scaffold built specifically for hanging and was located at the shoreline, symbolising the sea and the Admiralty's watery jurisdiction. Its last executions were in 1830.

Here again, an execution at the dock meant crowds would line the river's banks and even charter boats to get a better view of the killings. An execution of a pirate was considered a particular treat. This was done with a shortened rope, which meant a slow death from strangulation on the scaffold as the drop was insufficient to break the prisoner's neck. The death throes of the condemned man were known as the 'Marshal's dance' because of the twitching of the limbs during asphyxiation. Look at the funny man, Daddy! Happy birthday, darling! Pass the olives!

Unlike hangings on land, the bodies of pirates at Execution Dock were not immediately cut down following death. These corpses were left hanging in the nooses until three tides had washed over their heads. Food for thought. And eels.

There are three pubs on the river at Wapping: the Town of Ramsgate, the Prospect of Whitby, where there stands a commemorative scaffold complete with noose, and another named after the famous pirate, Captain Kidd, who was convicted of piracy and murder and executed at the dock in 1701. During his execution, the rope broke and he was hanged on the second attempt. His remains were then put on display by the river Thames at Tilbury for three years.

'His big mistake was getting caught,' said Half-life, as we sat by the river at the back of the Town of Ramsgate, raising a glass to the Captain.

'To err is human,' I said.

'To 'arr' is pirate,' said Half-life.

This final leg of my execution crawl is, of course, north of the river. Nevertheless, all three Wapping pubs afford terrific views across the water to the Glorious South, which, depending on the wind, would have been the last thing seen by the wretches who were hanged there. What a way to go.

Indeed, in William Kidd's case, he not only got to gaze over at Rotherhithe while he struggled for breath, he also had a boozer named after him. And which of us would not gladly embrace death in return for lending our name to a pub?

I Did it the Quietway

Of London's seven planned 'Quietways' – the city's network of back-street cycle routes – four will be in South London. The idea of getting somewhere on a bike, without the threat of being crushed by a fat truck, is a liberating one. But, would there be any pubs on the way to save it being a giant waste of time?

Only the other day, we'd cycled from Charlton to Bermondsey and discovered a publess four-mile stretch that had shaken our confidence in planners regarding this sort of thing. What if the Quietways were mapped by Quakers?

To find out, Half-life and I mounted our steeds at the beginning of Quietway 1, just under Waterloo Bridge, by the National Theatre. The big man was unusually gloomy. Something was on his mind, other than my refusal to let him travel the Quietway in a Hummer stretch limo. (I had at least told him there was no better way to show the world that he's an utter penis, which he'd seemed oddly pleased with.) He liked to ride, though. Not in a cycle club kinda way – you had to like the countryside and possibly people for that. He had to ride for his 'work'.

There's no notice to mark this momentous station. No fireworks to announce the start of this little triumph of the silent. Soon though, you come to a sign directing you to turn down Cornwall Road, where, not two minutes after our departure, we stopped for a pint, at the White Hart.

Ah, the White Hart. Pretty enough, but often overlooked for the seductive charms of the King's Arms, round the corner, in her Georgian glory. The White Hart is still well worth an entry on your dance card, mind. It has a slightly younger crowd than the KA and they've upped their game on the beer front. Half-life plumped for a kegged white IPA, on the grounds that it was 'more expensive'. I figured carbonated beer wasn't the way to go when you've got miles of pedalling ahead and had a simple pale ale. What a start to a day's exercise.

We'd only been back in the saddle for another couple of minutes when we came across the Stage Door, which we couldn't ignore because it has a lovely roof garden. The barmaid had never heard of Quietway 1 and had no idea she was on a cycle route to Greenwich. Despite a wealth of ride-based smutty gags at his disposal and the barmaid's full attention, Half-life smiled politely and went upstairs. He wasn't even tempted to thrash me at pool.

'You OK, hun?' I asked.

'I'm fine,' he barked, then moaned about all the flowers on the roof terrace that stopped him having a proper lean with his fag so he could enjoy the view of the arse end of the Old Vic.

With a little beer buzz, we continued to plough through the backstreets. A kindly truck driver waved us through onto Great Suffolk Street. This must be what it's like being pretty, I thought to myself.

'I feel pretty,' I told Half-life.

'That's nice,' he muttered.

At last, three minutes later, we arrived at The Libertine, another decent SE1 pub that we rarely visit. They do a stellar pizza.

'No, ta,' said Half-life. He wasn't even tempted to win money off me at darts either. Now I was thinking I should take him to A&E.

Next, whether due to a lack of signage or a lack of attention, we went wrong. We'd crossed Borough High Street onto Trinity Street and didn't notice anything suggesting that we should turn left on Swan Street. If you get to the agreeable Trinity Square, you've gone too far. We went as far as The Roebuck, a pub unnecessary for the purpose of the day's research, but a pub all the same. We had a lovely local pint and wondered why we don't go wrong more often.

Had we gone the right way, we would have instead visited the Dover Castle, which is a hostel (from £15 a night) and therefore aimed at those passing through, rather than those who require lifelong friendship, as all pubs should be.

'Good pubs are all about commitment, like a relationship,' said Half-life, warming up.

We'd had four pints by now, no breakfast and still hadn't left SE1. Plus, once we had rejoined the Q1 at Tabard Street, we had to pass the Royal Oak – and there's no frigging way that was going to happen. It's a lovely Victorian corner pub, made all the more welcoming by the slightly eccentric landlord. Their Harvey's Best is one of life's certainties, but Half-life surprised me by having Tom Paine, Harvey's dry-hopped export ale. But then he's as keen on the Rights of Man as he is on strong beer.

The Oak's menu is full of timeless hearty food from the '70s. There's not a *jus* in sight. Half-life smiled for the first time today. 'I'll have the pork pie and Scotch egg salad,' he beamed, which turned out to be exactly as described. 'Followed by a knickerbocker glory.'

Cycling is not an ideal post-lunch occupation but the Q1 beckoned and was separated from car traffic sufficiently at this stage for us to be safe, even while swaying and dawdling. I was thinking how much I liked the low-rise social housing of Waterloo and Borough when it started to tip down. This England and her alleged summer. The shower became almost torrential as we crossed Tower Bridge Road and we really had no choice but to stop at The Victoria, a favourite Bermondsey boozer, or risk our health in the wet rain.

Another Victorian cracker, another welcoming landlord. Some lads were having one for the road, repeatedly, until their road had been liberally hydrated. They talked about politics with that man-in-the-pub certainty that confirms they'd be running the country if only they weren't so damn busy.

Half-life was nursing a Mad Goose, looking glum. At least he wasn't goosing a mad nurse. At last, his woes spilled to the surface. 'My Cassie is doing my head in. She won't even *consider* a threesome. She's got some kind of problem with it. I mean, where's the commitment?'

Having a threesome with another woman is a vital part of a loving relationship in Half-life's world and he is baffled by anyone unable to see the benefit.

'Is that it? It that why you're such a grouch today?'

171

'And I've had to give Big Jen the heave-ho too. Kids today don't know what a real mistress is. I told her not to get attached. I'm addictive. Like butter.'

I began to despair of him, but now the sun was coming out. We still hadn't left SE1. It was time to ride. We had been to six cracking pubs but on the rest of the Q1 we wouldn't see a single one. It was almost like it had simply been designed for riding a bike from one point to another.

The housing became more modern and less interesting as we trekked through Bermondsey, past the New Den, towards Deptford. All was not lost though, as the Q1 took us through Folkestone Gardens, a little urban park on the site of WWII bomb-damaged high-density housing, where 50 people had died one terrible night. There, we smoked one we'd rolled earlier, kept calm and carried on. This small speck of green became a tree-lined paradise in the middle of an industrial estate. Plus, the drugs massively helped our cycling technique.

Again, either the signage was insufficient, or something had affected our minds; we got a bit lost. I still think it was the former, but we reached Deptford High Street regardless and in desperate need of a drink after our struggles. By straying off the path – always a good idea – we found ourselves at the Job Centre pub. Unfortunately it wasn't open till four.

'It's not a pub, then,' fumed Half-life, before storming off back towards the path.

'What about...?' But he had gone. My plan B for this stage had been to carry on up the High Street to London Velo, a licensed cycling cafe where we could watch the Tour de France, now that we were kindred spirits with the Froome Dog and all.

Back on the Q1 there was another lovely spliff-spot opportunity at St Paul's churchyard, by one of London's finest baroque churches, but I was still trying to catch up the drug-tainted front runner. We diverted off the Q1 again at Deptford Church Street, for the comforts of the Birds Nest, still a world leader in its own specialist field: circular intersection booze stops. Afterwards, we paused for a smoke at the Ha'Penny Hatch on Deptford Creek.

'Cassie did ballet there,' said Half-life, nodding towards the Laban music and dance school, a Stirling Prize-winning building, now dwarfed by ugly luxury flats.

'Pointe?' I asked.

'There's no need to be like that. I was just making conversation.'

We pressed on to Greenwich Station, the end of the Q1, where we high-fived like we'd climbed Mont Ventoux.

'Great work, mate. Fancy a pint?'

Not tempted by the bar by the station, we headed to the craft beer haven of The Union for some mad beer from a vast selection and a well-earned sit down. When I reached the beer garden with our Japanese ales, I heard Half-life's deep, resonant laugh for the first time today. He'd met a beautiful woman from the Netherlands who was giving as good as she got.

'A threesome?' she declared. 'Why stop at three?'

'Have the clouds lifted, mate?' I asked Half-life.

'You what?'

'You know. The black dog.'

'No idea what you're on about. Anyway, Mila, this is Dirts. He won't be joining us for afters.'

Every cloud and that.

My Day with a Dealer

Investigative journalism is hard, committed work, so not the kind of thing I'd get involved with voluntarily. So I have to confess that the day I spent following Half-life as he plied his trade – furnishing South London with narcotics – was an accident. A bad accident.

Half-life had borrowed the keys to my flat so he could retrieve the stolen cheese he'd stashed there on a previous visit. He was already cross that I was taking my girlfriend to lunch without him, but even more so that it meant he had to get his own shit out of my place, when he was so busy and all – just so he could turn a tidy profit with his substitute cheese fence, Two Thumbs Tony.

I should have known better than to let him have my only keys, especially as that's how I lost my spare set. He needed *them* when I was away recently, so he had somewhere to entertain The Actress where he wouldn't be found. Now The Actress has them, but wasn't returning his calls, which he put down to 'love paralysis'.

We arranged to meet later at The Rake in Borough so I could pick up my keys.

'What keys?' he said.

After searching his bag and shorts he said he must have left them at his place. Apparently this was my fault because there was nothing attached to my keyring to make them conspicuous.

'I never lose my keys,' he said, proudly, showing me his set, chained to his belt, attached to a purple butt plug.

He offered to fetch them, but I knew better than to let him out of my sight. It was Thursday, the day he had to score for his weekend trade. He'd be visiting his supplier before packaging and distributing the goods to his clients, like a pillar of business, and could end up any-where but where my keys were. I had to get them tonight as I was being picked up the next morning for a long-planned mucky week-end. My only chance was to become Half-life's shadow for the night, God help me.

'As long as you don't put it on that fucking website of yours,' he said. 'What's it called again?'

'TripAdvisor.'

'That's it.'

Half-life was cycling, which meant I had to keep up on a Boris Bike. Luckily, he was held up on the Old Kent Road as he dragged a driver out of his window, by the throat, to make a point about road safety. At least the window was open, this time.

At New Cross we were buzzed in to a heavily secured hallway that smelt so powerfully of skunk I felt immediately dizzy and self-con-scious, then hungry and incoherent and, finally, sexy. And this was before I'd even made it into the lair of the man known as No Name.

Half-life apologised for my presence but assured No Name that I was alright, 'For a cunt, like.'

No Name was polite and welcoming, but he was guarded by Angel, a monosyllabic colossus straight from Central Casting, perpetually on the verge of 'roid rage, willing me to make a faux pas so he could crush my bones to powder and then snort them. Angel passed Half-life a large bag of weed, a ball of coke, ketamine and some marinaded chicken.

Half-life complained about the previous consignment and refused to pay for anything until he'd had a free line and a joint for quality control purposes. Time was getting on as Half-life borrowed No Name's scales so he could bag up and short-change his friends. Bored at the lengthy process, I pulled out my phone, only for Angel to cough and lift up his shirt. At first I thought he was showing me his abs, so I was almost relieved to realise he was letting me see his handgun. I put my phone back in its holster and got patient, fast.

'How long will it take us to get to Brixton?' I asked Half-life once we'd made it out and my sphincter had recovered its equilibrium.

'Brixton? I've got work to do, pal,' said the man with a vocation to serve others. He rode off towards the Elephant to deliver his bounty to grateful customers, who had all, I've no doubt, been waiting for hours and shortly we were welcomed into a world in which Half-life was Lord, kissing, hugging and shaking hands like the Mayor of Ganjaville.

He left the last place richer, a couple of pints happier and with a whole salmon, bartered from the kitchen on favourable terms, which he strapped to my reluctant back. A keen gourmet, he'd happily trade low-quality drugs for high-quality fish, meat or veg, like he was Warren the Buffet.

'Gastrotwat,' I called him, almost within earshot, as we headed to a Waterloo boozer for his final delivery of the night, where Martina, a new, beautiful, Euro-barmaid had the misfortune to serve him.

'What would you like?' she asked, sweetly.

And he told her, in pornographic detail. The Guvnor intervened to save his momentarily stunned staff.

'This is Half-life,' he said, pulling his complimentary pint. 'You get used to it.'

It wasn't the only time that evening that Half-life would introduce himself with unexpected indecency. For him, it was the equivalent of a firm handshake. He takes the measure of women by their reaction to unsolicited intimacy, rather like, I imagine, Vladimir Putin does with bears.

At least we were in a pub that closed at 11. I could be home by one, away from the madness, skinning up in the garden in my pants. But I hadn't figured on the lock-in, the usually welcome entreaty to go on and on and on. Getting Half-life out of a pub that is still serving is impossible, especially when my own resolve was being tested by a free bar.

By the time the Guvnor turfed us out, it seemed like a good and logical idea to go to the river. On the beach at the South Bank I held the salmon still while Half-life snorted a livener and declared himself roadworthy. He climbed on his steed as I ordered a cab to his gaff.

While he sped home, I was tortured in traffic by Anodyne FM. You don't need pliers to get me to talk, just plug me into duets of the '90s. By the time I arrived he was already expertly cooking, preparing the salmon which we ate in the shed that stood in his living room.

'Keys?'

'Alright, alright, I haven't even had fucking dinner, yet. I've been working all night. Jesus, it's like hanging out with Jacob fucking Rees fucking Mogg's uptight fucking brother, Fuckface Rees-Mogg.'

It was past late. The food was welcome though, and superb, but the bottle of stolen Château Margaux was wasted on palates defiled by hops, herbs and unknowable chemicals.

'It's four, I'm out. Keys and cab time,' I declared.

'What are you on about? I haven't got your fucking keys. Crash on the sofa. I'll break in for you tomorrow.' In a pitiful attempt to calm my fury, Half-life told me he had searched for the keys when he got back and couldn't find them.

'Why didn't you tell me that two fucking hours ago?'

'Because I knew you'd be a fucking bitch about it. And I was right. Again.' Speechless, I huffed off and got a cab. If this idiot could break in, so could I.

Back home, I spotted an open bathroom window. All I had to do was lose two stone and cover myself with butter and I was in. Then I saw what had happened to my keys. There they were, dangling in my front door where Half-life had left them, mocking me and, worse, the entire home security industry.

Man's Best Friend

There is nothing better for a light MDMA hangover than a stroll by the river.

'A spliff?' countered my companion, Dirty South, channelling the wild wisdom of weeds.

I was happy to be corrected. There is nothing better for a light MDMA hangover than a stroll by the river and a massive little spliff. Particularly after work.

We had just completed a solid hour's graft in Borough. We don't record our podcast often, we acknowledge that. Why not? Well, to sum it up in three words: pure laziness. But when we do, we like to unwind with a quality ale outside The Rake pub, enjoy a long lean on the bins provided for such a purpose and consider our options and commitments.

After a brief discussion we had concluded that we had nothing in particular to do and had set off to the river to get on with it immediately. As devotees of the Deserter Way may already know, one of the wonderful things about having nothing in particular to do is that you never know what's going to happen next. And so it was as we skinned up on the exposed foreshore of the Thames in the pale late-afternoon sun, near Tate Modern.

We are often drawn to this special place, this ribbon of wilderness that lies at the heart of the city, offering unheralded views and unusual angles of the familiar. Right in the middle of it all and yet, at the same time, away from it all. Just how we like it. They can't build their shit flats here, we like to think, though they will probably find a way soon enough.

We breathed in the fresh riparian air. We breathed in the sweet-smelling smoke. We started to notice things. I saw it first. I gave Dirty South a nudge and nodded my head in its direction.

'Oooh,' he said.

'Isn't it?' I replied.

For there, nestled amongst the ragged stones, worn tiles and rounded house bricks, sheltering beneath Blackfriars Railway Bridge, lay a familiar yellow orb, bright but forlorn, as if it knew it was lost, out of place.

It were only a bloody tennis ball.

Men, generally, are delighted by balls. Perhaps because we speak so much of it. And Dirty South and I are no different. Freeing the blessed globe from its watery resting place, we began kicking it to one another as we strolled along the shore; knocking it off a wall here or a post there; using the banked sands to curl inch-perfect passes. Once we almost lost it to the waters but Dirty South, with a shriek, risked a wet foot to save it. Hero, plain and simple.

'What shall we call him?' asked Dirty South.

'Simon?' I offered, it being our go-to name for inanimate objects: a bifter, perhaps, or our shared Spotify playlist. But Dirty South didn't look keen. I could see he was working on something. Something big.

'Let's call him... Bally,' he said. And it was so right there was no point in further discussion. The man has an uncanny knack with words.

'And let's kick him all the way home,' I said, my eyes now wild with delight. And possibly skunk.

'Yes,' said Dirty South. 'To Wimbledon.'

'Wimbledon,' I breathed. '*Of course.*'

We passed the Oxo Tower and after several failed attempts (that might have forced lesser men to concede defeat) finally managed to flick-kick Bally up the steps at Gabriel's Wharf. Having lain alone on the Thames shore for so long, we figured he would appreciate the people and lights of the Southbank. And how right we were. He was the belle of the ball as we booted him, now, along this handsome riverside boulevard, past the ITV building and the challenging multiple levels outside the National Theatre.

The early-evening crowds were swelling and strangers joined in with our game, knocking Bally back to us or laying him off into our paths with a smile and a wave. We got the impression that some of the more skilful touches were performed by our European brethren and sistren, primed by years of tiki-taka. The more clumsy attempts to join in – by the shinners, the ball-treaders, the toe-stubbers – all seemed to be by English speakers, a sad indictment of something akin to our national game.

One man, sporting brogues and flamingo-pink chinos and facing a firm pass from the Dirty One, simply froze in his tracks and watched as Bally bounced off his shoes. I will never forget the withering look he received from his girlfriend, who had clearly seen this unforgivable side to him for the first time.

'I give it a month,' I said to her, not without sadness. One's approach to street football defines one. She knew that, and he'd just defined himself out of a relationship.

Heading now to Hungerford Bridge we approached pop-up beer stop the Hop Locker.

'I wonder if Bally might be thirsty,' said Dirty South, and we stopped to try their mighty Simcoe Pale Ale.

'Hello. Do you serve men with balls?' I enquired of the barman.

'I expect so, mostly,' he said.

'Excellent. Three pints of the Simcoe then, please,' I said, and we flicked Bally up onto a table to people-watch in the fading light.

One of London's finest viewing spots is the fifth-floor balcony of the Royal Festival Hall and it was here the three of us headed next, keen as we were to show Bally some sights before home time.

When you've a ball on the crew, you are only ever the discovery of a 'natural goal' away from a quick game of three-and-in and we paused at the external lift doors – which offered the perfect goal and excellent lighting – for some light exercise in order to build a thirst.

At the RFH bar we were presented with the choice of Theakston's, cider or 21 taps of Red Stripe. I went for a cider, Dirty South had a Theakston's and Bally surprised us both with a large rum, ice, no mixer. What a character!

Upstairs we gazed across London for a while and then took a table on the balcony next to some young women. Who can say who was first attracted to whom, but very soon we were all chatting and when they heard about Bally's evening they were thrilled to take some selfies with him, which he seemed to enjoy.

A quick look at Google Maps told us that Wimbledon was still, somehow, a two-and-a-half-hour walk away. We decided that it might make better sense, given the hour, if we escorted Bally onto a train at Waterloo instead. On the way out we popped into the gents and let Bally admire his own reflection in the mirror while we took a leak.

'I wonder if he might be hungry?' said Dirty South, as we rolled him down six flights of stairs and across the busy lobby.

'Very good point,' I replied, admiring his thoughtfulness and sensitivity to the needs of others.

Ordinarily, Dirty South and I might treat ourselves to a budget-conscious cheese–egg burger at Waterloo Grill after an evening out, but Bally had other ideas. On the way to the station he took an unexpected ricochet off a parked car and settled onto the terrace of upmarket grill bar Black & Blue.

'I think he wants a steak dinner,' I said.

'Well, it is his night,' said Dirty South, and we chipped him through the restaurant door, leaving the hurly-burly of the traffic behind.

'Table for three, please,' I said.

'Certainly, gentlemen. I like your ball,' said the maître d', making us fall in love with her. We told her his story and she laid Bally a place at the table and brought him a napkin.

The three of us tucked into a côte de boeuf and shared a powerful bottle of red before heading up the steps into the bright lights of Waterloo Station. At the ticket barrier for the Wimbledon train we found a good man who agreed to take charge of Bally and ensure he alighted safely at Wimbledon station.

'It would be an absolute fucking honour, boys,' he said, and we waved them both off.

Feeling a little emotional, we decided a pick-me-up might be in order and headed round to Penny, the late-night bar beneath the Old Vic. Penny may pass muster as a cafe (which it is in the daytime) but as a dive bar it's a bit short on atmosphere. We do end up there a lot, though. Mainly because it's so, you know, open.

There we raised a glass of continental lager to our dear, departed friend. We'd given a tennis ball probably the best night of his life, and in the process had had one of our own.

It made me realise that, really, all you need for a fine evening out is a humble ball, man's best friend. Plus a mate, to be fair. Perhaps some beer. Nice food. Spliff. Girls. London. But apart from that, nothing. Except maybe a fat dab of molly.

One at the Railway

'I thought you said you were just going for one at The Railway?' said Roxy's incredulous boyf, Jan.

'I did,' slurred Roxy, as she stumbled into her flat. 'I did just have one at The Railway.' Jan sighed.

'If you can't be honest with me, Rox...'

Poor Jan. Roxy wasn't lying, exactly. We'd had one at The Railway, alright. One in The Railway at Tulse Hill. One in The Railway at Streatham. One in Clapham. And so on, until we'd had enough of trains. You're never far from The Railway. Perfect for that swifty on the way home, on the way out or when there's still eight minutes till your train.

They used to be desperate, sticky-carpeted, last-resort pubs, but that's no longer the case. The Railways of Blackheath, Bromley North, Clapham, Forest Hill, Gipsy Hill, Lower Sydenham, Thornton Heath, Tulse Hill and Streatham Common are all worth more than a pint of your time.

Starting at Peckham Rye, we were in Tulse Hill in eight minutes for our first 'one'. It was a great place to begin: a big, hip boozer, open at 11, like all pubs should be, with a large conservatory and two outside spaces. It had the cricket on, a good beer selection and lovely staff, though David Gower did have to battle with Lauryn Hill to be heard – not a clash I ever expected to witness. I had a joyful Hophead and settled down for the Test when Roxy downed hers and exclaimed: 'Let's go have one at The Railway,' to the confusion of the barmaid.

In six minutes we were at The Railway, Streatham Common, with an even more impressive beer list and a sign declaring: 'Proudly Serving London Brewed Ales'. The Portobello, from North Kensington, was probably the farthest travelled beer there. People were already having lunch in what was probably their only Railway pub of the day, the simple creatures.

We popped into the large back room to find it almost full with chocolate brownie-eating mums and their babies. We had unwittingly stumbled into the Tea Room, serving coffee, cake and brunch, making use of the pub's space to broaden its appeal to parents needing adult company and baked vices.

'Shouldn't be allowed in pubs,' groaned Roxy.

'Bit harsh, Rox. You might have kids of your own one day.'

'Not babies. Cakes shouldn't be allowed in pubs. Not until we can get pissed in a patisserie.'

Though we were right by the station, we took a detour to the rather lovely common, an open space and nature reserve with views made for the afternoon toker. There's an old well in the Rookery garden reminding you that Streatham spa water was once a thing, known for its healing properties.

'So was this,' said Roxy, passing me her hip flask of Irish whiskey, in exchange for a J. I enquired if she'd thought of inviting Jan, her boyfriend, along.

'He's on a bloody health kick,' she replied, shaking her head. 'Cut down on booze, gave up the gear. Lost three kilos doing Hot Bikram Yoga. Mostly from his mind.'

That didn't sound right, Roxy with an exercise mat-botherer, though she'd recently taken up vaping after a friend warned her it was addictive.

'It's not right!' she went on. 'If you must exercise, the least you can do is shut up about it. He asked me to come along, to sweat out my toxins. Like they're a bad thing.'

By the time we'd strolled back, the munchies were upon Roxy. As we passed the pub, she exclaimed: 'Cakes!'

'Shouldn't be allowed in pubs,' I told her, as she plundered the stickies. 'Flip-flopper.'

One stop to Balham and the Northern Line to Clapham North took us close enough to The Railway at Clapham High Street. It's bright and open at the front, but mercifully dark at the back. I found it mostly notable for its pig's cheeks. You can have pig's cheeks on your burger, in flatbread or on a jacket potato. It's a lovely tender, meaty flourish, but there's no getting away from it – you're eating animal face.

Changing at Denmark Hill, next we went to The Railway at Blackheath, whose best feature is a roof terrace where you can get away with a doobie doo to accompany a pint. Non-smokers have their own garden downstairs, where they breathe the virtuous air and are closer to the bar, but I prefer the elevation, even if the stairs felt like exercise.

'Don't mention exercise,' said Roxy. It sounded like Jan was on the way out. 'Shit in bed. Shit at the causes of bed.'

They were no longer getting drunk together, as he eschewed the very glue that made them sticky. Roxy reckoned she hadn't had sober sex since she was 15, her first time – the very night she discovered the microsecond. I suggested she talk to him.

'Oh, do fuck off,' she said, as if I'd just suggested healing crystals and an enema.

She had been considering heading home, but I'd inadvertently made her determined to go to more Railways, for one.

Three trains and 35 minutes later and we were at the Railway Tavern in Bromley, a gorgeous Victorian tiled boozer, now run by Antic. Good food, good ale, stylish surroundings in what would be a perfect location, if Bromley North station could take you anywhere. Trains go to Sundridge Park and Grove Park. That's it. Sort it out, isn't it? It's cruel to have such a picturesque Railway pub mocked by one of the least useful stations in the country.

And so despite being beside a station, we had to get a bus to Penge to go to the Railway Telegraph in Forest Hill. Madness, on a day punctuated with sound logic.

The Telegraph is another good-looking pub, right on the South Circular, but, oddly, it's eight minutes' walk from the station (though it took us 25). It has a good rep for food, but we were past that point and dined on nuts and Whitstable Bay.

'The thing is, being tipsy around people who are sober is fine. They're the ones that get bored. I couldn't give a stuff,' said Roxy. 'It's being *high* around people who aren't that's shite. It's like hanging out with your parents.'

'Your parents are great,' I said.

'No, your parents.'

Roxy's list also included another Railway Telegraph, the best pub in Thornton Heath, the Railway Tavern in Lower Sydenham and the Railway Bell in Gipsy Hill. But although I could have managed another pint, I couldn't handle the travel. We trundled back to Peckham to finish on a high note – a fat one on the Rye before Roxy headed home to tell Jan the truth.

Streetlife: Tower Bridge Road

Sometimes your body tells you it's time to take a day off. God knows, you've put in the hours. You're first in and last out, just like the Marines. So I listened to my body and heard it say: 'For pity's sake, man, no pub today.'

It was unfortunate that this point coincided with my plan to spend an entire day on Tower Bridge Road (TBR), with all its interesting watering holes, but successive unscheduled booze-ups had led me to look at the bigger picture. I wanted to be able to see my youngest grow up and, one day, buy me a pint.

I was drawn to tour the road as it leads to and from our famous river, headed at one end by one of the most iconic bridges in the world. And yet it has been a shabby thoroughfare for much of its life, permanently clogged with traffic and devoid of the grandeur of the bridge that lends it its name. It's a road that doesn't add up.

Half-life had already made it clear he would not be joining me on a tee-total tour. 'It's unnatural,' he cried. 'A rank abomination.' So I was surprised to bump into him outside London Bridge relatively early in the morning as I made my way to Tower Bridge. His red-rimmed eyes told me he was still up, not up early. He was coming down and being visited by that fearful hunger that's left behind once the fast drugs have worn off. At least he could join me for the most important meal of the day.

Breakfast

The Cat & Cucumber Cafe is not named after the scaring-cats-with-cucumbers Internet sensation but it is a prescient name. It is also a classic greasy spoon and a Bermondsey institution.

'Got any liver?' slurred Half-life.

'For breakfast?'

'Unless you can do me a transplant, yeah. With bacon, two eggs, mushrooms… I dunno, whatever you want.'

'No vegetables?'

'You're right. Mushrooms are not a vegetable, are they? They're a fungi,' he said. 'Like me.' She looked at him like he'd just shat in her hand. '*I'm* a fun guy,' he persevered.

'Take number. Sit down.'

Satisfied by the breakfast we deserved, I thought we were about to part, when Half-life said, 'You'll be wanting a coffee then. Let me show you round,' and started marching towards the bridge.

Post-Breakfast

Unfortunately, he marched straight into the Pommeler's Rest, the local 'Spoon's.

'Pint of Bow Bells, pal,' he told the barman before turning to me. 'You want a coffee, yeah?' Fuck it.

'Make it two pints.' My day of abstinence was in tatters by 10.30am.

'£3.50 a pint! It's £2.35 at my 'Spoon's. You'll have to get this one, Dirts.'

We settled in with the other morning imbibers, long since shorn of shame. They're such regulars I'm surprised they're not carpeted. The beer was refreshing though, even at that time of day. So much so, in fact, that we had to have another to take us to opening time at the Draft House.

I make no apologies for liking the Draft House chain. The beer is excellent, the staff are lovely and having thirds of beer means you can take a punt on a mad motherfucker, like a 7% French Oak Vanilla Porter. Madness. But only a third of madness.

Now I felt immortal.

Coffee

Implausibly, a Twitter poll of Deserter readers found that coffee was their second favourite drug, after booze, so I felt duty bound to find a recommendation. The main contenders were: Hej, the Scandi-inspired cafe; Sobo, an old favourite; and Machine, the bike cafe and repair shop. All are excellent in their own way.

Machine is pretty groovy. It's cool yet welcoming, sorting out your ride for you while you wait with a fine cup of java. But I went for Hej, because, well, Sweden. Plus it was the nearest to the churchyard where we accompanied the caffeine with some herb. Half-life had a disco nap on somebody's grave, as I dozed in the sunshine on the grass, as happy as pie.

Lunch

Speaking of pie, even though it felt like we'd only just eaten, Half-life was starving again, probably as a consequence of not eating at all the day before. He was even prepared to shell out £4 of his own money for pie and mash at Manze's. I was almost tempted, but not having a steak and kidney option still chafes with me in what claims to be London's oldest pie-and-mash shop.

It does have a proper Bermondsey vibe though and also attracts visitors eager for some authenticity, and possibly eels. Manze's (est. 1902) is a striking example of the old rubbing shoulders with the new, being next door to Lechevalier (est. 2017), a wine bar that offers cheese and charcuterie along with exceptional wine. Manze's looks like it will always thrive, but I hope their neighbour does too. Along with the other food options on TBR, which include Indian, Lebanese, Turkish, Japanese, Argentine, Chinese and Spanish, it gives us what we love about London – the world on our doorstep. Posh options for when you're minted and meat-in-pastry options when you just need some carbs with a bit of animal. Long live le London.

Beer we go again

Over the road is the Other Room Beer Bar. A lovely little place, it is essentially a micropub, without casks. You might connect it to the new Bermondsey, but there's nothing wrong with that. It's got taps that represent the Bermondsey Beer Mile, which is only right and proper. And Bermondsey's ale explosion only echoes the long history of brewing in the area.

It's perfect in the afternoon for a quiet drink and simple grub and has deckchairs and tables outside so you can take in the sunshine and pollution. It's owned by Joe Lowe, the son of the artist, Jeff Lowe – known to the artists of Forest Hill's Havelock Walk as Lord Havelock – and his business partner.

From the Other Room to The George lies a very odd collection of shops. You've got a beer bar, a bookies, a charity shop/food bank, a Thai massage, a mountain-climbing shop and a pub. Half-life had a go in all of them. He was happy in three, baffled in two and ejected from the other.

A food bank, though? Three miles from Buckingham Palace. It's like a lump of coal in London's crown; a sad and stark reflection of our days, though hardly unique in our history. There's always someone under the window when the royal pot gets emptied.

The George is a throwback boozer and although it's a locals' gaff, tourists and strangers are also welcomed. It's sort of the opposite of the Other Room, but, like Manze's and Lechevalier, we need them to coexist. What's wrong with liking them both? You can't make me choose. I won't.

Some would call it a 'proper pub', yet it's odd that the modern version is the one with the great beer. The George has Courage Best, which is OK-ish, plus Sky Sports, which is welcome, as it was the only time we'd see it all day. I recall many years ago watching England v Switzerland in there with England 3-0 up, and Osman leading a chorus of, 'You can stick your Nazi gold up your arse.'

It can get a bit raucous at the weekend, but only in a knees-up kind of way. The music gets loud, the punters get louder, but the overwhelming sound is that of laughter.

Cocktails

My move towards temperance was going really well. Thoroughly enjoyable. The only trouble was I was six pints down and Half-life was braying for more. He insisted on one in the Bermondsey Arts Club, where he and the Raider had recently nightcapped. It was just opening so it made sense to us that a cocktail would lively us up.

Housed in an old public toilet, the BAC has undergone a thorough and tasteful art deco makeover. A gay friend, Roberta Slack, loves the place but remains sad that you can no longer get pulled off there by a passing tradesman. You can get fine aperitifs though, if you're a member, or with Half-life. He had one with absinthe, benedictine and lillet blanc, while I was naturally drawn to one called South of the River (sloe gin, lemon, sugar and prosecco). The BAC is also owned by Joe Lowe and pal, who in addition have an interest in Peckham's Bianca Road Brewing, recently relocated to Bermondsey.

Now we were ready to take on the world. Instead, we tried to get into another subterranean bar – Bump Caves, underneath the Draft House. Unfortunately it was closed, despite signage to the contrary. Though gutted, we were at least in The Drafty, where we consoled ourselves with a pint of Juicebox and where Half-life proposed matrimony to the barmaid.

'So when we getting married, love?'

'Sorry, my diary is all full up,' she told him with a smile.

'Till when?'

'Let me check. Oh, the end of days,' she said, which Half-life seemed strangely encouraged by.

Change is upon Tower Bridge Road, we noticed, with local legend Hasan selling his kebab joint to, erm, Mr Lowe and his pal. They are, by all accounts, a couple of super nice guys, trying to do exciting things in SE1, but it struck me that the liveliest places we'd been in all day were Manze's and The George. The old school has some life in it yet.

It's funny how that first drink can return you to 'health', or at least something approaching normality. Maybe the body knows nothing. Though I knew it would be shouting its message to me again, the very next day.

Half-life Comes Clean

It all started when I received a text message from an unrecognised number that read: 'This is my new number. Lose the old one. I'll be around Fri & Sat if you want cheese. Half-life.'

Was he tripping again? I put in a call to find out.

'You branching out, mate?' I asked.

'Contacts cock-up,' he said. 'Fucking technology. Now every fucker wants a piece of me. I'm going into hiding for the day. Coming?'

'Where to?'

'The spa.'

'The spa? I don't know. Isn't it all fat people sitting around staring into space?'

'Yeah. You'll fit in fine.'

And so it was that I found myself waiting for Half-life outside Brockwell Lido, Herne Hill, the art deco Grade II-listed building in Brockwell Park that houses a gym and a hydrotherapy unit as well as an outsized swimming pool. Just standing outside it was making me feel healthy. Or was it simply hot and tired? I took a seat on a bench and tried for a nap.

I dreamed a giant man in yellow micro-Speedos and mid-calf Doc Martens was prodding me with a cane and shouting 'Arise, sloth!', until I realised that I was in fact awake and Half-life had arrived.

'Follow me,' he commanded.

We strode to the front of the long queue for the pool where Half-life announced to all staff present that he'd brought me along for the 'free trial' and that I'd be 'doing the form' on the way out. Someone nodded and, with this simple exchange, we were in. We headed down to the changing rooms.

'Alright, big man,' said a chap with a mop to Half-life.

'Believe,' replied Half-life. 'Anyone asks, I'm not here.'

I felt honoured to be witnessing yet another facet of Half-life's mysterious existence, even if I was in a glorified bath house. In the changing room I stripped, put on my swim shorts and collected together my stuff for the locker.

'That's weird,' I said, 'looks like you have to bring your own padlock for the lockers. Who carries around their own padlocks?'

'Take your pick,' said Half-life, unzipping his bum bag and tipping out half a dozen onto the bench, along with two Nectar cards and some King Size Rizla. 'Never know when you're gonna need to lock summat.'

We went through to the hydrotherapy room where the jacuzzi groaned at us and an elderly man was, despite the racket, asleep on one of the loungers. Through the internal window was the disconcerting sight of people exercising in the gym. I looked away.

'Jacuzzi, sauna, steam, crash,' said Half-life doing a lot of pointing, and I wasn't sure if he was showing me the ropes or if this was the itinerary. I stepped into the jacuzzi.

'Have a fucking shower first, you filthy dirtbag,' said Half-life, horrified.

I duly showered and had just about got used to being wafted about in the jacuzzi like a dead horse when the water-groaning stopped and, to my surprise, a waterfall began.

'Get it on your back,' said Half-life. 'It's a free massage, innit.'

After a good pummelling, we padded over to the sauna to breathe boiling air and sweat out our own organs.

'So what was with the cheese text?' I asked Half-life as we sat in the yellowy gloom. He sighed.

'Look, I may as well level with you,' he said. 'Dirty knows, so I'll tell you an' all. Truth is, I'm not a cycle courier.'

'Ri–ight.'

'At least, I am, only I'm not delivering fucking planning apps and court summonses or shit like that. And it's not cheese either. You get me?'

'Erm...'

'It's drugs, Raider. I'm delivering drugs. Top quality drugs. Well, not top quality, but lots of 'em.'

I didn't have the heart to tell him that this has been blindingly obvious to everyone for years, nor that Dirty South had regaled me at length about their night out together, dealing drugs and fish. Next Half-life would be telling me that those months he disappeared weren't, after all, spent on a 'silent meditation retreat somewhere outside Aberystwyth'.

'So I have my clients, yeah?' he went on. 'And they have my number, which I change every month. Only this month I've been floating around in K-land like a fucked balloon and I sent it out to the wrong contacts, didn't I? To my girlfriends, my mother, my fucking dentist...'

'Tricky.'

'Tell me about it. Now I've got normals ringing me on my drugs number and no cunt using my private number. It's a shambles, Raider. Is it any wonder I'm stressed?'

To be honest, he looked the least stressed person I could imagine as he gave his jumblies a good jiggle about in his Speedos with one hand and waggled his little finger in his ear with the other, before smelling it. By now, sweat was running in rivulets down my ruddy folds.

'I'm hot,' I said. 'And not in a good way.'

'Come on, let's cold-shower,' he said.

If shouting is good for the soul then my shower shrieks filled up the tank good and proper and I was more than ready for the tropical wet heat of the steam room.

'Phew. It's like a sauna in here,' I said.

Afterwards we dripped our way round to reception where Half-life nodded at the gate man and we were let through to the lido. Here we swam, had an intense game of 'Bottle-top' that involved flicking a bottle-top to one another and a bewildering scoring system that Half-life was loath to fully explain. Then we ate fig rolls as we dried off in the sun.

'What now?'

'Now,' said Half-life, 'we do it all again.'

Our body temperatures dropped as we headed back round to the hydro room and wading back into the warm jacuzzi was most welcome. And that's when it happened. There we were, lying on the tiled loungers, the water lapping around our ears, when I thought to myself, *I bloody love this*. Right there in the dreamy half-light, relaxed and carefree, I became a spa convert.

'I feel magnificent,' I said.

'You think this feels good,' said Half-life, 'wait till your first pint.'

'I really didn't have you down as a spa man,' I said.

'You're kidding, aren't you? It's where all the big deals are done these days.'

'Right. Where else do you go?'

'The big new gaff is the Elephant. Very popular; 65p with an Axess card. Every cunt's in there. That Aphex Twin was in the sauna the other day.'

'Ever go in the gym?'

'Don't be daft. I did the yoga here for a bit but the teacher was so peng I started seeing her after hours and gave it up. Why pay for what you get at home, right? Namaste.'

We fell silent again, possibly thinking about sexy yoga teachers. I know I was.

Back in the changing room I realised I hadn't brought a towel.

'Don't worry, I've got one,' said Half-life, pulling a bottle-green Wimbledon bath towel from his rucksack.

'Nice,' I said.

'Used to be Gabriela Sabatini's.'

'Oh, yeah?'

'Had a little thing with her in the '90s.'

'*What?*'

'Yeah, I was on the squeegees, she was an international tennis star. Was never gonna last. Somehow I ended up with the spider plant, her godawful CD collection and this towel. You can still smell her arse on it sometimes. Here, wanna share?' he said, offering it to me.

'You're alright, thanks.'

'She was all like, "would you be with me if I was just a squeegee girl?". On and on. Did me bonce in. In the end I was like, "No, love. Sorry, but no." And that was it, she had a fucking meltdown, right there in Habitat.'

Out in the bright sunshine, Half-life grimaced at his phone.

'Fuck-a-doodle-doo, 22 messages,' he said. 'I'll have to get another phone. Right, beer. One in The Regent, one in The Nanny and two in The Effra. We've earned it. Your round, plus you owe me 15 quid for the spa.'

Half-life took a call and we sauntered over the road to the Prince Regent. As I stood at the bar I marvelled at how refreshed I felt. I wasn't sure if it was just down to taking some time out – absconding from life for a bit – or simply the thrill of spending some time in an unusual element, but I felt rebooted. Ready to top up my toxins. And Half-life was right, that first sip of beer was tremendous, like tasting it for the first time.

I took our pints outside, where Half-life was finishing his call.

'That was my dentist,' he said, shaking his head. 'She wants a pound of Stichelton and some Cornish Yarg.'

Holiday on the South Circular

When John Hanning Speke discovered the source of the Nile at Lake Victoria in 1859, he ended centuries of wonder and speculation. From where had the mighty river sprung forth, that nourished the abundant life teeming in its wake?

It was in the same pioneering spirit that four intrepid explorers – Half-life, Dulwich Raider, Roxy and myself – set out to discover the source of the South Circular Road. A voyage of discovery that would reveal the very genesis of the orbital corridor that once girdled South London. I say once, because now her love handles (yes you, Wimbledon, Streatham, Crystal Palace) overspill the confines of its belt.

Our four heroes gathered where legends, whispered rumours and Google Maps had suggested the fountainhead might be: underneath the Chiswick Flyover. Yes, as oxymoronic as it sounds, the source of the South Circ was said to be *north of the river*. It's no wonder it had lain undiscovered for so long. None of the world's great explorers had claimed this breakthrough. Where was our Scott? Our Shackleton? Our Neil Armstrong? Well, Half-life was probably being shaken awake by the cleaners at his local.

The three of us waited for him at the roundabout underneath the flyover where the North Circular meets the South, flicking the Vs northward, towards Gunnersbury-Wherever-The-Fuck-That-Is. The two semicircular roads were designed, or more accurately, cobbled together, to bypass London. Now they are most definitely London – at least if pollution maketh the city they are.

'Doctor Livingstone, I presume,' said Roxy, extending her hand to the arriving Half-life resplendent in pith helmet, welder's goggles and his 1960s Dukla Prague away shirt.

'Speke,' said Half-life, bowing to kiss her mitt.

'Erm, OK,' said a confused Roxy. 'Think I'll go and speak to someone nicer.'

'So, this is it,' beamed the Raider, waving a stick he'd found on the roundabout, as the cars buzzed about us, like fat bees around a circular traffic junction. 'The source!'

'Speaking of which, they're open in five,' said Half-life. 'There's no time for your fucking ruminations.'

'But look at it,' said the Raider, from behind his sunglasses, in wonder at the life that surrounded us. Grass, trees and flowers in bloom. 'Is that... is that a rabbit?'

Closer inspection proved that it was a crisp packet hopping in the faint breeze, but the roundabout did indeed abound with nature. And though there was no neon sign declaring it the source of the South Circular – no souvenir shop selling trinkets from the mouth of the beast – there was a street sign planted in the ground that read, simply: 'It's a sweet little flyover – Jayne Mansfield, 1959.'

What must have seemed a wonder of modernity back then, had indeed been opened by the Hollywood star, who was filming *Too Hot to Handle* nearby at the time. 'The Queen of Sex and Bosom' – as one catchy nickname styled her – died tragically in a car crash eight years later. She is remembered with a star on Hollywood Boulevard and at the starting point of the South Circular – a rare double.

Day One

From Chiswick we set off to walk the entire South Circular Road – a gruelling two-day, 20-mile journey in the summer warmth, all the way to the Woolwich Ferry. A walking holiday like no other, on what Wikipedia describes as 'one of the least popular roads in Britain'. A voyage that would take in new sights, strange creatures, alien flora and, if there was a god, pubs.

After eight hellish minutes we spied a sign: 'The Express Tavern – Ale, Cider, Food'.

'Thank fuck for that. I was about to give up,' said Half-life, quickening his pace.

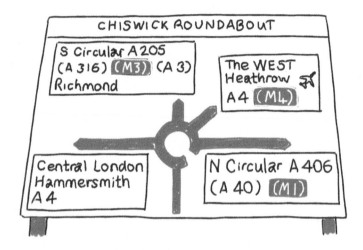

'North of the river though, Raider,' I said, turning to find him gone, along with Roxy. Half-life and I looked at each other for a moment. Half the crew dead, swallowed up by unknown beings not half a mile from departure. Better have a pint, we agreed, without words.

Just then Raider's head popped out of the door of Roastery, next to Kew Bridge station. 'Just grabbing a pastry,' he said. Half-life looked at him like he was speaking Klingon and pointed at the Express.

'Pub!'

Opening the door of the Express we began to see why no one had managed to complete this trip before: too many hand pumps to count, a stellar line-up of breweries, bar snacks fit for kings and queens on a budget... This was heaven – why ever leave?

'Here, you'll like this breakfast stout,' said Half-life, sniffing his pint as the Raider and Roxy joined us. 'Mmm. Notes of croissant.'

'This must be the best pub north of the river,' declared Roxy. 'And it's on the South Circular,' she said with some satisfaction. 'What more proof do we need?' We weren't sure what had been proven, but we all agreed that it had.

Eventually, we tore ourselves away from this northern belle. And moments later we were in South London, overlooking the river from Kew Bridge. This was a different Thames to the one we were used to. No light industry, aggregate or tourist boats, just people rowing in unison; humans straining to be machines, navigating past the uninhabited wooded isle of Brentford Ait, where Half-life claims he once lived for a month while evading the gaze of the law, surviving on 'seeds, grubs and takeaways'.

'I feel magnificent,' said Raider, buoyed by his recent spa day and looking out on the strangely peaceful Tideway. 'I *am* magnificent!' he cried, before a juddering coughing fit.

Safe on the South side of the river, the South Circ then rudely bisected Kew Green, but just before we bade farewell to the grasslands we were offered a choice of pubs. On one side, The Botanist, on the other, the Coach & Horses. We chose the latter, as The Botty looked a bit restauranty. The Coach is a hotel, but felt, happily, like a pub: brown and soothing. We tried to have a half there but the words wouldn't come out right and we ordered beautiful pints of something local.

The next stretch tested us. For more than 20 minutes it was somehow like walking next to a busy, smelly road through an entirely residential area. The Raider's new-found health was being challenged by petrol fumes and he broke out the surgical face masks he'd brought with him. Half-life refused to wear one.

'What the fuck are you doing? Look at you. How are you going to smell South London with that on?'

Raider tried to convince him that he should put aside aesthetic concerns and consider his lungs for a moment. But it was access to his lungs he was worried about, as you can't smoke while wearing a mask.

By the time we reached Mortlake Cemetery, we had wearied of roads and popped in to cheer ourselves up, away from traffic. After more trekking we reached the Bear Kick in East Sheen, having gone 45 minutes without a pub. OK, the Bear Kick isn't a pub, but it had Kernel beer in the fridge and we were sure we risked scurvy if we didn't get some in us quick.

One advantage of a walking holiday on the South Circular is

that you never have to wonder where you're going. The path is laid out, for better or for worse. Fortunately, it wasn't long before more refreshment opportunities revealed themselves to us. Still in East Sheen, we had the choice of the Hare & Hounds, a splendid-looking Young's pub in an old coaching inn, or Micro Beers, a craft beer bottle shop. We chose craft for its variety of intense, powerful flavours from some of the most creative brewers around. It felt every bit as welcoming as a pub, and all the beers it sold were special, like children. Also like children, I believe they are our future.

The narrow focus of our mission began to challenge us at this point. Half-life moaned there was nowhere he could 'bun a zoot', so we went slightly off piste to skin up in the woods by the side of the South Circ between East Sheen and Putney. After getting a little lost in woods, where zoots were well and truly bunned and Roxy's magic cannabis convection machine was put to use, we returned to the world and the road at the oldest pub in Putney.

The Arab Boy was built in 1849 by Henry Scarth, who bequeathed the pub to Yussef Sirric, an Arab servant he had brought back from

Turkey. We sat out front, with the traffic, enjoying the simple pleasures of a hiking holiday.

'This is the scene you'd put on the brochure,' said Half-life, his
words almost drowned out by a passing lorry. Roxy lifted her face
mask to take a sup of ale. She's a happy hayseed at heart; it was like
watching a caged bird trying to look on the bright side.

Onward we strode, to the Putney interior, where a group of young
lads on bikes stopped to ask why some of us were wearing masks.

'It's the end of the fucking world, innit?' said Half-life. The boys
gave us a knowing look and warmly shook our hands, like everything
had suddenly become clear to them.

We stepped past the Fox & Hounds and the Prince of Wales, in a
clear breach of protocol, though the PoW did describe itself as a 'dining room', which suggests a pub that serves food on slate, bits of wood
or dustbin lids. Instead we entered the Beer Boutique, another shop
you can drink in, where a punter admired Half-life's Dukla Prague
shirt.

'I got it for Christmas,' he confirmed. 'It's funny how many people
want to buy me a pint when they see it.' Which set the stranger fumbling for change.

Hunger came crashing down on us all of a sudden, but we were
incapable of going backwards for fuel at the dining room. As
serendipity would have it, we found ourselves just metres away from
a Morley's chicken shop.

'So we are in South London, after all,' declared Roxy. Having
eschewed a place that we suspected of being plate-less, Roxy and
Half-life then ate ribs from a cardboard box by the side of a busy road.
And yet, they were happy. Happy and free, but with sticky fingers.
There was only one thing for it – we would have to find a pub in
which they could wash their hands.

We found ourselves in Wandsworth and in a classic English boozer,
the Spread Eagle, with its dark wood, ornate glass, maroon walls, pen-
sioners and regulars. It would have been rude to visit Wandsworth
and not have a pint of Young's. And we are nothing if not polite, I
thought to myself, just as Half-life belched, 'Jamie Vardy' when the
England striker appeared on screen.

'How to make friends and repulse people,' commented Roxy.

After finding another spliff spot by Wandsworth Common, we were in a position to pick and choose our bars. We passed on The Roundhouse, Northcote, Hawkin's Forge and Tequila Mockingbird in favour of The Merchant, where we caught the end of the England game with the luxury of sitting outside, looking in. Too tight to dine on Battersea prices, we grabbed snacks from the Sainsbury's Local and ate, drank, smoked and watched footy – a truly executive experience for a trekking holiday.

We were torn over whether to have a drink in The Brewdog bar, unsure whether they're pioneers or shitesters, but the prices and chain-ness of the place convinced us to head on to Clapham Common for another toke and some giggles. Whatever you think about Clapham, you can't take away its common – a place of pleasures, whether for strolling, playing football, cruising or having 420 fun in the relatively fresh air. We opted for the latter, which opened another hole through which time fell in, before we reached the south side of the Common.

Not, strictly speaking, actually on the South Circular, Gigalum is a bar with an outside deck that overlooks the SCR cutting through the Common. The lack of enticing beer options persuaded me it was time to 'just say no'. And have a large dark rum and ginger. A feeling of satisfaction grew over us. We couldn't quite see Everest's peak, but we had broken the back of the journey. One more pub and we would have to think about setting up camp for the night.

That last pub was the Crown & Sceptre, at Streatham Hill, the first Wetherspoon's of our journey. At last, some real value for money, though as it was our tenth bar of the day, it was a little late for budget considerations. And what we saved on cheap drinks was more than swallowed up by our accommodation for the evening.

Halfway along the South Circular lies the perfectly placed Tulse Hill Hotel. Ideal for a two-day walking holiday on the A205. The plan was for me and Raider to share, Roxy to have her own room and for Half-life to pitch a tent in the car park. However, Half-life forgot his tent.

'It's OK, love,' Half-life told the manager. 'I'll just sleep in the bar.'

'I'm afraid you can't sleep in the bar.'

'Balls. I've done it dozens of times,' he said. 'Give us a pint and I'll talk you round.'

'The bar is closed.'

'Closed? In a hotel? No, no, no, no. The bar closes when the last guest goes to bed. That's the law. Strange Martin told me – and he's been in court more than any lawyer I know.'

'I'm afraid your friend is misinformed.'

'He did also tell you that iron was a vegetable,' chipped in the Raider, before Half-life opted for the exit. His promises to return in the morning were not met with a great deal of belief.

Our room was perfectly fine, but the best feature was a small, frail metal balcony on which we took turns with Roxy's magic machine, just in case we hadn't had enough intoxicants for the day. Needless to say, it took mere seconds to fall into a deep, dreamless sleep, but the South Circular traffic woke me early, reminding me just where I was. On holiday.

Day Two

The Raider and I made it downstairs in time for breakfast, feeling terrible and looking worse. Imagine our surprise when Roxy and Half-life emerged from upstairs to join us. I did a genuine double take.

'How did...?'

'What?' said Half-life. 'There was no cunt here, so I went looking for youse lot. Ran into this one, innit.'

'Ah. So where did you stay last night, then?'

'What are you, my fucking probation officer?'

'I'd save your questions till after midday,' suggested Roxy, wisely.

The rooms at the Tulse Hill Hotel may have been pricey, even after lengthy negotiation, but the breakfast was top notch. It even had a strange little garnish. Watercress, or nettles, or something.

'What are you supposed to do with it?' I wondered. 'It's all over my bacon.'

'Chuck it on the floor. That's what I did,' advised Half-life.

A couple of coffees and ibuprofens later, we were ready to take on the second half of our expedition: Tulse Hill to Woolwich.

I can't say it wasn't a struggle walking towards Dulwich, though thankfully it was nowhere near as sunny or warm as we'd been promised, such is British summertime. Roxy and the Raider soon donned their masks again. Every slight incline felt like a mountain. Nobody said a word until we reached Belair Park, when the Raider mentioned: 'There's a bar in that park.'

'Well, what are we waiting for?' said Half-life, perking up.

'Opening time?'

'Gaaaah!' yelled Half-life, in a primal expression of frustration, terror and sheer hatred.

While the road remained busy, we were at least passing playing fields and grand buildings. On our right was Dulwich College, a selective independent and boarding school that accepts stinking-rich children from all backgrounds. Opposite, humongous houses are set back from the road behind lawns and crunchy gravel drives.

'You still live on the fucking South Circular,' shouted Half-life to no one in particular. It's a fact that may chafe when you've spent millions on a house in leafy Dulwich.

Past the riding school, Dulwich Park and 'The Menace' of Peckham Town FC we came to one of the saddest sights on our journey: The Grove, a once-proud pub that lay boarded up, silent and impotent. It remains a monument to deadlock between the owners, the lease-holders and the council, with none of them considering the welfare of poor holidaymakers.

If there's one thing you don't want to face after finding a closed-down pub, it's a mahoosive hill. The steepness of the A205 up to the Horniman – a wonderland ranked in the Top 10 Coolest Museums by the *New York Times* – is ball breaking. We could at least step away from the road and into Horniman Gardens, part of the way up. Usually we'd try and get even higher at this point, as the views over the city are something special, but at 10.45 no one felt like skinning up, not even the big man.

The relief of reaching the brow of the hill had us tumbling down into Forest Hill with a measure of enthusiasm. We knew what was coming next: the Eighth Wonder of the World – The Capitol. A pub housed in a glorious 1920s cinema building. Now a 'Spoon's, it opened in 1929 with the film *Man, Woman and Sin*. These days it opens with much the same, plus breakfast.

I wasn't sure I felt like a drink, but I did feel like I'd earned one after that hike. We had arrived at the beginning of the crown jewels of the South Circular – the pubs of Forest Hill and Catford. One taste of fresh beer and I knew it was the right thing to do. One by one, we supped, exhaled and felt revived, sitting in the splendour of The Capitol, us adventurers – heroes all.

Unfortunately it was only 351 feet to the next pub, so the Raider and I decided to skip The Signal and plough on. Half-life and Roxy felt compelled to have one, though, and said they'd catch us up at the Railway Telegraph. The Telegraph is a stately Victorian pub that Roxy and I had visited on our railway tour, so I had no excuse for forgetting that The Signal had the more exciting beer. Fool.

'Half?' said the Raider, reading my mind.

'Half. They can catch up with us at the Blythe.'

'Oh my. The Blythe…' he breathed, in awe. We may have been to the source of the South Circular, but now we were headed to its sexy parts.

It's not that long a walk from The Railway to the Blythe Hill Tavern, but it felt it. And yet, the anticipation of its geniality and the consistent perfection of its offering led to optimism, not impatience. There was no fear of disappointment. Only expectation of possibly the greatest pub in South London.

And yet, when you open the door, there's a sense of ordinariness. There's nothing showy about The Blythe; no crazy beer list, no secret gigs by hot new bands or models behind the bar (with all due respect, Terry). But it makes a fine home for good times.

The beer is so exceptionally well kept it is virtually impossible to have just one, so we were on our second when Roxy came through the door, laughing, followed by a smirking Half-life.

'Anyways, there was these three blind nuns in a sausage factory…' he was saying.

They were unable to just have one either, so we had to have a third. Although we still had a long way to go, there was no hurry as our next two pubs didn't open till 4pm – frankly, a disgrace. Eventually we were persuaded out of the door to seek out a late lunch in Catford. But we'd soon smoked our appetite under Catford Bridge, near the graffiti art of the Lewisham Natureman: a customary white stag painted amongst the urban blight, by the fenced-off stream of the River Ravensbourne.

'How did he even get down there?' I wondered, peering through the barrier.

'It's not a "he",' claimed Half-life. 'It's a spirit. It lives along the railway lines and reminds us of what we've lost.'

'Right. You've seen this "spirit", have you?'

'I have. I owe it a score, as it goes.'

Back in the earthly realm, we stopped by the Catford Bridge Tavern. It's good to see the CBT return to life after it burnt down in 2015, even if it does lean towards diners more than sweary giants and explorers. It's also revived the Catford Beer Festival, so can only be regarded as a force for good.

I didn't expect to be surprised at this leg of the journey. In fact, I never expect to be surprised. But surprised I was by another watering hole in Catford, before the next pub, the Bottle Shop and Bar, on Catford Broadway. While they sell craft beers that you may consume on the premises, their main retail focus is cocktails that they've made and bottled for your pleasure.

'Nice one,' said Half-life. 'Mans cannot live on beer alone. I'll have a bottle of Twisted Old Fashioned. How 'bout you, Rox?'

'That'll do us, Half-pint.' And then something strange happened. Half-life actually paid for the booze.

'I believe in miracles,' said the Raider.

'Something for the long walk ahead, innit,' said Half-life.

'You sexy thing,' replied the Raider.

We had one more Catford stop to make before we hit the South Circular's equivalent of the skeleton coast: the barren six-mile stretch between Catford and Woolwich, with only closed pubs and tempting side streets for company. Why no micropub, so we can enjoy the traffic?

First though we had the Catford Constitutional Club, Antic's atmospheric conversion from the old Conservative Club. The phrase 'shabby chic' is often used in relation to Antic's boozers and the CCC is much more shabby than chic – which suited us. It has been said that Maggie Thatcher would be turning in her grave if she could see how much fun people have here, which is another good reason to enjoy their excellent booze and food menu. Unwilling, or unable, to deal with cutlery at this point, we went for charcuterie and cheese, though sharing plates with Half-life is a lead-weighted lottery. Roxy said the Con also has the finest ladies' loos in South London. And Half-life concurred.

Next we set off to tackle the desolate outback, through Lee and Eltham, all the way to Woolwich. We passed the first of the closed pubs, the Black Horse and Harrow. It's been there since at least 1700, but rebuilt twice, most recently in 1897. Though this former gin palace is a distinctive building with an impressive facade and original features, it traded on cheap beer and food, rather than a history that included early beard star Karl Marx among its patrons. Happily, Laine Pub Company have bought it, but not in time to nourish us on this year's holiday.

We stopped at Mountsfield Park to prepare our minds for the struggle ahead with cannabinoids, before donning our masks and heading into the urban desert.

'Are we really going to do this? How will we survive?' I asked, doubting the wisdom of this holiday rather late in the day.

'With a twisted old-fashioned,' said Half-life, proudly producing his bottle of bourbon, vermouth and the rest. 'Nothing can go wrong with an old-fashioned.'

So with booze and Roxy's magic machine we set out, with Half-life telling barely believable tales of incarceration, poetry tours and being probed in the K-hole by aliens, or similar.

We reached Lee and looked mournfully north and south, knowing civilisation lurked off the highway. The road widened. This was how the South Circular was originally intended, as a spacious dual carriageway, great for cars and hideous for humans.

'What's that up there?' asked Roxy hopefully, spying something that wasn't a double-glazed house.

'That's the World of Leather roundabout,' I answered.

'My kind of roundabout,' said Half-life. The World of Leather has gone but its name remains. It has more of a ring to it than Big Yellow Self Storage roundabout, to be fair.

The next roundabout was even more of a disappointment. It used to house a pub, the Yorkshire Grey, once one of South London's most infamous boozers. Its rough-as-guts reputation was largely down to the unlicensed boxing that used to go on in the hall attached to it, and the crowd that attracted. Now it's a McDonald's. We swallowed our despair. Half-life swallowed a Quarter-Pounder with Cheese.

We were out of the old-fashioned. We'd drained Roxy's hip flask of brandy. We were close to madness. Not only had we walked for an hour and a half, we had increased our altitude by 300 feet. It's little wonder there was mutiny.

'Fuck this! I'm never going on holiday with youse again,' railed Half-life.

'Not far now!' I pleaded. But it was useless.

'Follow me,' said Roxy. And Half-life did, as she turned onto Shooters Hill.

'Holiday traitors!'

'It's one thing being stubborn, mate, but it's another to find a pub at the earliest opportunity,' said the Raider, consolingly.

We joined them in the Red Lion, for a pint, a rest and another pint in the garden. We got chatting to some walkers who'd just come on the Green Chain Walk from Bostall Woods to see the triangular folly, Severndroog Castle, in the nearby Oxleas Woods.

'Why, woman, why?' said Half-life. 'Fuck me, it's like a pub for walka-fucking-holics, this. Let's get out of here!'

I was pleased to leave though, as it had looked as if we might come up short of the finish line, after coming so close. We walked across Woolwich Common, where Half-life insisted on a number by Ha-Ha Road, and on at last to The Castle, the Top Ghanaian Pub on a Roundabout.

Outside The Castle you can see the river, where the Woolwich Ferry hauls its burden over to North Woolwich. It was our first sight of the Thames since Kew. We had come full half-circle. We drank Guinness in the gloaming, congratulated ourselves on our victory over common sense and waited (quite a long time) for our fish and plantain. We had made it where the likes of John Hanning Speke had feared to tread. And unlike Mr Speke we didn't have to travel 4000 miles for some decent African food.

Top Six Pubs in Pollution Blackspots

Innocent drinkers outside several South London pubs are being exposed to dangerous amounts of air pollution, if reports on illegal levels of toxic gas at nearby schools are to be believed.

When Boris Johnson was accused of burying reports that showed hundreds of schools were in areas that breached EU pollution limits (40 μg/m^3), instead of getting rid of the pollution, he got rid of the EU, revealing the kind of lateral thinking that only a private education could inspire. But what these so-called reports don't tell us is which pubs are nearby and should be treated with caution. After experiencing the dangers of pollution first hand recently, on our forced march along the South Circular, we have put together a list of hostelries in pollution blackspots so you can make an informed decision on where to spend your afternoon.

If you should find yourself in one of these establishments, our advice is to stay inside until closing time. On no account should you leave the pub, even if you receive a text telling you dinner is ready. Not even if it's toad in the hole. You can't take chances with your health.

6. Flowers of the Forest, Lambeth

At first glance, the name of this boozer by slow-moving traffic on Westminster Bridge Road seems ironic. But it is named after the ancient Scottish folk song commemorating the defeat of the Scottish army at Flodden. A lovely melody – often accompanied by bagpipes, unfortunately – it is a lament usually heard at funerals. Still, it's a lovely name for a pub, even one with the highest pollution in South London.

It does have a beer garden and outside tables at the front, which you take to at your own risk. In summer the front of the pub is wide open, revealing a devil-may-care attitude to nitrogen dioxide. A welcoming locals' pub with Sky Sports, it unfortunately doesn't sell any great ale, so avoidance is conceivable.

5. Prince of Wales, Elephant & Castle

Sky Sports and a pool table make the PoW tempting for the indoor athlete; however, ale drinkers will be disappointed, if not incredulous. Formerly the staff room of choice for lecturers at the nearby London College of Communication, the drive towards professionalism in education has left it quiet at lunchtime. Students paying nine grand a year don't expect tutors to stink of booze and be in need of a nap in the afternoon. That, after all, is a student's role.

They make a big play for the food crowd with a surprising menu, though it remains one of those pubs that you are amazed is still going.

4. The Beehive, Vauxhall

With its mock-Tudor exterior, you might expect an olde-worlde-ness inside The Beehive. But no, it's all clean lines, modern art and neat leather seating aimed at the numerous Sky screens. Great for sport, even if the pub design resembles the calm of a psychiatrist's waiting room – but one with a bar, as all waiting rooms should have.

It's right by The Oval and gets rammo when there's a match on. It's the home of the Barmy Army – or the battalions that haven't travelled with the team – so it can get lively, even at 9am, when they're open for tour matches played on the other side of the world. It earns big bonus points for opening at unsocial hours for such matters of national importance.

3. The Horse & Stables, Lambeth

Hostel pubs are not a distinguished genre but the Horse & Stables has been nicely spruced up, has a decent beer selection and the Jolly Roger's comedy club upstairs.

In summer, the Stables' doors remain open, along with the windows, as if it were an Alpine chalet bar looking out over a tranquil lake to the mountains beyond, rather than a highly congested highway pumping shite into the naked air. It's perfectly located for many of London's tourist landmarks as well as noxious gases, so it's got the lot.

2. The Albert Arms, Elephant & Castle

As we found on our Boris Bike tour, the Albert Arms' Victoria bar now leans toward fine dining. The little Albert bar remains as cosy as ever, however, though now with tributes to lost music legends, instead of the trad-pub shizzle. The beer is fine without being spectacular, as it's still a Brakspear pub. The Brakspear family are distantly related to Pope Adrian IV, England's only pope, though there's no discount for Catholics, even if you're a guilt-ridden, repressed inebriate with a predilection for spanking (I was asking for a friend).

1. Crown & Cushion, Lambeth

What a treat it was to discover this gem, having walked past it so many times. A classic old-skool Irish pub, with its nods and winks and great accommodation for seated sports enthusiasts. Guinness is to the fore, of course, but it often also has a local ale, along with pub grub. Upstairs there's a Thai and Lao restaurant, so you can take up a pint to pair with some *paht nam prig pow*, should you fancy.

It gets lively for the footy and they will accommodate more than one game at a time, just like we assume they do in heaven (but with better air quality and free Mini Cheddars). And being Irish, there's plenty of horse racing on, so you can get rich while enjoying the black stuff. Smokers can get their kicks in the beer garden out back, where the air might be a microgram or two better than at the front.

Studies have offered evidence that long-term NO_2 exposure may decrease lung function and increase the risk of respiratory disease. Add that to smoking 20 Rothmans and you've got a health time bomb coming at you like last orders on wheels.

'It is a scandal that in a wonderful, modern world city like London, thousands of people are dying because the air they breathe is toxic,' said Mayor Sadiq Khan, announcing clean bus routes to add to a larger Ultra-Low Emission Zone. Buses are much better for getting to pubs than cars. They come with a designated driver and many bus stops honour pubs by being named after them.

The Mayor's initiative is a good start, but in the long run pollution surcharges don't save lives. Just like the Congestion Charge that no longer reduces congestion. It just raises money. And as we are painfully aware, you can't buy a round when you're dead.

Sadly, the problem is that we have too many people who don't give a stuff, driving large cars, alone, unnecessarily. People who are too good for public transport, who think nothing of the ugly air our smokers are forced to breathe outside our beautiful pubs.

Taking the Ps

'Thirty quid each? Fuck that. It's not even got a roof,' said Half-life, recounting how he had refused his own mother her lifelong dream of a ride on an open-top London sightseeing bus.

'Was she miffed?' I asked.

'Nah. I gave her my Oyster and stuck her on the RV1 at Covent Garden. She saw the sights, I had three pints in The Harp. Job done.'

The RV1, for those unfamiliar with the more obscure forms of London transport, is a cheeky single-decker bus that runs from Covent Garden to Tower Gateway via Waterloo, London Eye, the South Bank, Borough Market and Tower Bridge. For the price of one journey, the sights are all yours to be seen.

'Did you know that the RV stands for 'Riverside'?' I said, but Half-life had found an insect in his pint and ignored me.

'Twat,' he said, to the bug. Probably.

'I wonder what the P stands for in the P buses,' I continued. 'You know, the P4, P5, P12...'

'Strange Martin says it stands for "Pubs",' said Half-life.

'*Pubs?*'

'Yeah, like, the pubs on the routes. P4's got four pubs. P5, five pubs...'

'Yeah, but Strange Martin says King's Lynn is the lost city of Atlantis,' I reminded him. Half-life shrugged.

'He also said Hedy Lamarr invented Wi-Fi, didn't he?' he said, pointedly, referring to an unfortunate wager I'd recently got involved in, which ended with me having to hand over 20 notes to a man with the IQ of a pot plant.

'I'm looking it up on the Internet,' I said, reaching for my phone.

'Fuck the Internet.'

This, as we know, is Half-life's default position on the popular international network of computer networks. He's only ever owned one computer – an Amiga – and it's still in the box.

'It says here that the P of the P buses is there because they go through Peckham,' I said.

'Crock o' shit,' said Half-life. 'What does he know?'

'Or she,' I admonished, but let's face it, this was someone writing about bus numbers, on the Internet.

'What about the P5? Goes nowhere near fucking Peckham,' he continued.

'Fair point,' I said.

'Nor the P4. I don't know why you read that fucking thing. I'm telling you, it stands for Pubs. Strange Martin knows someone at TfL.' Then he leaned in for the kill. 'Get us another pint in and we'll work them all out.'

He knew he'd got me. Sitting on a velvet-covered stool, drinking beer and discussing the best pubs available on bus routes? It's the parallel universe they never told us about in Careers Advice. We knuckled down and within the hour had thrashed out – with the assistance of various reprobates at the bar – the four optimum pub stops on the route of the P4. Gold dust. This is the sort of public service the TfL website should be offering. Exhausted, we knocked off and agreed to meet the next day to test it out in the real world.

Bus mates

Buses are wasted on commuters. Commuters get grumpy because they stop all the time, get stuck in traffic or change their destination willy-nilly, while the drivers merrily wave at each other when they pass, like they're arriving at a cocktail party.

But there is nothing like being on a bus when the only place you're going is to the pub. Try it. It's very liberating. It becomes less of a journey and more of a ride, like in a theme park, a giant theme park filled with historic victualling houses. Moreover, the advent of apps like Bus Mate means you no longer have to wait around for buses in abject hope; now you can stay at the bar until the next one is due and order accordingly: five minutes – get a half in; 15 minutes – a pint; 25 minutes – a jug of Pimm's and two bags of pork scratchings.

You don't even need to worry about the cost – just hop on and hop off as if you own the things. If you already have a Travelcard on your Oyster, you're laughing – work that thing, baby. If you're Pay As You Go then you can take as many bus journeys as you like and your daily rate is capped. After your third hop, you're already up on the deal. And that's even before you factor in the multi-hop discount.

Perhaps the best thing about the P buses in particular is that they take wilfully obscure routes, giving the afternoon Deserter a chance to visit some out-of-the-way places, including that dying breed, the backstreet boozer.

Anyway, here are our four pubs for the P4.

Trinity Arms, Brixton

Stop: Brixton Station

Trinity Gardens is a good-looking square tucked away between Brixton Road and Acre Lane, and in one corner you will find the Trinity Arms. It's always a-buzz, day and night, with a convivial local crowd who appreciate the laid-back vibe, evidenced by armchairs and the presence in them of pub cats Woody and Horatio. It's a Young's pub so the ale can be quite ordinary (literally, in the case of Young's Ordinary) but they do have the occasional guest ale.

Fittingly, it's a pub in three parts. There's the seating out front with its view of the pretty square; there's the roomy, comfortable, three-sided interior; and then there's the Secret Garden, a great spot in the winter with its fire pits and heaters. For someone like Half-life, who is drawn to fire like it's the first time he's ever encountered it, the fire pits provided a few moments of serenity as he poked about, burning leaves and stones, until he burnt his fingers, spilled his pint and insisted on helping me finish mine.

Just down Brighton Terrace on Brixton Road is the start/end point of the P4 route, Brixton Station. We were setting off from here and a little rudimentary Bus Mate action allowed me to watch Half-life finish my pint and then saunter down the road just in time to catch an empty bus heading east (warning, do not attempt this between 5pm and 7pm, when it most assuredly will not be empty).

The Cambria, Camberwell

Stop: Deerdale Road / St Saviors School

You know that pub that you've heard is nice, somewhere around Loughborough Junction – and you're sure you went to Karen's drinks there once about five years ago – but can never quite remember how to get there? It's The Cambria.

Alight at the above stop on Herne Hill Road, walk down the hill to Kemerton Road and you will find another fabulous backstreet boozer with the most chandeliers we have ever seen in a pub.

It features outside seating and a garden as well as glamorous interiors and there are plenty of music performances and events – some held in the spacious upstairs room – which are enjoyed by a loyal local clientele who all realise what a treasure they have on their doorstep.

Beer-wise, the choice of cask ale is limited. In fact, on our visit there wasn't even a choice and we forsook the Doom Bar for a decent Guinness.

Back on the P4, you are taken over Herne Hill and down into the rarified gloom of Dulwich Village, with its overpriced cake and white post-and-chain-link fences. You might be tempted to stop off at the Crown & Greyhound (known locally as The Dog) at this point, but we stayed firmly put on the bus because we knew what was coming next.

London Beer Dispensary, Brockley

Stop: Brockley Grove / Horsmondon Road

With apologies to the Brockley Jack pub (we're only allowed four, see? No one said it would be easy) our next recommendation is Brockley's finest. The London Beer Dispensary is a bar-less brown-wood beer room with more cask and keg beers than you will ever be able to get through on a single visit. Which is why we go back to it a lot. Indeed, this is already the third time we've mentioned it in this very volume, so we'll push on to our final stop for the day.

The Ladywell Tavern, Ladywell

Stop: Ladywell Station

This was a new one on me. Half-life recalled it from his musician days (maracas, if you're interested. Or rather, maraca – he needed one hand for his pint) and I'm glad he did – it's great: a warm welcome, lovely tiled floor, a sensational fireplace and great beers. As well as regular live music, it also has a large gallery that plays host to exhibitions, classes, recitals and movie nights.

When we arrived it was filled with a convivial mixture of after-workers, locals, dog lovers and a couple of first-daters we overheard from the bar:

'I really liked *Breaking Bad*.'

'So did *I*…'

Beyond Ladywell, heading west to east, the P4 passes through Lewisham which of course offers further delights. But, having done our four pubs, we decided to stay put, ordered a platter of chicken wings and toasted ourselves on a job well done. Roll on the P13.

Romance must have been in the air that night because, inexplicably, Half-life was later able to swap phone numbers with a woman he got talking to over a rolly in the garden.

'How did you manage that?' I asked him at the bar. 'Not the old "What's the point of winning the Lottery when you've got a dodgy ticker?" routine.'

'Nope. I was just telling her about who invented Wi-Fi.'

'Right, listen, Lamarr held one of a wide range of patents that, *all of which, together,* allowed the development of what we now know as–' I started, but Half-life interrupted.

'Let's have another pint. This one's on me,' he said, and I was so startled I forgot what I was talking about.

A Game of Three Halves

When there are three top-flight games on in the pub of a Sunday, it's hard to look beyond the simple pleasures of an autumn afternoon in a boozer, watching men kick a ball, in the company of your favourite idiots. Indeed, the Raider had just left home with a cheery, 'Back in six hours, darling!' when he got my text: 'Heading to three-sided football, Fordham Park. New Cross v Deptford v Philosophy.'

He was powerless to resist.

We arrived at the little grass oasis behind New Cross Station with our bag of tinnies as the players were setting out two pitches. It was a double header. Bonus. The adjacent pitch would host Strategic Optimism v Husaria v Athletico Aesthetico. We were going to watch the top six sides of the Deptford Three-Sided Football League. Or to put it another way, the bottom six sides.

It was refreshing to see the players didn't mind interacting with members of the public during their warm-up routine.

'Is that a gin and tonic?' I asked Chris of SOFC as he downed a can.

'Gin and *diet* tonic.'

'Silly me. I forgot you're an athlete.'

What is Three-sided Football?

Three-sided football is a match between three teams: three teams of five players, with three goals and one ball on a hexagonal pitch. They play for three 20-minute thirds and the winner is the team that concedes the fewest goals. All teams attack both their opponents' goals, unless they form an alliance with one of them. Teams form temporary unions within the game to attack the third side but can be subject to sudden betrayal and attack from both the other teams, leaving five players defending their goal against ten. There is no offside and there are rush goalies. Teams get no points for a win, one for coming second and two for coming third, so the team with the fewest points wins the league. It's as simple as that.

The game is the brainchild of Asger Jorn, the Danish artist and author who co-founded the Situationist International along with, among others, the French philosopher and proto-Deserter, Guy Debord. Jorn devised it to illustrate his theory of triolectics, a three-sided logic system that goes beyond the focus on true or false outcomes, by adding a third option. And what better way to manifest the refinement of dialectical materialism than with an impenetrable, three-sided game of soccerball?

Jorn never got to play the game he invented – I'm not even sure he was the sporty type. It is thought the first game was played in 1993 in Scotland as an offshoot of a Glasgow anarchist gathering. The match was chaotic and the players swiftly decamped to the pub, but a seed had been planted and games continued to crop up around the world, often in unlikely places: tenement roofs, town squares, Lithuanian woods.

Mark Dyson played in that very first match and in many others since, before starting Deptford Three-Sided Football Club (D3FC) and founding the league in 2012, which some know as the Luther Blissett Three-Sided Football League.

Silkeborg, Denmark – Jorn's hometown – hosted the first Three-Sided Football World Cup in 2014, with teams from England, France, Germany, Poland and Lithuania (who chose to represent Uruguay). The competition is held every three years, naturally.

Today, brilliantly, South-east London is the hub of the three-sided game in the UK, with New Cross hosting games on the first Sunday of the month from September to June. In theory the game is free of the kind of 'us and them' aggression of regular football, but with added treachery and connivance. Some players and teams take it more seriously than others, but with the pitches free and everyone welcome to watch or play, it retains a kind of purity that our long-sullied national game has lost.

Match Report: New Cross Irregulars (0) D3FC (3) Philosophy Football FC (3)

It was only the second game of the season, but PFFC and D3FC seemed determined to gang up on last year's champions New X, attacking their goal together, but to no avail. The orange shirts of New X held firm, prompting shifting alliances. One moment Deptford were attacking New X's goal, but seeing the path blocked, they quickly switched to a surprise attack on PFFC. Even though the emphasis, in theory, should be on defence and possession, all teams are more intent on attack, which makes for a much better game.

Though all sides display a level of skill and commitment, New X were well organised and attacked more purposefully as a team. With Philosophy and Deptford both having conceded two goals, it was clear neither was likely to overhaul New X, so they began to attack each other. No one wants to come third in a game of football. They both conceded again, which meant they shared a losing draw and picked up two points each.

Elsewhere in the league, Strategic Optimism performed their trademark tactic of conceding a netful of goals early doors. This meant their goal was pretty much disregarded late in the contest and they were able to mount a stirring comeback that saw them come second to the Polish team, Husaria FC. It was both a strategic and optimistic manoeuvre. The match finished Husaria (1) SOFC (4) Athletico Aesthetico (5).

Over to you, Barry.

Post-game analysis

Some of the players trooped to the Marquis of Granby, the only proper football pub at this end of New Cross, to catch the end of a two-sided game and then sit outside chatting to the smorgasbord of strangers who had settled on the table out front.

It's a fine pub for the footy. The beer is OK, the staff are nice and there's a big screen at the back, one telly at the front and a little TV for the racing by the side of the bar. There were plenty watching, the sound was up; it were proper. After watching the match, we caught up with some three-sided footballers and were joined by an eclectic mix of wanderers.

There was an ex-raver in his late forties for whom the beat goes on and on. He sat down in the middle of the crowd and introduced himself to everyone, talking non-stop, quite pissed, but warm and chatty and cheeky. There were people having their first night out in New Cross at the start of their life at Goldsmith's, but holding their own and showing great judgement by sitting outside a pub on a Sunday afternoon when their fellow students were busy nesting in halls. It was an inspiring confluence of humanity's oddness, not unlike three-sided football.

The three-siders spoke of legendary games of the past: the stone circle at Hilly Fields, Marx's grave and Tate Modern. They tried playing in the Tate's Turbine Hall, but were stopped by security, who weren't too heavy about it. They were told to just email in and ask for permission. They did so the very next day and got an immediate response asking when they wanted to do it. They replied: 'Yesterday'.

Is it any wonder we're drawn to such genius? As Mark Dyson puts it: 'We're just trying to work as little as possible and play as much as possible.'

Heroes, all.

Town and Country

When I arrived at the Wood House pub on Sydenham Hill, Half-life was at the bar frowning at the crossword.

'Alright, mate?' I said.

'This place is in the middle of fucking nowhere,' he said. 'You owe me for a cab.'

'Lovely to see you, too,' I said, looking around. The Wood House had been completely rearranged since my last visit, with the bar back up top where it should be, the main rooms given over to drinkers and diners moved down to the conservatory.

'Wow, this is better, isn't it?' I said. Half-life shrugged.

'Is it?'

'Yes, remember when we were in here last, when we were doing Beer Triangle?'

'No,' he said, 'I've got no memory. It's what keeps me going.' And he went back to his paper. 'Listen, here's one for you. Eleven across: post or mail man.' I thought about this for a moment.

'Post or mail man,' I repeated. 'How many letters?' Half-life looked up.

'A fucking great sackful!' he ejaculated and, laughing like a mad-man, high-fived the barmaid. I ordered a pint of the strongest beer on offer.

We took our drinks out into the garden and set up camp in one of the huts that had appeared. Sadly all the grass had been taken up and replaced with some kind of AstroTurf, which is a shame. To be a proper garden you need grass, in my book. My book about pub gardens.

'Which do you prefer?' I said to Half-life. 'Grass or AstroTurf?'

'I don't know, I've never smoked AstroTurf,' he said, without missing a beat, and this time he high-fived me.

'You're on fire today, mate,' I said.

'You line 'em up and I'll knock 'em over,' he said. 'So, what's the plan and who's paying?'

Today's journey was to take us by train from the wilds of Zone 3 to the heart of the empire in less than 15 heady minutes. From the wild autumnal splendour of Sydenham Woods, the last remnants of the Great North Wood, a natural oak forest that once dominated the area, to the UK's second-busiest railway terminus, Victoria – or 'London Victoria' as it now seems to be called – just three short stops away.

'London Victoria?' said Half-life. 'So is London Bridge now 'London London Bridge'?'

'I know,' I said. 'It's the sheer inconsistency that's unbearable.'

Back in the bar for a pair of pints for the road, we got chatting to some of the mixed crowd beginning to roll in for lunchtime: an elderly hiker couple from Upminster, two Spanish tourists, a businesswoman and a grizzled '70s hippy waiting for his chums.

'Y'know, I could live with this,' said Half-life. 'I could come here when I'm retired.'

'You are retired,' I said. 'And, come to think of it, here.'

As we walked past the grand houses of Crescent Wood Road and down into Peckarmans Wood, a wan sun came out, picking out the yellows and browns of the leaves underfoot. We paused on a bench in Sydenham Woods in order to enhance the colours still further with some of Half-life's own magic leaves.

Sydenham Hill station, situated in a cutting as the line disappears into Sydenham Hill Railway Tunnel, was opened in 1863, primarily to facilitate visitors to a bloody great greenhouse that someone had left nearby – it was originally called 'Sydenham Hill (for Crystal Palace)'.

It, like the Wood House, also appears to be in the middle of nowhere, though Kingswood Estate lies hidden on the other side of our approach. Nevertheless, the station itself remains a quiet and leafy oasis. It's difficult to believe you're in a city at all, let alone the sprawling metropolis of a London. And the marvellous thing about this train journey is that over the course of a quarter of an hour you can watch the dramatic transition from country to town. And then, of course, get another beer.

The first thing we noticed as the train pulled out, apart from, in my case, Half-life fiddling incessantly with his industrial-sized vapouriser, is how green this part of London is. First the playing fields and dreaming spire of Dulwich College slip by, the seat of learning for one Nigel Farage:

'Just goes to show, money can't stop you being a tosser,' said Half-life, handing me his device. 'Here, try this one. Strawberry Astronaut by Jimmy the Juice Man.'

'Not bad,' I said, exhaling the sickly steam.

'Roxy gave me that one,' he said. 'It's her favourite.'

'Have you cut down on the fags then?'

'Have I fuck. I just use this for pubs, clubs, trains and bar mitzvahs.'

Then, after a stop at West Dulwich, we looked out over Belair Park and the playing fields of Edward Alleyn Sports Club to the right, while Brockwell Park appeared on the left, bathed for us today in weak sunlight.

'How beautiful,' I said, but Half-life was busy changing vials.

'Vanilla caffè latte?' he said, as we drew into Herne Hill.

'You're alright, mate,' I said.

After Herne Hill the green disappeared to be replaced by increasingly concentrated housing, including, as you reach Brixton – the penultimate stop – the renowned 'Barrier Block', Smethwyck House, the unusual shape of which was down to it being built to minimise noise from a planned six-lane urban highway that was to run alongside it and which, thank God, never got built.

At Brixton Station we spotted Karin, one of three lifesize bronze statues that stand on the platforms there. As we headed on towards Clapham and Battersea we rode upon a sea of roofs, an urban visual poem of timber and scrapyards, house-backs, graffitied walls, tower blocks and industrial estates, all presided over by the distant Shard (quite the best kind of Shard, in our view).

Just past Battersea Dogs Home – 'And cats,' said Half-life unexpectedly – you are treated to the disappearing vista of Battersea Power

Station, the largest brick building in Europe. Be quick, though, as it's gradually being obscured by a wall of shit flats, part of the area's ongoing redevelopment into Wankland.

After a glimpse of the bright river and, to the east, the ornate mansard roof and tower of the Western Pumping Station, the train scythes through the estates and tenement blocks of Pimlico and into Victoria Station, which opened in 1862, having been built on the site of the basin of the old Grosvenor Canal (a small portion of which remains to this day on the north side of the river near Chelsea Bridge).

'I hope there's a bar near,' said Half-life. 'All this water is making me thirsty.'

Grand Central Station it ain't, but considering that 15 minutes ago we'd been in a forest kicking leaves at each other, Victoria Station was still a startling outcrop of urban sophistication to our hillbilly eyes. We looked around at the chain outlets and up at the immense vaulted roof.

'Fuck me, there's a 'Spoon's!' said Half-life, pointing up to the Wetherspoon's on the first floor of the concourse.

'With a neon sign!' I said. And without further consultation, we headed up the escalator to beer heaven. Yes, it has an escalator.

If your local is a bit quiet after lunch on a Monday afternoon, you really should consider the London Victoria Station Wetherspoon's, with its fine ales, friendly staff and constant flow of travellers having one for the road or finding their feet on the balcony after a journey to the capital. For some it's obviously a handy central meeting point too, giving it the air of a local, with little pockets of regulars.

'Hold all the reels, press cancel and let them spin to get the feature,' said Half-life to a group of fellers playing the fruit machine. They turned out to be postmen, mostly Irish, and Half-life merrily told them his crossword joke. Twice.

When an armed policeman walked through the automatic sliding doors, like we were in a 'Spoon's from the future, Half-life was prompted to say to them:

'You know, it doesn't seem like yesterday that it was you lot planting the bombs.' And a lively conversation ensued while Half-life disappeared to the lavs.

'There's a word for your mucker,' said one of the Irish lads to me. 'It begins with "G" and ends with "ite".'

'Gcuntite?' I offered, and we parted the best of friends.

From Victoria you could visit Tate Britain or get a fine meal at legendary caff, The Regency, off Horseferry Road. But we had other ideas. Or, rather, I did.

On the main concourse, we headed over towards the north-west corner. There, sandwiched between an Accessorize and something called iSmash (not, sadly, selling modern mashed potato) is a door to a bureau de change marked, oddly, 'Grosvenor Hotel'.

We entered and strode straight past the bureau, almost as if we were going to a posh London hotel through an – if not secret, then little-used – passage. Which, in fact, we were. We headed up a small flight of steps, through some double doors and down a short corridor to emerge, agog, into the opulent lobby of the aforementioned hotel, where you can take an aperitif in the Grosvenor Arms bar before dining in the cavernous surroundings of the Grand Imperial.

'I know this place,' said Half-life, puncturing the magic. 'Used to have the best lavs for sniff.'

Walking through the wood-panelled rooms to the bar, beneath magnificent chandeliers, it came as something of a shock to find Sky Sports silently flickering on a giant TV. *More Than a Woman* played on the loudspeakers as Kirsty Gallacher gazed down from the screen. It seemed to sum it all up for me. I realised I was quite delightfully squiffy.

Seasoned drinker as I am, I'm not accustomed to drinking four pints before lunch, particularly when two of them were 6.2% ABV Camden India Hells Lager. I couldn't remember the last time I'd done such a thing and mentioned as much to Half-life.

'Bollocks,' said Half-life dismissively. 'Don't you remember that cider in First Class on the way to Haydock Park?'

'No,' I said, truthfully.

One of my superpowers is spotting at a glance what the best value booze is on the menu of potentially expensive places – especially if I'm paying – and we were able to order two glasses of Argentinian Malbec at a fiver a pop and take a seat at the bar to watch the tourist buses head up and down Buck Palace Road.

The Grand Imperial restaurant, at the other end of the hotel, offers two cracking courses of Cantonese cuisine for £16 per person, or in my case, £32 for one person, with one person eating free. The dim sum platter is freshly prepared each morning, we were told, and is worth twice the price – which in fact it is after 5pm.

Our meal dispatched, we repaired outside to Grosvenor Gardens for a restorative spliff in the shadow of Marshall Foch's statue and near a sign that read 'No Alcohol'.

'Doesn't say owt about sparking up though, does it?' said Half-life, happily.

Appropriately enough, the vista looked particularly *Parisien* as darkness fell and the street lights popped and fizzed around us.

'Remember last time we had one here?' said Half-life.

'No,' I said.

'Me neither,' said Half-life.

I wondered if Half-life was concerned about how little impact our experiences were apparently having on our memory.

'My memory's full, that's all,' said Half-life. 'If I have to fit anything more in there, I'll forget something important like my name. Or your credit card number.'

And with that we wandered back into Victoria and got the 16.49 back to Brixton to beat the rush hour. After that it's all a blur. What I remember of it.

Magic Bus

The London Borough of Bexley might not be the most fashionable area in sexy South London, but it scores big beer points for playing host to eight micropubs; plus bonus balls for providing a designated driver to six of them – the 51 bus. Even better, thanks to the Mayor's Hopper Fare, many of the journeys are free, making an afternoon spent micropub-hunting not only fun, but wise.

With the help of a tetchy Half-life, I aimed to visit the micro eight before hopping back on the 51 to go on to Taproom SE18, Hop Stuff Brewery's very own bar. It's not, strictly speaking, a micropub, but nonetheless it's a room on the route with fresh beer – surely the best kind of room there is.

The Hopper's Hut

Our journey began in Sidcup High Street, where Half-life arrived an hour late, panting and holding his hand to his heart before plonking himself on a stool. I ignored him.

'I'm dying here, Dirts. It's a miracle I even made it. Get us one in, will you?'

The perfect start to any pub crawl is a flavourful ale with a modest alcohol level – after all it's a crawl, not a sprint, and we'd yet to face the marathon of Christmas jollies. Luckily, the Hopper's Hut had a cracker. Riding Ale, an unfined session beer from Hackney's Howling Hops, is light but so fruity and hoppy it's hard to believe it's only 3.0%. As an achievement I'd put it on a par with time travel.

Half-life's pint was gone in seconds before he reported: 'That's better. I've been getting these dizzy spells... Ooh... here I go,' as he rocked on his stool. 'It's quite nice, actually. Like free drugs.'

'When did you last eat?'

'I ate a couple of pills last night, but they were tiny.'

Conversation with the locals took in the entire panoply of human experience, from other much-loved micropubs, favourite beer, the characteristics of American and Kentish hops, other planned pub crawls – everything.

The Hackney Carriage

The Hackney Carriage is in the Lamorbey district of Sidcup, a slice of pure suburbia that prior to all the housebuilding was home to fields of hops. Wild hops still grow on the allotments nearby, as if nature were winking at us, calling us to feast on her flesh.

The Carriage, like The Hopper, is a smart shop conversion (formerly selling school uniforms), the work of a tidy mind. Micropubs are bound to be quiet when empty, as there's no music, TV or distractions. They're perfect places to do nothing in, if only we could remember how. The Hackney Carriage has some interesting books to stave off that infuriating instinct to reach for the phone when conversation fails. Micropubs often have mobiles nailed to the wall to warn newcomers of the 'no mobile' rules. Texting and surfing is tolerated, but phone calls are not. With Half-life down to grunts and groans, I found myself chuckling at *The Ladybird Book of The Hangover*.

'That's just fucking rude,' he exclaimed at my reading in his company, when one of his phones blared out a cascading horn motif, followed by James Brown singing 'Paid the cost to be The Boss'.

Half-life not only answered it, he soon bellowed out: 'You are pulling my cunting pisser!'

After ending the conversation with a profane, yet imaginative flourish, I mentioned that the lady behind the bar might not be too pleased with his flouting of the micropub ethos.

'Has she just had her car nicked?' he railed.

'You haven't got a car.'

'I borrowed Jam's Nissan. And the cunt has only found it and nicked it back.'

Despite drinking nice, well-kept beer at someone else's expense, Half-life was in one of his dark moods. I suggested we treat his dizzy spells with a marijuana cigarette in the park opposite. Often we have to find a nice quiet spot to smoke a joint, away from people. At The Glade, we had to avoid groups of kids smoking smelly skunk and playing frenetic tunes. But what else would they do in Sidcup? They're not going to fancy the area's silent beer temples.

We stopped at the lake, opposite the grand home of Rose Bruford College, the drama school whose alumni include Gary Oldman and Tom Baker. Sidcup seems such a strange place for this branch of the arts, though it made more sense in the gloaming after a doobie, watching intense young luvvies reading parts on the lawn, gesticulating wildly to an audience of swan.

Halfway House

Diverting us off the bus route slightly, the Halfway House Craft Beer bar has a small but solid range of cask and keg in another converted shop. On our visit we witnessed a guy getting told off by his good lady for having enjoyed four lovely pints from Beavertown, when he had only nipped out for a pint of milk.

The owner, Danny, is originally from Bermondsey and, in a nice touch, has pictures of his granddad on the wall, picking hops in Kent – a popular working holiday in his day.

It was good to see some younger types in there, but also an old boy giving his Zimmer frame a rest, sitting at the bar with a bottle of wine to himself. Despite having the good fortune to have a pub land round the corner from his home, he seemed to enjoy having a moan about, well, everything. Half-life was unusually diplomatic, saying, 'It's been nice meeting you Tom, even if I disagree with every fucking word you just said.'

Back on the 51 bus, we travelled to our next port of call.

'Tell you what, this knocks the spots off the P4,' said Half-life, from the upper deck's back seat, recalling a recent bus tour with the Raider. 'For a start it's got an upstairs. You can't have a shag and a smoke on those fucking diddy little hoppers. People look at you funny.'

Luckily, it was a short ride and he didn't have time for either.

The Hangar

The micropubs come thick and fast on the 51 and such was our inattention that we went flying past The Hangar, another converted shop, at The Oval. Yet in moments we had arrived at another.

The Broken Drum

No sooner had we realised our mistake than we arrived in Blackfen, an unremarkable part of South London's borderlands, blessed by the award-winning Broken Drum.

Once upon a time places like Blackfen and our next destination, Welling, were 'somewhere'. Somewhere with a great cinema or dance hall, where people would go out, meet other people and have fun. I wonder how a community reaches a point where it no longer needs fun. 'Just an Asda and a plumber's merchants will do us, thanks,' they seem to be saying. 'We've got a radio.' It's little wonder that this crawl was accompanied by great wafts of weed stink that were not our own, as people are forced to roll their own fun.

Named after a bar in Terry Pratchett's Discworld series, The Broken Drum is housed in an old nail bar. Andy Wheeler knew he was about to be made redundant and immediately set about making a pub, like a hero. It's simple and unfussy, in the micropub tradition. We enjoyed an excellent £3 pale ale served at the perfect temperature – plus sausage rolls on the house. Really, anyone would be happy. Well, almost anyone.

'Thank fuck it's nearly over,' moaned Half-life.

'What, the year? Tell me about it. It'll be nice to see the pubs left to the professionals again.'

'No, this pub crawl. I haven't seen a woman since Lewisham.'

The Door Hinge

The 51 took us up the road to Welling High Street and the much-loved Door Hinge, London's first micropub. It feels a little more pubby, festooned with hops as it is and with a little snug at the back that looks like your nan's living room.

As it was also empty, the wisdom of this crawl at this time of year was in doubt. I don't need a pub to myself very often. It had started to resemble a pub crawl after the apocalypse, I thought to myself, which warmed me to it again. However, three empty pubs in a row made me miss the sound of music and people. I began to long for a chat about the weather or the pathetic screams of partly devoured zombie victims. Once again, the beer was splendid, but it was time for the hustle, bustle and bright lights of the great metropolis. We were back on the 51 – to Woolwich.

Taproom SE18

Hop Stuff's Taproom is pretty slick, in keeping with the grandeur of the Royal Arsenal, and its hubbub was welcome after the silence of the suburbs. Normally there's a greater cask selection, but this time it was mostly their own brews, though that's hardly a problem.

Starving by now, I found their White Pony pizza exceptional. Half-life's appetite suddenly kicked in and he ordered the pizza-and-salad combo: 'But with twice as much salad and twice as much pizza.'

'You want two?'

'No. I want one fucking massive one.'

Sadly, when the Greek salad arrived it grievously offended him. 'Olive,' he muttered, before raising his voice to a passing waitress. 'Olive!'

'It's Phoebe,' she said, meekly.

'Where are the fucking olives, Phoebe? What kind of Greek salad doesn't have olives?'

'Of course, I'll just...'

'It's an insult to Zeus, to Plato, to Aristotle and to Demis fucking Roussos, love,' he said, as she carted the offending greenery away.

We'd been to five bars and had high-quality beer in each, most of them around the £3 mark – and spent around £3 on transport. We hadn't had much to complain about until the salad incident. Phoebe returned with his salad festooned with the bitter fruit. 'Cheers, Pheebs,' he said, passing her his number. 'And don't ring before mid-day, alright?'

As the bemused waitress left us for more personable customers, Half-life sat back in his chair.

'You know, I think I'm feeling a bit better.'

I'm the Bishop of Southwark

If you find yourself in and around the bars of Borough as November slips into December, listen out for a seasonal call-and-response drinking toast peculiar to the area, in which folk declare that they are – despite all appearances to the contrary – the 'Bishop of Southwark'. You may even spot a mitre or two. For it is the anniversary of the Night of the Lost Bishop, a welcome reminder that religion can still be as relevant today as it was, say, yonks ago.

With the march of so-called 'science' – now relentlessly taught in schools and blatantly promoted on primetime TV by the likes of 'Professors' Brian Cox and Alice Roberts – it is hardly surprising that people have turned their backs on religion. Cold, hard facts have, it seems, replaced the warming succour of blind faith and murmured superstition. Religion is now characterised as somehow odd, out of touch, even elitist.

So it is reassuring that, in such times, one man was able to humanise our Anglican orders, to break with episcopal protocol, to reach out to the layman and bring Christianity to the commoner. To – quite literally – find God in the gutter. That man was the Right Reverend Thomas Frederick Butler, the Bishop of Southwark, 1998 to 2010, and this is his story.

On 5 December 2006, after giving a eulogy at Southwark Cathedral at a memorial service for the late John Young (head of the famous brewery family – which we're certain bears no relevance to the tale), the bishop, Dr Butler, made his way to the Irish Embassy in Grosvenor Place, near Buck House, to attend the ambassador's legendary Christmas drinks, at which Guinness, spirits and wine are freely dispensed.

Less than five hours later Dr Butler, a regular on Radio 4's *Thought for the Day,* arrived at his home in Tooting with head wounds, bruises and a black eye. He was missing his crucifix, mobile phone and a briefcase full of confidential church papers.

What happened in between has been the source of much conjecture, with the Bishop initially reporting to the police that he had been mugged somewhere between the Embassy and his home, but later stating that, in fact, he had absolutely no recollection of the period in question and may have experienced some sort of 'blackout'.

Fortunately, there were other witnesses to help fill in some of the blanks.

Instead of returning directly to his home from the Embassy, it seems Dr Butler, for reasons unclear, headed back to Borough. Here he managed to set off a car alarm outside the Suchard Bar in the aptly named Crucifix Lane, a dark and windy outpost by the railway arches of London Bridge.

Hearing his car alarm go off, a Mr Paul Sumpter, who was playing pool in the bar, dashed outside to investigate. He saw the hazard lights flashing on his Mercedes and a pair of legs protruding from one of the open rear doors. Inside, he discovered the 66-year-old Dr Butler 'sprawled' across the back seat, tossing out his child's soft toys. 'He was completely out of it,' reported Mr Sumpter.

Bewildered, he asked: 'What are you doing in my car?' At which point Dr Butler gave his legendary reply: 'I'm the Bishop of Southwark. It's what I do', the phrase that now accompanies the Yuletide raising of glasses throughout the area.

When Mr Sumpter enlisted the help of others to attempt to remove Dr Butler from his car, Butler became 'aggressive and arrogant', according to Mr Sumpter. Apparently unable to stand, Dr Butler then fell to the ground, striking his head, and spent some time sitting in the gutter, where he declined the offer of an ambulance from the bar manager, Paul Sathaporn.

'He got up and staggered under the railway bridge,' said Sathaporn.

'We were laughing because he was staggering so much as he walked off.'

At this stage, it is claimed that Dr Butler told onlookers he was in fact the Bishop of Woolwich, but the personal belongings he left behind in Mr Sumpter's car told a different story – a story that was to come out when Sumpter saw press reports of the 'mugging' of a Bishop and came forward with his side of the tale.

Was the Bishop pished out of his prelatial bonce, as witnesses claimed, or was it simply a period of divine intervention which sent him out amongst the people on that famous night? We may never know for sure. But either way, we applaud the man for taking the night off to walk with his flock.

Indeed, we enjoy plotting potential routes from Grosvenor Place to Bermondsey to commemorate the event, although ours tend to take in pubs on the route. And sometimes, not on the route.

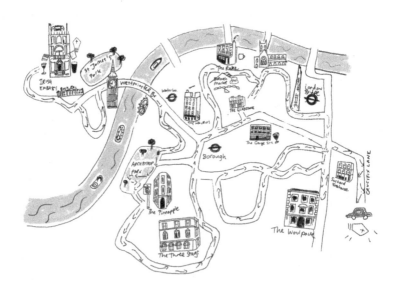

Dr Butler acknowledged that he drank two glasses of red wine at the ambassador's reception, but was subsequently unable to recall if or what he drank after that – though, it should be said, he was absolutely certain that he was not drunk. Just as well, as he had a fearsome reputation for dealing with the alcoholic transgressions of his own clergy, which might have left him open to accusations of hypocrisy.

But that won't stop many making the pilgrimage to Borough in December and raising a glass to honour the man. Let the bell of joy and goodwill ring out for Dr Butler at Christmas, and never let the bell end.

Dirty Southbank

'Fifteen degrees in December!' read Roxy's message. 'Taking the afternoon off. Dirty Southbank day?'

Spend the last T-shirt day of the year messing about in a brutalist playground? How could I refuse? Unlike many of our daytime destinations, the South Bank – and in particular the Southbank Centre – was actually designed to have fun in: captivating interiors, vast terraces, secret nooks, river views, music, art and – perhaps most importantly – all bars and no cars.

The Southbank Centre's genesis was as part of the 1951 Festival of Britain, hailed as a post-war 'tonic for the nation' by Herbert Morrison, the government minister responsible for the gig. Now it's more 'gin and tonic for the nation', but still has enough about it, enough rough edges, thankfully, to draw us to it.

Queen Elizabeth Hall

I was leaning outside the Queen Elizabeth Hall, holding a pint and enjoying the clatter of the skateboards beneath me in the Undercroft, when I spotted Roxy approaching on the level below. Who was that bloke she was with?

'Who was that bloke you were with?' I said, when she joined me.

'Oh, that's Ricky. He asked for a pound and we got talking,' she said.

'Oh, right.'

'He's 40 next week and he still sucks cocks for rocks, he said.'

'Dear God.'

'And he carries his guinea pig around in a shopping trolley.'

'Imagine not living in London,' I said, in wonder.

'Exactly. So I invited him up to join us.'

'What? Are you kidding?'

'I'm the Bishop of Southwark. It's what I do,' she said, referencing the T-shirt she was wearing. 'What's wrong with that?'

'What if he wants to suck my cock?'

'Believe me, no one wants to suck your cock.'

'What about that girl in Herne Hill?'

'She was deranged.'

Sure enough, Ricky soon appeared, pulling his trolley behind him, and joined us at one of the high tables on the terrace. Roxy went to buy them both a drink.

'I'm 40 next week and I'm still sucking cocks for rocks,' he said, with a smile that revealed several absent teeth.

'So I understand,' I said.

'It's not what I had planned,' he went on. 'I was going to be an artist.'

As is often the case when you start a conversation with low expectations, there followed an enjoyable and salutary discourse on ambition, parental support, self-confidence, depression and, ultimately, poverty and addiction. It wasn't what I'd come out for, but with a pint in my hand, I'm very adaptable.

As soon as he'd finished his drink, Ricky jumped up.

'Well, I can't sit here chatting all day,' he said. 'I've got to get back to Sussex.' Blimey, I thought, even the tramps are busier than me.

'You don't live in London, then?' said Roxy.

'No, but I get up here every chance I get. The people are so much friendlier.'

'Hope to catch you again, sometime,' I said, and I meant it.

'Have you got a boyfriend, love?' he asked Roxy and – to my surprise – she shook her head. 'Well, someone's gonna be very happy to find you,' he added, and waved goodbye.

'I hate it when they say that,' said Roxy.

National Theatre

The National Theatre is a softly lit warren of escape and dreams, with plentiful seating areas and, as we've mentioned before, several delightful balconies on offer. The only problem is that the bars don't open till five. And when they do, a decent bottle of wine is £30.

So, ever budget conscious, we first picked up a bottle of chilled plonk from the Costcutter on York Road, then helped ourselves to a couple of glasses from the thoughtfully provided NT water points and settled down on the catchily titled Bank of America Merrill Lynch Terrace. With the trees losing their leaves, the river was reappearing and I was encouraged to see plenty of like-minded shirkers had bunked off for the afternoon to enjoy the view and the last of the sun.

'So, what happened to Current Boyfriend?' I asked Roxy.

'Jan?' she said.

'Yes, if he must be given a name.'

'Oh, he had to go,' she said. 'I found one of his wrist sweatband things clogging up the Hoover.'

'Little bit harsh,' I said.

'That's not the half of it,' she went on. 'It was one of those ones with a little zipped compartment in it, you know?'

'No.'

'I looked inside and there was a little note he'd written.'

'Uh-oh.'

'I know,' she said, and poured us some more wine.

'Well, what did it say?'

'It said "Sweat is fat crying".' I looked at her, dumbfounded.

'He had to go,' I said.

'Had to go,' she agreed. 'Cheers!'

Before our next stop I took the opportunity to visit one of my favourite toilets.

'You off up the velvet tunnel?' said Roxy.

'You know it!' I said, as I went through the auditorium doors and into the dark soundproofed passage that led round to the gents. All sound was hushed, even my tread softened on the lush carpet. The senses dimmed as I moved forwards, as if in a film with no sound;

alone, in blessed quietude, meditating on life and love... Then I had a quick piss and fucked off out of it. Textbook.

Hayward Gallery

Next, we planned to have a nose about in the refurbished Hayward. The portents weren't good, when we noticed that Concrete, the characterful cafe-bar that once sat in the corner and spilled out onto the concrete walkway, was now a shop. Things got worse when we tried to go inside.

'We're closed Tuesdays,' said a man in a hi-vis security jacket, whose sole job it was to disappoint people.

'Oh, that's a shame,' I said. 'Is there still a bar on the premises?'

'Yes, it's on the first floor,' he replied, 'but it's not very good.' We could but admire the man's honesty.

Royal Festival Hall

Thwarted, we headed round the corner to reliable old favourite, the RFH, the beating heart of the Southbank Centre. Open all day from 10am, it offers a cafe, a bar, free Wi-Fi and leccy, plus the odd free live show in the Clore Ballroom by the main bar. As we bought drinks a small jazz band started up.

'Oh, Jesus,' said Roxy, 'a thousand chords for three people.' We didn't hang around and took the 'Singing Lift' up to the fifth floor where we found a table on the balcony.

'Last time I was up here, I was on a night out with a tennis ball,' I said.

'So I heard. No offence, but you two are weird.'

'None taken.'

At that point a uniformed security man asked Roxy to stop vaping. But as soon as he'd disappeared, she ushered me to the end of the balcony, through a little gate marked 'No Entry', where we stood out of sight, vaping and drinking. Rubbish lay strewn about and I pointed out a not-quite-finished half-bottle of gin. An overhead vent puffed out a sick-making melange of food smells. It was where we belonged.

The daylight doesn't last long in December so we headed down to the riverside for a sundowner at The Understudy, the welcome, if pricey, craft beer bar at the National Theatre, to get one in before the Christmas dos arrived. It's a lovely spot and we sat at one of the outside tables.

'Did you hear about Osman's new job?' I said. He was relocating (again) to 'run New York'.

'I did. Still got to work though, hasn't he?'

'Ha ha! True. Who needs more money when you can sit here instead?'

'Even if you're a millionaire, you can still only drink 30 pints a day,' said Roxy, and I laughed, despite having heard it somewhere else.

'Sounds like something Half-life would say,' I said, and Roxy blushed. Then I remembered where I'd seen her T-shirt before.

'Roxy! Is there something you're dying to tell me?'

'Not really,' she said, sheepishly.

'Oh, what?! I knew it! Where *did* he sleep that night in Tulse Hill?'

'He's just a friend,' she chuckled. 'A friend with benefits.'

'A friend *on* benefits, more like,' I said. I was still processing the news when my phone rang. It was Dirty South.

'Why can't you text me like a man?' I said, adding, to Roxy's annoyance, 'Mate, have I got some goss for you!'

'I've got some news as well,' he said.

'I bet it's not as shocking as mine,' I said.

'I think it might be,' he said. 'Are you sitting down?'

A South London Funeral

At five minutes to opening time on the day of the funeral, I peered through the door of old favourite the London Beer Dispensary, frustratingly close to a nerve-settling pint. Instead, I stepped into the bookies to nick a pen, to put the finishing touches to my eulogy.

Something drew me to the far corner of this temple of slender hope and broad despair, to the newspaper plastered on the wall. And there he was, running in the 2.10 at Kempton: Brother Bennett, at the tempting odds of 7/2. It was a sign. A sign that I had learnt fuck all about gambling.

Buoyed by my tiny wager respecting an irreplaceable friend, I returned to the LBD, where I was joined by the Raider and some other mates, all holding back the terror and the tears, dealing with grief in their own ways.

'You wanna see a picture of my new bird?' asked Spider. The dress code for the funeral was 'Colourful, with hats'. Spider was sporting an electric-blue turban.

Meticulous planning is not my forte, but I had timed the walk from pub to Honor Oak Crematorium the previous day, in order to ensure I could get one in before kick-off. Now we walked the route again, for real. We gathered by a small chapel, smoking rollies in a futile and frantic effort to stay calm. We were surrounded by stern faces in black suits. Must be family, I surmised.

'Or, we're at the wrong funeral,' laughed Spider.

We were at the wrong funeral.

The other chapel was surrounded by dresses that could wake the dead, spectacular hats and suits and the smell of strong weed. We were in the right place.

The passing of Bennet Merlin Arthur Roscoe was unexpected but, in truth, entirely predictable, given his dedicated consumption of delicious poisons. All the poisons. Between swigs from hip flasks, the congregation speculated on why the cause of death was still unknown:

'They're still printing out the toxicology report.'

'NASA want to weaponise his liver.'

BMAR was, appropriately, hopelessly late for his own funeral, which started 30 minutes after the allotted time. The speeches were warm, funny and moving. Everyone had just about recovered their composure when they were asked to belt out 'You'll Never Walk Alone'. Everyone lost it again. People spilled out of the chapel in tears, lighting up anything that came to hand and wailing into heartfelt embraces.

The 'after-show party' was at The Sheaf in Borough. The place was packed, on a Monday afternoon, with sharp sisters and herberts in hats. The Raider stood outside, wearing a stovepipe hat that turned out to be an inverted ice bucket. Roxy sported a fascinator that doubled as an ashtray. Everywhere people were ready to chat, to commiserate, to reminisce.

BMAR chose his friends carefully, so I knew that I would be in good company whoever I spoke to. He chose them so well, it was still full at closing time. People from all chapters of his life in Liverpool, Bristol and London merged, telling barely believable true stories of guns, poetry, drugs, prison, girls, theft, violence and inappropriate use of the word 'cunt'.

Funerals do strange things to people. There's a need to remember, a need to laugh and, surprisingly, a need to flirt; life protesting death. Hardy souls headed down to the Blue Eyed Maid in Borough High Street in the small hours, where a few minor injuries were sustained, not least to the ears of other punters as we reprised a quite terrible but shameless 'You'll Never Walk Alone', without a Scouser between us.

The mourning after, a Chernobyl of a hangover was ably treated at Maggie's Cafe in Lewisham, where Maggie amused herself by giving me a heart attack with her 'Irish sauce' gambit – a mustard jar that propelled a giant penis jack-in-the-box to whack me in the face. It was a surreal post-funeral moment, but oddly appropriate.

An almost automatic, drone-like instinct led us back to The Sheaf for a hair of the dog. It felt like Borough days of old, where a heavy night was followed by opening time in the same pub with the same characters. You went for one; you stayed until you could stay no more.

It was an inevitable continuation of a goodbye to our mate, an extraordinary man and funny fucker, who reached the extremities of charm and rudeness, but never of dullness. He had patrolled his manors, around Brixton and SE1, dressed as a vicar, a cowboy or officer of the Third Reich, but always dressed to kill, with a ready wit and an eager thirst.

He was a true Deserter; a fugitive from society's expectations and a ferocious ally in the struggle against the dullification of life. He considered mornings an affront, barely worked a single day and was available at a moment's notice for any adventure that veered from the path of rectitude. He saw equal beauty in art, violence and fermentation. He shed tears at children's cartoons, spilt drugs and unforeseen punchlines. And he believed to his core that there is no higher calling than fucking about.

At Kempton, Brother Bennett came in fourth. Late again, the cunt.

RIP Bennet Merlin Arthur Roscoe. You lived a great life. Even if half of it was spent in prison. Which is why we called you Half-life.

Epilogue

London, 2218

First, I noticed her industrial boots; second, the face of an angel once removed. But before I got to her five-alarm curves, there was a flash of silver as she poured something into the two drinks on the bar in front of her. Risky. You could get three months for full-strength booze in the capital.

She looked like the perfect mess, even down to her misshapen bag, into which she slipped the flask.

'What else you got in there, hun?' I asked, nodding at the holdall, letting her know I'd seen, but wasn't telling. She turned her mocha eyes on me with a look beyond disdain.

'The head of the last guy to call me "hun",' she said. Gulp.

Next to her, in a silver cap and space-jodhpurs, her lanky pal was talking loudly at the lady behind the bar.

'I'm not paying for that,' he barked, as he necked one of the pimped-up purple liquids and belched. He didn't have enough credit in his retina to pay for it anyway. The security bots started to hover. Their little displays agitated, spoiling for action.

'It's on me,' I said, on a hunch. They must have heard the same thing I had: that this new bar had a secret stash of beer over the legal limit of 1.5% ABV, ten years after London's last pub had closed and been turned into luxury flats. Luxury empty flats. Ten years in which brewing had become a lost craft, frowned upon from above as an anti-social, anti-work crutch for lowlifes like me. But no, this place had the same watered-down schmuck juice that was in every joint owned by the Big Three Barcos. That is to say, every joint in the Smoke.

'I would thank you, but it was shithouse,' he said, introducing himself as Demi-vie and his beautiful friend, appropriately enough, as Risky.

'Don't mention it,' I said. 'Maybe we have the same thirst. Is it too much to ask for just one *pint*?' The room fell silent. All eyes were on me. 'I mean, pie...' The crowd looked suspicious. '...napple smoothie.'

Phew. The hubbub returned. My smoothie arrived. Whoop de fucking doo.

'The Dulwich Impaler told me this was *the place*,' moaned Demi-vie.

'He's not fucking here though, is he?' said Risky. Demi-vie tried to reach his source, this Dulwich Impaler.

'Cunt never answers his iMind when you need him,' he said. When he did get through, we got Demi-vie at full volume.

'I want to fucking spew, Impaler. It's full of chinless dead-eyed cunts, apart from me, Risky and some speccy twat in a trilby.'

'Clean South,' I said, introducing myself, 'pleased to meet you.'

With all the bar looking on, insulted by his rant, Demi-vie loudly arranged to meet up by some bins in South London. Yes, every inch of the town had been developed, redeveloped and regenerated but they couldn't take away our bins.

'Hold on,' said Risky, spotting something. 'Follow me, fellers.' In a secluded part of the bar, Risky reached towards a fridge door.

'They're fruit cocktails, Risk. An insult to liquid,' said Demi-vie.

Risky twisted the handle and the door opened to reveal a hidden tunnel. Demi-vie bundled me in. I thought I was being kidnapped till I heard the unmistakable sound of a secret bar: laughter.

'Let's get paralytic!' exclaimed Demi-vie.

'I don't know about this,' I warned, as I eyed the place. Something was wrong. The spaceyacht-shaped bar was decorated in a gaudy Boy Georgian style, yet the furniture was clearly late Jedwardian. I looked around me. These tasteless clowns didn't know what they were doing. They were drinking cocktails made of leather and sapphires served in puce trainers with model aeroplanes on the side and mini-burgers floating in them. This had to be it: the secret lair of the property developers, the people who had sold London's soul to the highest bidder.

It was too late. Demi-vie had made it to the bar.

'Three double whiskeys, lad,' he shouted, before turning to us. 'And what do youse fancy, seeing as you're paying and all?' Suddenly we were surrounded by ray guns.

'You're not in the property game,' someone said. I knew exactly what to do. I started to whimper.

Risky had a better idea. She made a serious no-chain enquiry about condominiums. The developers relaxed, and Risky asked about their weapons: 'Is that the Foamball XL-5 you're packing?' she purred. 'Do you mind if I...?'

The enchanted developer handed it over and Risky duly covered the cream of the London property industry in fast-setting foam before Demi-vie took the opportunity to draw a penis on a vice-president. We then did what was once known as 'a runner'.

'Sector SE1,' Demi-vie told a cabbie-bot.

'Is that south of the river?' he bleeped back. It was hard to tell now the river had been paved over and covered in flats. 'Only I don't go south of the river at this time of...'

'Shut it and fly, bot boy,' said Risky, firmly. Demi-vie flung an arm round her shoulder.

'That's my girl,' he said.

We were dropped off near where the river used to be and Demi-vie led the way into the south. I'd heard it was full of ferals and that the houses were all caravans, but in fact it was just like the rest of London, except that there were still some gaps between the buildings where people could walk, if they remembered how.

They led me through alleys to the sewage works where we found the Dulwich Impaler leaning on a bin. He was a long-haired freak with a four-day stubble, sporting cargo trousers and sandals, admiring the beauty of the drainage system with the help of some powerful skunk. Risky took out her hip flask and we shared some potcheen. It was the strongest thing I had drunk in a decade; an utterly foul potato-based booze.

'Delicious!' said the Impaler. 'What a versatile vegetable.'

Stoned, drunk and lost, I felt brilliant again.

We wandered and wondered, until we came across Drinkme Street. Irresistibly drawn, we found the buildings had doors at ground level. Weird. And we weren't alone. Others were walking towards what looked like a dead end, except they didn't return. The last door had a light above and a key in the lock. We entered without a word to find the legendary secret taproom, Southey 451.

'Just closing, guys,' said the cheery, bearded man, standing over a hand pump, next to a plate of Scotch eggs. Our faces, so previously wide-eyed with fervour, dropped like gutted stones.

'Only kidding!' said the barman. 'What can I get you?' Risky unzipped her bag and took out a dimpled pint jug, which she handed to the barman.

'Respect, madam,' he said, as he filled her dimples. 'That'll be £4300 please.'

'Do you accept Tastecard?' asked the Impaler.

With 50% off we drank twice as much, followed by a pint to celebrate. Because no matter how they mutilate our town, there are always little victories, nights of joy, lost afternoons and well-earned sickies.

Into the future, comrades!

Acknowledgements

First of all, many thanks to all the people who pledged cash money to make this book a reality and whose names now grace the pages of this book. You are the real heroes of this enterprise, in a way, although let's face it, you didn't have to sit in your pyjamas writing the thing when you could have been out in the sunshine. So, think on.

Thank you also to the many friends and supporters of Deserter. In particular, those who have contributed with advice or suggestions to the website or podcast, or even joined us on an excursion. Sorry about your livers:

Ian McClelland, Mike Taylor, Janine Smith, Helena Burnell, Robert Marsh, Sarah Bowles, Lloyd Shepherd, Tim Wright, Duncan Palmer, Duncan Hart, Chris Pressley, Mark Slater, Emily Power, Anthony Medley, Sam Potter, Paul Whitehead, Emily Medley, Tom Cullen, Fiona Scurlock, Dulwich Hamlet FC, David Rogers, Sarah Thompson, Alex Manson-Smith, Mike Fairbrass, Liam Bailey, Cara Church, Jason Cobb, Llia Apostolou, Darryl Chamberlain, Bruce Dessau, Zoe Ellsmore, Chris Lockie, Will Clunas, Rachel Holdsworth, Megan Eaves, Iain Gordon, Dan Jestico, Luke Eastney, Steve Overbury, Ben Sibley, Bibi Lynch, Will Noble, James Drury, Mark Blakeway, Jess Tyler, Matt Hall, John Tackley, Andrew Finnerty, Rob Dickinson, Brendan O'Duffy, Sam Barber, Darren Macrae, Steve Keegan, Zelda Rhiando, Paul Chapman, Karina Bidault, Anna-Louise Ukairo, Rima Patel, Ade Clarke, Anji Clarke, Tom Witcomb, Bernadette Lintunen, Nigel Proktor, Bob Millar, Jess Coleman, Bridget Duffy, Bear Hawkins, David Moger, Noel Blanden, Ralph Raison, Corinna Silk, Billie Mae Ukairo, Ella Ukairo, Unbound, James Attlee and Wolfie.

And our old friend Mally.

Thank you also to the hostelries of South London without whose help and ceaseless encouragement this book would have been completed in half the time.

The creation of this book has been a joint and cooperative endeavour. Each author would like it noted that any errors in this book are the sole responsibility of the other.

Versions of some of these pieces first appeared on the Deserter website (deserter.co.uk) and are re-presented here alongside the new material that the publisher insisted upon.

DIY index

Clapham

Croydon

Crystal Palace

Denmark Hill

Deptford

Dulwich

East Dulwich

East Sheen

Elephant and Castle

Eltham

Forest Hill

Gipsy Hill

Greenwich

Hither Green

Herne Hill

Honor Oak

Kennington

Kew

Kidbrooke

Ladywell

Lambeth

Lee Green

Lewisham

London Bridge

Loughborough Junction

Merton Park

New Cross

Nunhead

Peckham

Putney

Rotherhithe

Shad Thames

Shooters Hill

Sidcup

South Bank

Streatham

Sydenham

Thamesmead

Thornton Heath

Tooting

Tulse Hill

Vauxhall

Wandsworth

Waterloo

Welling

West Dulwich

West Norwood

Wimbledon

Woolwich

Patrons

Ziad Al-hasso
Caroline Bourne
Chris Carus
Graham Cornish
Alison Craig
Bruce Dessau
Mike Fairbrass
Sarah G
Bart Hallett
Heideewickes Heideewickes
Simon Hemsley
Patrick Horgan
Tom Howard
Louis Jagger
Chris Lockie
Lard Longfield
Stuart McLellan
John Moss
Carlo Navato
Mick Paterson
Chloe Raison
David Rogers
Jake Seaman
Maggie Simpson
Susan Simpson
Linzi Sinclair
Emma Snaith
Lisa Suiter
Bert Trautmann
Alistair Twiname
Murray W
Will Walker

Heide Wickes
Will Wilkins

National Theatre

The National Theatre is a softly lit warren of escape and dreams, with plentiful seating areas and, as we've mentioned before, several delightful balconies on offer. The only problem is that the bars don't open till five. And when they do, a decent bottle of wine is £30.

So, ever budget conscious, we first picked up a bottle of chilled plonk from the Costcutter on York Road, then helped ourselves to a couple of glasses from the thoughtfully provided NT water points and settled down on the catchily titled Bank of America Merrill Lynch Terrace. With the trees losing their leaves, the river was reappearing and I was encouraged to see plenty of like-minded shirkers had bunked off for the afternoon to enjoy the view and the last of the sun.

'So, what happened to Current Boyfriend?' I asked Roxy.

'Jan?' she said.

'Yes, if he must be given a name.'

'Oh, he had to go,' she said. 'I found one of his wrist sweatband things clogging up the Hoover.'

'Little bit harsh,' I said.

'That's not the half of it,' she went on. 'It was one of those ones with a little zipped compartment in it, you know?'

'No.'

'I looked inside and there was a little note he'd written.'

'Uh-oh.'

'I know,' she said, and poured us some more wine.

'Well, what did it say?'

'It said "Sweat is fat crying".' I looked at her, dumbfounded.

'He had to go,' I said.

'Had to go,' she agreed. 'Cheers!'

Before our next stop I took the opportunity to visit one of my favourite toilets.

'You off up the velvet tunnel?' said Roxy.

'You know it!' I said, as I went through the auditorium doors and into the dark soundproofed passage that led round to the gents. All sound was hushed, even my tread softened on the lush carpet. The senses dimmed as I moved forwards, as if in a film with no sound;

'And he carries his guinea pig around in a shopping trolley.'

'Imagine not living in London,' I said, in wonder.

'Exactly. So I invited him up to join us.'

'What? Are you kidding?'

'I'm the Bishop of Southwark. It's what I do,' she said, referencing the T-shirt she was wearing. 'What's wrong with that?'

'What if he wants to suck my cock?'

'Believe me, no one wants to suck your cock.'

'What about that girl in Herne Hill?'

'She was deranged.'

Sure enough, Ricky soon appeared, pulling his trolley behind him, and joined us at one of the high tables on the terrace. Roxy went to buy them both a drink.

'I'm 40 next week and I'm still sucking cocks for rocks,' he said, with a smile that revealed several absent teeth.

'So I understand,' I said.

'It's not what I had planned,' he went on. 'I was going to be an artist.'

As is often the case when you start a conversation with low expectations, there followed an enjoyable and salutary discourse on ambition, parental support, self-confidence, depression and, ultimately, poverty and addiction. It wasn't what I'd come out for, but with a pint in my hand, I'm very adaptable.

As soon as he'd finished his drink, Ricky jumped up.

'Well, I can't sit here chatting all day,' he said. 'I've got to get back to Sussex.' Blimey, I thought, even the tramps are busier than me.

'You don't live in London, then?' said Roxy.

'No, but I get up here every chance I get. The people are so much friendlier.'

'Hope to catch you again, sometime,' I said, and I meant it.

'Have you got a boyfriend, love?' he asked Roxy and – to my surprise – she shook her head. 'Well, someone's gonna be very happy to find you,' he added, and waved goodbye.

'I hate it when they say that,' said Roxy.

Dirty Southbank

'Fifteen degrees in December!' read Roxy's message. 'Taking the afternoon off. Dirty Southbank day?'

Spend the last T-shirt day of the year messing about in a brutalist playground? How could I refuse? Unlike many of our daytime destinations, the South Bank – and in particular the Southbank Centre – was actually designed to have fun in: captivating interiors, vast terraces, secret nooks, river views, music, art and – perhaps most importantly – all bars and no cars.

The Southbank Centre's genesis was as part of the 1951 Festival of Britain, hailed as a post-war 'tonic for the nation' by Herbert Morrison, the government minister responsible for the gig. Now it's more 'gin and tonic for the nation', but still has enough about it, enough rough edges, thankfully, to draw us to it.

Queen Elizabeth Hall

I was leaning outside the Queen Elizabeth Hall, holding a pint and enjoying the clatter of the skateboards beneath me in the Undercroft, when I spotted Roxy approaching on the level below. Who was that bloke she was with?

'Who was that bloke you were with?' I said, when she joined me.

'Oh, that's Ricky. He asked for a pound and we got talking,' she said.

'Oh, right.'

'He's 40 next week and he still sucks cocks for rocks, he said.'

'Dear God.'

tation for dealing with the alcoholic transgressions of his own clergy, which might have left him open to accusations of hypocrisy.

But that won't stop many making the pilgrimage to Borough in December and raising a glass to honour the man. Let the bell of joy and goodwill ring out for Dr Butler at Christmas, and never let the bell end.

'We were laughing because he was staggering so much as he walked off.'

At this stage, it is claimed that Dr Butler told onlookers he was in fact the Bishop of Woolwich, but the personal belongings he left behind in Mr Sumpter's car told a different story – a story that was to come out when Sumpter saw press reports of the 'mugging' of a Bishop and came forward with his side of the tale.

Was the Bishop pished out of his prelatial bonce, as witnesses claimed, or was it simply a period of divine intervention which sent him out amongst the people on that famous night? We may never know for sure. But either way, we applaud the man for taking the night off to walk with his flock.

Indeed, we enjoy plotting potential routes from Grosvenor Place to Bermondsey to commemorate the event, although ours tend to take in pubs on the route. And sometimes, not on the route.

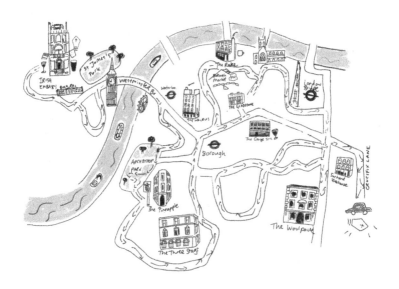

Dr Butler acknowledged that he drank two glasses of red wine at the ambassador's reception, but was subsequently unable to recall if or what he drank after that – though, it should be said, he was absolutely certain that he was not drunk. Just as well, as he had a fearsome repu-

legendary Christmas drinks, at which Guinness, spirits and wine are freely dispensed.

Less than five hours later Dr Butler, a regular on Radio 4's *Thought for the Day,* arrived at his home in Tooting with head wounds, bruises and a black eye. He was missing his crucifix, mobile phone and a briefcase full of confidential church papers.

What happened in between has been the source of much conjecture, with the Bishop initially reporting to the police that he had been mugged somewhere between the Embassy and his home, but later stating that, in fact, he had absolutely no recollection of the period in question and may have experienced some sort of 'blackout'.

Fortunately, there were other witnesses to help fill in some of the blanks.

Instead of returning directly to his home from the Embassy, it seems Dr Butler, for reasons unclear, headed back to Borough. Here he managed to set off a car alarm outside the Suchard Bar in the aptly named Crucifix Lane, a dark and windy outpost by the railway arches of London Bridge.

Hearing his car alarm go off, a Mr Paul Sumpter, who was playing pool in the bar, dashed outside to investigate. He saw the hazard lights flashing on his Mercedes and a pair of legs protruding from one of the open rear doors. Inside, he discovered the 66-year-old Dr Butler 'sprawled' across the back seat, tossing out his child's soft toys. 'He was completely out of it,' reported Mr Sumpter.

Bewildered, he asked: 'What are you doing in my car?' At which point Dr Butler gave his legendary reply: 'I'm the Bishop of Southwark. It's what I do', the phrase that now accompanies the Yuletide raising of glasses throughout the area.

When Mr Sumpter enlisted the help of others to attempt to remove Dr Butler from his car, Butler became 'aggressive and arrogant', according to Mr Sumpter. Apparently unable to stand, Dr Butler then fell to the ground, striking his head, and spent some time sitting in the gutter, where he declined the offer of an ambulance from the bar manager, Paul Sathaporn.

'He got up and staggered under the railway bridge,' said Sathaporn.

As it was also empty, the wisdom of this crawl at this time of year was in doubt. I don't need a pub to myself very often. It had started to resemble a pub crawl after the apocalypse, I thought to myself, which warmed me to it again. However, three empty pubs in a row made me miss the sound of music and people. I began to long for a chat about the weather or the pathetic screams of partly devoured zombie victims. Once again, the beer was splendid, but it was time for the hustle, bustle and bright lights of the great metropolis. We were back on the 51 – to Woolwich.

Taproom SE18

Hop Stuff's Taproom is pretty slick, in keeping with the grandeur of the Royal Arsenal, and its hubbub was welcome after the silence of the suburbs. Normally there's a greater cask selection, but this time it was mostly their own brews, though that's hardly a problem.

Starving by now, I found their White Pony pizza exceptional. Half-life's appetite suddenly kicked in and he ordered the pizza-and-salad combo: 'But with twice as much salad and twice as much pizza.'

'You want two?'

'No. I want one fucking massive one.'

Sadly, when the Greek salad arrived it grievously offended him. 'Olive,' he muttered, before raising his voice to a passing waitress. 'Olive!'

'It's Phoebe,' she said, meekly.

'Where are the fucking olives, Phoebe? What kind of Greek salad doesn't have olives?'

'Of course, I'll just...'

'It's an insult to Zeus, to Plato, to Aristotle and to Demis fucking Roussos, love,' he said, as she carted the offending greenery away.

We'd been to five bars and had high-quality beer in each, most of them around the £3 mark – and spent around £3 on transport. We hadn't had much to complain about until the salad incident. Phoebe returned with his salad festooned with the bitter fruit. 'Cheers, Pheebs,' he said, passing her his number. 'And don't ring before midday, alright?'

The Hangar

The micropubs come thick and fast on the 51 and such was our inattention that we went flying past The Hangar, another converted shop, at The Oval. Yet in moments we had arrived at another.

The Broken Drum

No sooner had we realised our mistake than we arrived in Blackfen, an unremarkable part of South London's borderlands, blessed by the award-winning Broken Drum.

Once upon a time places like Blackfen and our next destination, Welling, were 'somewhere'. Somewhere with a great cinema or dance hall, where people would go out, meet other people and have fun. I wonder how a community reaches a point where it no longer needs fun. 'Just an Asda and a plumber's merchants will do us, thanks,' they seem to be saying. 'We've got a radio.' It's little wonder that this crawl was accompanied by great wafts of weed stink that were not our own, as people are forced to roll their own fun.

Named after a bar in Terry Pratchett's Discworld series, The Broken Drum is housed in an old nail bar. Andy Wheeler knew he was about to be made redundant and immediately set about making a pub, like a hero. It's simple and unfussy, in the micropub tradition. We enjoyed an excellent £3 pale ale served at the perfect temperature – plus sausage rolls on the house. Really, anyone would be happy. Well, almost anyone.

'Thank fuck it's nearly over,' moaned Half-life.

'What, the year? Tell me about it. It'll be nice to see the pubs left to the professionals again.'

'No, this pub crawl. I haven't seen a woman since Lewisham.'

The Door Hinge

The 51 took us up the road to Welling High Street and the much-loved Door Hinge, London's first micropub. It feels a little more pubby, festooned with hops as it is and with a little snug at the back that looks like your nan's living room.